Stephen Taylor was born in South Africa in 1948 and grew up near Johannes-burg. At the age of twenty-two he made his home in Britain and travelled for four years in the Middle East and South Asia. From 1980–87 he was a foreign correspondent for *The Times* and the *Observer* based in Africa, South East Asia and Australia. Both his previous books have had African subjects, including *Shaka's Children: a History of the Zulu People*. He works for *The Times* and is married with two children.

Livingstone's Tribe

A Journey from Zanzibar to the Cape

STEPHEN TAYLOR

Flamingo
An Imprint of HarperCollinsPublishers

Flamingo
An Imprint of HarperCollins*Publishers*
77–85 Fulham Palace Road,
Hammersmith, London W6 8JB

www.**fire**and**water**.com
This paperback edition 2000

1 3 5 7 9 8 6 4 2

First published in Great Britain by
HarperCollins*Publishers* 1999

ISBN 0 00 655069 X

Maps copyright © Duncan Stewart 1999

Set in Postscript New Times Roman by Rowland Phototypesetting Ltd,
Bury St Edmunds, Suffolk

Printed and bound in Great Britain by
Omnia Books Limited, Glasgow

CONTENTS

To my children, Wilfred and Juliette

Acknowledgements

To SAY THAT MY biggest debt is to the people of East and southern Africa may sound facile, but I must say it anyway, for it was the unfailing humour and humanity of those among whom I travelled in 1997 that made this the most joyful, fulfilling journey of my life.

Neither the journey nor the book would even have been attempted but for Caroline, my wife, friend and travelling companion for more than twenty-five years. On our journeys she taught me to go further, to look closer. This time, as a reader, she was my constant guide, encouraging, lighting the way when I was lost and again helping me to discover more.

Over the years, it has been my fortune to have in Tom Fort that rare thing, a close friend and an honest, perceptive critic. He too has accompanied me in learning about each subject of which I have written, and has shown me how to do it better.

Many people helped before I took steps towards Zanzibar. I must specially thank Randal Sadleir for advice on the languages and people of East Africa. I am also obliged to Michael Holman, Trevor Jaggar, Nick Westcott, Mark Cocker, Richard Dowden, Michela Wrong, Shelby Tucker, Hugh and Yvonne Dinwiddy, Mrs. A. Sajiwa of the Malawi High Commission in London, and, for guidance from British diplomatic missions, Victoria Stickland in Dar es Salaam, Lesley Craig in Kampala and Rod Pullen in Nairobi.

Many people welcomed me kindly. I must mention: in Tanzania, Daudi Ricardo, Chief Justice Francis Nyalali, David and Marion Bartlett, Wolfgang Dourado, Marius Ghikas and the late Gosbert Rutabanzibwa; in Uganda, Keith and Tereza Anderson, Abubakar Mayanja, Father Damian Grimes, Peter Bewes, George Lugalambi, Professor Apolo Nsibambi, Mansoor Esmail and John Nagenda; in Kenya, Nancy Riley, Fanie and Carol Kruger, the Lord and Lady Delamere, Tom Cholmondeley, Robert and Judith Shaw, Charles Harrison, George Mbugguss, Richard Leakey, Dominic Martin, Fergus and Angela Macartney, Allen and Jean Harries and Dr Julius Kiano; in Malawi, the Reverend Anthony Luhunga, the Lady Roseveare and Stephen Drew; in Zambia, Tony and Gabriel Ellison, Jane Jellis, and Rosemary Pope and her late husband, John; in Zimbabwe, Felicity Wood, Judith Todd, Musa Zulu, Alan and Lesley Windram, Malcolm King and Zwide Khumalo. In South Africa, I was sustained by old friends, Michael and Wendy Lyall, while Vivien Barnes did valuable research on my behalf.

There are others who spoke to me or helped in other ways who cannot be named, or whose identity is concealed in the text. They know who they are, and I thank them.

I am also grateful for the encouragement and professionalism of the team at HarperCollins, Michael Fishwick, Rebecca Lloyd, Richard Collins, Kate Johnson, Annie Robertson and Caroline Hotblack.

Stephen Taylor
February 1999

Preface

THIS IS AN ACCOUNT of a journey in search of a dying tribe. Even at the time I was travelling, in 1997, it was clear that whites as an ethnic minority were doomed in most parts of Africa. It seemed as though the colonial era had belonged to another century rather than to the previous generation. In Tanzania, Uganda, Malawi and Zambia the whites had all but disappeared; in Kenya they clung on diffidently. In Southern Africa, however, there remained hope. Although politically redundant, their economic influence appeared to assure them a future.

My interest in the whites who stayed on in what used to be rather quaintly known as 'Black Africa' dates back to the imperial retreat. From the bastion of South Africa, I grew up in the 1960s observing what became a familiar process. As each new African state acquired its independence, the old colonial hands would decamp. Some returned to Britain, but most flinched from the prospect of rationed sunlight and costly alcohol. Ultimately, much of this human debris was borne by the winds of change to South Africa.

The fact that the withdrawal coincided with the seemingly unstoppable rise of apartheid helped shape my own response to these events. When self-styled refugees from African rule came among us, bursting with the same racism as the dour, resentful xenophobes in charge of our own society, it seemed only natural to identify with those they had left behind. Even when the promise of *uhuru* gave way to cupidity, corruption and worse, the whites who continued to identify with African aspirations to the extent of sharing their fate acquired a certain defiantly heroic status.

At the same time I confess my own attitude to the continent was ambivalent. When I felt compelled to leave South Africa, in the 1970s, it was not to the black states to the north that I looked to make my home but to the motherland of my British antecedents. Only in 1980, and the coming of independence to Zimbabwe, did I feel the summons to test years of conviction by going to live in an independent African state. In the end I stayed for four years.

Since the first publication of this book, Zimbabwe has returned to the headlines. On page 203 I describe visiting a farmer friend, Alan. His efforts had brought him prosperity and his workers conditions that were the envy of all who knew them. I was intoxicated at the time by a heady fusion of landscape and memory, wondering whether I might not yet return to Africa again. Alan – sceptical and pragmatic – was, however, more alive to the precarious status of whites. His words were to be prophetic. The tide of venomous racism whipped up by Robert Mugabe in the election campaign of June 2000 led to almost a thousand white farms being invaded by squatter gangs. Alan and his family were among hundreds forced to flee their homes. His workers paid a severe price for their loyalty; a third had their homes razed.

The land seizures in Zimbabwe had an eerie echo of events in post-independence Tanzania and Uganda. There too white farmers and planters were dispossessed in the name of agricultural and political reforms that proved to be disastrous. In Uganda, at least, lessons were learnt. In the midst of the turmoil in Zimbabwe, an official Kampala daily newspaper said that Uganda needed commercial growers and proposed that land be offered for white Zimbabweans to settle.

Nevertheless, the overall effect was devastatingly harmful. Africa watched helpless as one of its last productive economies was ruined by the same instincts, and the same methods, that had proved so self-destructive in the past.

At the end of my journey I reflected that only time will tell whether whites are capable of enduring in Africa. In just three years the prospects look less auspicious than they did even then. Increasingly parents, not only in Zimbabwe but also in South Africa, see their children attempting to make lives abroad. Inevitably, it is those with abilities and qualifications who are best able to leave. And as the brightest and most adventurous depart, the chasm between Africa and the developed world continues to widen.

PART ONE

GOING OUT

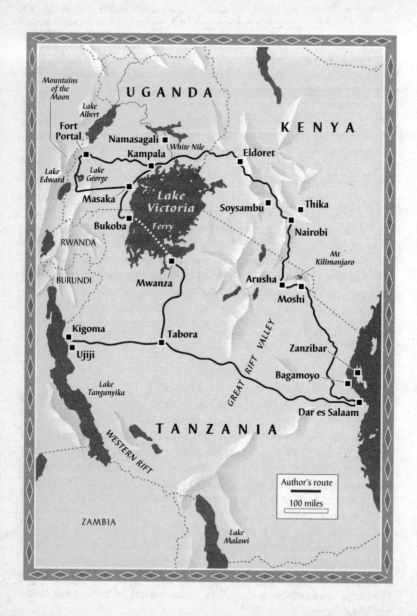

THE DIRT ROAD FROM Dar es Salaam petered out at a hedge of bougainvillea. Off to one side lay the shell of a deserted hotel amid palm trees that hung darkly at the edge of the Indian Ocean like bats. Beyond the purple blossoms, on the verandah of a cottage, stood a tall, grizzled white man in a T-shirt, sarong and sandals made from car tyres. 'And you must be Stephen,' he said.

He motioned to a seat on the verandah which looked out over the pale sea. A pot of pitch-like coffee was produced and served, in the Muslim manner, in tiny cups. He looked at me intently, a rather forbidding figure with the head of a patrician, a great beak of a nose, thinning white mane and beard, and watchful eyes. I felt apprehensive. My letters had gone unanswered and my presence was unbidden. Now I was expected to explain myself.

I was interested, I said, in whites who had stayed on in Africa. I was starting a journey in the footsteps of the explorers, missionaries and settlers, along the routes of imperial advance and retreat, looking for those who had made their home in post-independence Africa, who had lived through coups and wars, and learnt to live with the corruption, the collapse of services and the generally miserable lot of the African citizen. In particular, I was interested in those who had faith in Africa and its people, and who believed it still had something to offer the world. And now that the last protective white *laager* had fallen, I was looking for lessons on how they might endure in South Africa.

It sounded desperately earnest.

'Well,' he barked. 'It helps to be a little mad.'

I had heard of Daudi Ricardo long before the flight landed me that morning in Dar es Salaam. In Britain, where old district officers reminisced in their twilight on exotic human specimens who had crossed their paths, and in tales of post-colonial diehards, Daudi's name had resonance. Once an English grandee, born David Ricardo, he had sacrificed everything on the pyre of Tanzania's hopelessly inept experiment with socialism. Now in his seventies, he lived in genteel poverty in a shanty beside the beach twenty miles north of Dar es Salaam.

A single large palm tree stood in front of the whitewashed cottage. I took in the interiors of two adjacent rooms. They were of incongruous, almost paradoxical, character: a bedroom of missionary simplicity; and a book-lined study with a roll-top desk and leather chair. The shelves contained a near-complete set of G. A. Henty novels in the original gold-embossed covers.

'Meshack, more coffee,' ordered Daudi.

Once there had been a few other whites living in a ragged little colony at Kunduchi beach. But the major who used to see non-existent thieves in the dark and shout 'I've got my artillery, Sir, and I won't hesitate to use it', had died, and the couple who smuggled birds and small creatures to foreign zoos had been forced to make a run for it. Daudi was the last *mzungu* at Kunduchi, sharing his roof with Meshack, a smiling-faced young man, his wife and their baby.

In the days I spent there it became apparent that Daudi had a variety of roles. To Meshack, he was paterfamilias and opponent in hard-fought games of backgammon and Monopoly. To his neighbour, Saidi, he was friend and confidant. To most local folk he was simply the *mzee*, an ancient revered as sage and occasional benefactor.

One evening, I related two stories about whites in South Africa.

In 1686, a richly laden Dutch vessel, the *Stavenisse*, was wrecked off the south coast. For many months nothing was heard of the ship and it was concluded that it had gone down with all hands. Then, three years later, another ship called on this storm-blasted stretch of coast and found *Stavenisse* survivors, living contentedly among an African people. The Europeans returned to the tiny Dutch settlement at the Cape of Good Hope with elegiac accounts of life in an Eden among peaceful and generous folk, having left behind a Portuguese mariner, shipwrecked in the same place forty years earlier, who had acquired a wife and children and declined to leave his idyll. 'He spoke only the African language, having forgotten everything else, his God included,' wrote a would-be rescuer.

Almost a hundred years later, in 1782, an East Indianman the *Grosvenor* was wrecked along the same stretch of coast on a return voyage from India. This time, however, the survivors were not welcomed. Out of 123 men, women and children to reach the shore, fewer than twenty eventually got back to the Cape, bearing harrowing tales of murder and persecution by pitiless savages.

These two accounts represented for me a characteristic of the European experience of Africa: arcadia or inferno – it seemed always to be one or the other, as if the place chose to reveal only a benign face to some, and a malign aspect to others. Rarely had the world seen a more baleful side of Africa than now, over the horizon in Rwanda. Yet here was a modern equivalent of the shipwrecked mariner, loved and enfolded by a kinship network. His other family – his wife, Lady Barbara Montagu-Stuart Wortley, daughter of the Earl of Wortley, and children – lived in England.

'Africa has been kind to me,' he agreed. 'I won't be going back to England to die. My life is short now. I have cancerous waterworks. Collapsed recently and spent two days on the floor in the local hospital.' I knew enough about Tanzanian hospitals to marvel that, in the face of this final test, he had not submitted to the National Health Service.

The ambiguities were baffling: a white man who loved Henty, yet lived among blacks; a former settler serenely awaiting death in a land which old colonials saw as the final word in African failure. I asked him to start at the beginning.

DAUDI'S ANCESTOR WAS David Ricardo, the nineteenth-century economist whose prosperity built Gatcombe Park in Gloucestershire. The family was famously well-connected. 'I have an early memory of being given a hiding by George V. Grumpy old chap. He'd come to lunch and afterwards he was dozing in a comfy chair. I wondered if the beard was real, so I gave it a tug. He woke up quick enough. Queen Mary was very nice though.'

At the outbreak of war, then himself named David, he joined the family regiment, the Irish Hussars, suffered fearful wounds in the desert campaign and went to Tanganyika to convalesce. There, in the Southern Highlands, he turned to ranching, founding Matanana, a fabled homestead in the bush adorned with touches of Gatcombe – Sèvres porcelain, portraits by Sir Peter Lely, and green and gold livery for the African footmen.

Then he began to act oddly. He had always been considered an eccentric but when he started to consort with Africans, to dress in native garb and disappear into the bush for weeks at a time, even the relatively unconventional settler society of the Southern Highlands took notice. He announced his conversion to Islam and with it a change of name from David to Daudi. At *uhuru*, he took Tanzanian citizenship and became a member of Julius Nyerere's party. He handed over Matanana to his workforce and went to work for the people.

We mostly sat on the verandah because Daudi said it had a happy feeling about it. So it did, but I liked the study, with the sturdy oak desk, the swivel chair, its leather crackled and crisped by the tropics, and the walls of foxed and weathered books which ranged well beyond Henty. When he heard that I had written a biography of F. C. Selous, the Victorian hunter and adventurer, his face lit up. He dived into a pile of books and emerged delightedly with a distinctive green Bentley first edition of Selous's *A Hunter's Wanderings*, one of the great rarities of hunting literature.

I looked for other memorabilia – the odd picture, perhaps a piece of porcelain – in vain. 'All gone,' he said. Only one object did he mourn, a bronze of an Irish Hussar presented to his father by Edward VII. It had been stolen years ago, along with anything else of value. 'The burglars don't bother any more. They know there's no money.' He smiled with wry satisfaction.

Actually, there was not much food either. Once we ate fish and prawns at a small place down the beach and another time Meshack made a chocolate cake which fed five people, although one of them was Rodda, the baby. Daudi was down to his last fiver until he was paid some money owed to him. Not that there was anywhere to shop. Provisions came from Dar once a week.

'Thank God there's enough coffee,' he said. By then, however, there was no water. The rains had failed and the borehole had expired. There was also no electricity. His last luxury was a cheap, pungent snuff which he took from a plastic film canister.

Once, sitting on the verandah in his customary attire of T-shirt and sarong, he produced an old photograph album. A yellowing snap showed the master of Matanana at the Tanganyika Cattle Breeders' fair in 1958, a striking figure in plus fours, top hat and cravat. Now the homestead where liveried footmen had waited on guests was crumbling and Matanana had been reclaimed by the bush. 'I went back recently. It was a bit melancholy. But there were still some of the old families and we had a few laughs.'

After leaving the ranch, he worked for twenty-five years among peasants, a field worker for development projects. Most were doomed by incompetence and corruption. Yet he had found the work personally fulfilling.

'Well it opened up so many more *possibilities*,' he said. 'Getting involved, I mean. There were colonials who were frightened of the place. Before independence they would say to me, ''Do you think we're going to be all right?'' What I always said was ''Only you can answer that. I know that *I* am going to be all right.'' Then there were others who got involved. They cared for their people – some really loved 'em. They enjoyed the country and themselves. I did the same thing, in a different way.'

Had his work achieved anything? 'I've often doubted, and I still do, whether we have any business being here. All this advising and cajoling of people – who are we to say? But can we get out? No. It's gone too far for that. And there are instances where, yes, I think we did improve things.'

I went back to paradoxes. Just as Europeans had tended to see Africa as either Elysium or an abyss, it had often brought out in our kind extremes of either idealism or cynicism. What, I wondered, did Africans make of us;

I was not talking about any of those trite old clichés about colonialism. What did Africans *really* think about us?

In answer to this absurd question he told a story.

Germany's colonial wars were harbingers of the Holocaust. In 1904, the Herero people rebelled in German South-West Africa, killing about a hundred colonists. The authorities' response was to issue an order for the Hereros' extermination. Over the next year, General Lothar von Trotha hunted down the civilian population, driving them and their livestock further and further into the eastern desert. Of 80,000 Hereros, fewer than 16,000 survived. A year later, across the continent in what is now Tanzania, the Maji Maji rising began. Its suppression was equally pitiless. About 75,000 died of wounds or starvation.

In the aftermath of these terrible little wars, statues were erected in both territories to the power of German arms and the colonial dead. The hill in Windhoek, the arid but strangely appealing little capital of South-West Africa, was dominated by the triumphalist bronze of a rampant Teutonic cavalryman. Another monument was set up in the Southern Highlands, not very far from the Ricardo ranch at Matanana.

When *uhuru* came, Daudi anticipated the early removal of the statue. For more than fifty years it had stood as a grotesque affront to local sensibilities. Now, surely, it would be toppled, perhaps to be melted down and refashioned as a likeness of Mkwawa, the rebel leader. Time went by without any action, however. Eventually Daudi asked a local chief, a grandson of Mkwawa.

'Oh no,' said the chief, 'it is staying there. It is now our memorial, to *our* dead.'

A similar process, I recalled, had taken place more than twenty years later when South-West Africa became Namibia. To the astonishment of everyone, the Teutonic rider was left to flaunt his empty triumph from the hill above Windhoek.

Was that it? Was it that, even at our worst, we were recognised simply as a fact, an inescapable part of existence?

'Africans are endlessly tolerant but those of us who stay face a challenge. We have to learn a new cultural language and that can be very painful. Then, at some point, it just happens. We wake up to find we have been absorbed.'

He laughed. 'Anyway, the question is academic. We old *mzungus* are dying out. Soon we'll all be gone.'

I was thinking of South Africa, I said.

'Ah, yes,' he said.

When he got up I saw again how tall and thin he was. He leaned on a stick and walked with painful slowness while Meshack fluttered anxiously around. The cancer had left Daudi unsteady on his feet and in one bad fall recently he had broken a wrist. Long and gnarled, he might have been a bit of debris, an old tree, washed up on the beach.

We made our way down to the sea, passing the deserted hotel. In the late afternoon the sun had fallen behind a hill, casting a deep shadow across the building, now crumbling and streaked with decay. 'Used to be pretty lively round here,' Daudi said, 'all night parties, that sort of thing. I prefer it like this.' A solitary fat woman sat under one of the palm-thatched beach shelters, as if waiting for the party to resume. Beyond the shadow, the sea was pure and luminous. At the edge, a waste-pipe debouched into the shallows. For that moment all the ambiguities of the figure beside me were reconciled in the paradoxes of Africa itself – the white man, patrician yet humble, enduring in a place cruel but forgiving.

Before leaving I asked if there was anything he needed. He waved the idea away. 'I've got a nice library. I get the odd visitor. And Meshack lets me win at backgammon every now and again. It's just a pity he's hopeless at chess.'

As the car pulled away, heading back to Dar, the driver turned to me. 'I know him,' he said. Then he added, almost fiercely as if I might deny it: 'He is a *good* man.'

1. The Island

St Monica's Hostel, Zanzibar: Sunday, 9 March

I AWAKE IN AN enclave of Christendom to the muezzin's call. My room at the old missionary hospital is appropriately bare but spacious as well, with shuttered windows opening on to a sun-blasted courtyard and a lone palm tree beside Christ Church Cathedral. The cool, smooth floor offers more by way of relief than the fan, which wobbles and creaks alarmingly overhead. Even at dawn the air feels thick and moist beneath the mosquito net.

I can remember no Anglican building which has moved me more than the cathedral. The pale pink mortar of the exterior has been blackened by tropical mould, giving to the whole vastness of the structure the gaunt magnificence of an ancient ruin. The interior, showing similar signs of decay, is full of the incongruities and misunderstandings born out of a fusion of alien cultures. The materials combine African and Mediterranean elements – local coral and mortar for the walls, and twelve marble pillars at the rear of the nave which were shipped here from Europe and so confused the local builders that they were erected upside down. The apse strives for further classical effect, raised on a marble floor and lined behind the high altar by a ring of seats carved in African style from local wood.

Beneath a slab between the altar and seats lies the cathedral's builder and first bishop, Edward Steere. Above all, though, the place is a monument, and an apt one, to David Livingstone – big, flawed and craggily grand. As building began on Christmas Day in 1873, the missionary-explorer's embalmed body was being borne down to the coast by his companions, Chuma and Susi, on his most famous journey of all. The arrival of this touching little cortège in Zanzibar three months later captured the British public's imagination as no single act had during Livingstone's lifetime. On a pillar at the entrance to the sanctuary is a symbolic relic which encapsulates the whole episode, a crucifix made from the tree at Chitambo in Zambia under which his servants buried Livingstone's heart.

His work as a missionary had been a hopeless failure, but Livingstone's mission in the grander sense was complete. A month before his death, the Sultan of Zanzibar had submitted to pressure and signed a decree abolishing the slave trade in his dominions. Christ Church Cathedral, named after St Augustine's first cathedral in England, arose on the site of the old slave market. The altar was on the spot where once the whipping-post stood.

The service began with gusto, *Rock of Ages* sung in Swahili. The sermon that followed was barely audible. At an English parish church it tends to be the other way round – congregations singing softly, vicars talking loudly. Here the hymns are *fortissimo* throughout, unaccompanied but instinctively reaching for three-part harmony. Women and children sit on the left of the aisle in bright print frocks that challenge the sombre interior. Men and the older boys sit on the right. All efforts to break down this custom from the Islamic past have failed but neither side has any other inhibitions. They come and go, the well-off clattering noisily on leather-soled shoes, the humble passing soundlessly on bare feet.

Afterwards, a young man named Denis asked if I had found the old slave cells below my room. He guided me down steps descending from the courtyard of St Monica's to a subterranean chamber. We had to duck low to enter, and once inside remained in a crouch. In the dark I could just make out a cavern about 30 feet long and 12 feet wide. On either side was a raised ledge on which slaves had lain, chained to the wall. The clearance between ledge and ceiling was less than 2 feet. I tried to clamber on to a ledge but was almost physically repulsed by claustrophobia.

Crouching and breathing heavily, I was struck by a thought obvious but compelling. The profligacy of the slavers was one of the puzzles of the trade; like the ships on which the slaves were transported, this chamber created conditions so atrocious that their mere survival was a wonder. But what if the suffering was not incidental, was instead intrinsic to a design intended to crush those it did not kill? The slavers' reckless disregard for their merchandise made a perverse sense only if their ultimate concern was to extinguish the last flicker of the human spirit.

We are not used to coming across such crucibles of suffering intact. This death chamber of innumerable souls lies directly beneath the spot where I lie, under a mosquito net and a lazily turning fan.

'WHAT YOU HAVE to remember about Zanzibar,' said the Deputy Chief Justice, 'is that it might be Africa, but it is not of Africa. Persian, Arab, Indian – even British to some extent – but it is not African.'

After just a few hours, I could see what he meant. That morning I had walked the mile or so to Dar es Salaam harbour, hefting the unfamiliar weight of the rucksack and already regretting bringing so many books. Dar was raw African metropolis, raucous, ramshackle. On seething streets lined by general stores offering cheap, gaudy trifles, traffic was reduced to a boiling gridlock. Sweating and floundering along, I nevertheless felt a momentary sense of liberation for having foresworn a taxi. Now, ferried less than thirty miles out into the Indian Ocean, I was brought to the Orient.

Zanzibar belonged in that realm of the traveller's imagination occupied by phantasms, a destination from an opium dream. From a childhood stamp collection, that most potent of geographical stimulants, I recalled images of minarets and dhows, and bearded, turbaned potentates. To this world, the British were merely the last, and least tenacious, of the imperial powers to be carried on the trade winds.

The east coast was known to the geographers of Greece and Rome, most notably Ptolemy whose *Geography* referred to the region as Azania. Arab travellers called it Zenj, and were the first to explore it, al-Masudi in the tenth century, and the great ibn-Batuta on his voyage from Aden to Kilwa around 1330. The Shirazis brought the religion of Arabia and the culture of Persia. Reaching out across the Indian Ocean, they linked Africa with India, China and the Malay peninsula, trading slaves and ivory for glass and porcelain. The Portuguese came and went. Then, under the Omani sultans, Zanzibar entered its pomp.

No longer now did the traveller come to Zanzibar by dhow. These majestic and sinuous craft, the great *jehazi* of the Gulf trade and the cheeky little *mashua* plying the inshore waters, their lateens scything the sky like the crescent of Islam, were going the way of the transatlantic liner. Busy harbourside kiosks below the Lutheran church in Dar sold passage by motorised ferries which swept the visitor out to Zanzibar in hours.

At first sight the fabled shoreline was also disappointingly prosaic. Imagination prepared the visitor for a scent of cloves and ambergris coming off the sea, and a Sultan's palace – bombarded by the British in 1896 in the briefest of all colonial conflicts – worthy of the name. The old Stone Town sat at the water's edge, white and flat, just a few stubby minarets rising above the line of red-tile roofs. The harbour, once teeming with dhows, was deserted.

Feigning deafness to the imprecations of porters and hotel touts, I struck out towards the heart of the old quarter. Along Creek Road, lined with mango trees, the town sprang to life. At the market a crowd was gathered around a very large dead shark. Children gazed, transfixed, while men in skull caps negotiated noisily for cuts from the leviathan; even the flies seemed to abandon salted fish drying pungently in the sun for this new attraction.

Down in the Stone Town, alleys wandered among high lattice balconies.

Along these narrow lanes, domestic and community life merged. Children tumbled from doors at the feet of a passer-by. Women gossiped from behind bright veils. Mysteries and intrigue seemed to lurk among the maze of lanes, although the reality was that in this intimate jumble no household could retain its secrets.

The Deputy Chief Justice's house lay along one of the alleys. From Wolfgang Dourado's door hung the emblem of Amnesty International, as though it were a crucifix to ward off evil. Dourado, indeed, was a Catholic of Goanese descent, but the cool, darkened living-room that lay beyond the door was furnished in the Arab manner.

'So you're an Aussie, eh?' he said. Before I could correct him he went on, 'in that case you'll want a beer.' He returned with an icy can. I gulped gratefully and in the hope of being offered another decided against correcting the misunderstanding.

He was a tiny bobbing figure with a high-pitched voice and a gleam in his eye, one of that breed of combative lawyers with their origins in the Indian subcontinent, who have devoted themselves in Britain's ex-colonies to a good scrap and free speech with almost equal relish. For a member of the bench his pronouncements on his political masters were startlingly injudicious. 'Nyerere? That bastard. Never liked him – utter hypocrite. Karume was another matter. A peasant and a madman, but with a humane side. I pray for his soul but I fear he's sizzling like a kebab these days.'

Dourado had known both embrace and rejection by the British. On a legal scholarship in London, he learnt to love the collegiate rituals and stimulus, but was quickly reminded on his return that the same people who had invited him to their homes in London would not be seen with him socially in Zanzibar. 'The thing about the Brits was that they had a good eye for the best sites. Where there was a good view, there you'd find the British club. Our clubs had to be tucked away. We found it baffling because in Goa, the Portuguese assimilated. One never knew what the Brits were afraid of – did they really think we might roger their wives?' His eyes gleamed wickedly at this subversive thought.

'More beer? Forgive me if I don't join you, I'm getting over a bout of malaria.'

Other racial currents had drifted around the island. Under Omani Arab rule for centuries and a British protectorate for seventy years, Zanzibar was infiltrated in the last years of British control by mainlanders hungry for the island's prosperity. In 1964, within months of independence, an Africanist revolution saw the eclipse of the Arabs. The Sultan fled and thousands of

Arabs and Asians were massacred. Zanzibar was united politically with the mainland.

Nyerere's attempts to graft socialism onto an island culture rooted in enterprise were doomed. Dourado, then attorney-general and one of nature's Tories – 'absolutely dyed in the wool, old chap' – spoke out against the union and was first flogged, then detained. 'Three months, fifteen days. Not very long, but vile conditions. After I came out I said I would rather have been detained in South Africa.' He paused, then added with profound satisfaction: 'That *really* got up Nyerere's nose.'

For the time being, he was riding high again. 'I'm writing my memoirs. I think I'll call them *From Cell to Bench*.' He crowed delightedly. 'Boy, I'm a cocky bastard.'

BLACK IVORY WAS intrinsic to Zanzibar's rise. For centuries the rival Arab and Portuguese slaving empires maintained their strongholds along the coast, at Kilwa and Mombasa. Then in 1832, left supreme by the eclipse of the Portuguese, Seyyid Said, the Sultan of Oman, moved his seat from Muscat to Zanzibar. He had no territorial ambitions on the interior; his aim was simply to make the island the hub of a commercial network based on slavery. Within a few years, 40,000 slaves were being sold at Zanzibar's market annually.

Said was a man of high intelligence, but prosperity evidently stimulated no yearning in him or his successors to emulate the achievements of Arab and Persian culture. The town that grew up at the ocean's edge was functional rather than imaginative, with mosques as sturdy and unadorned as Said's fortress down by the harbour. Zanzibar's sole concession to the aesthetic traditions of Isfahan and Damascus were the ornately carved wooden doors of the merchants' houses.

Then, in December 1856, two British officers arrived on a sloop borne down from Bombay by the south-west monsoon. Richard Burton and John Speke were the first of a new wave of visitors to Zanzibar. From the quest for the Nile's source flowed everything else – the mission to Uganda, the opening up of East Africa and in due course the settlement of Kenya. Speke and Burton's expedition to the Great Lakes and, that same year, Livingstone's clarion call to the students of Oxford and Cambridge which summoned a generation to service in Africa – these were the first steps in the 'Scramble' for Africa itself.

Burton was in the full flush of his early brilliance and, in the six months he and Speke spent preparing for their journey, acquired enough information for a two-volume study of Zanzibar. His fascination with Islamic culture, and with matters outlandish or lubricious, had been kindled on army service in Sind and travels in Egypt, Arabia and Somaliland. Yet even he found Zanzibar strong meat. The port was 'a filthy labyrinth, a capricious arabesque of disorderly lanes, and alleys, and impasses, here broad, there narrow; now heaped with offal, then choked with ruins'. Of local sexual practices he was even more disapproving: gonorrhea was 'so common it is hardly considered a disease'; the Arabs were 'weak, effeminate and degenerate' due to 'excessive polygamy and unbridled licentiousness'.

Burton had been fired some years before by the talk of a German missionary, Johann Krapf, at Shepherd's Hotel in Cairo. Little more was known of the African interior at this time than had been advanced by Ptolemy 1,700 years earlier in a map showing the Nile taking its rise in two great lakes watered by the *Lunae Montes*, the Mountains of the Moon. From Krapf, the Englishman heard about a snow-capped mountain far inland, virtually on the Equator. Now, doing his rounds among the Zanzibari traders, he was given similar accounts and also of a great lake lying at the end of the main caravan route to the interior.

Many others were to be drawn to Zanzibar, which became the starting-point for all subsequent exploration. Livingstone made his first visit in 1866 when entering the lists to find the Nile; the newspaperman, Henry Stanley, followed five years later to find Livingstone, and again in 1887 to find Emin Pasha; the missionary, Alexander Mackay, passed through in 1877 on his way to find souls to save in Uganda, and was even more mortified than Burton: 'Zanzibar is an island no greater than a county of Scotland but as great in crime as the Babylon of the Apocalypse', he declared fervently; above all, perhaps, there was Sir John Kirk, the British Resident in Zanzibar.

Kirk was one of Livingstone's acolytes, a member of his Zambezi expedition who had been shattered by what he had seen of slavery. From the whitewashed and shuttered British consulate beside the Sultan's palace, Kirk worked to advance Livingstone's mission to eradicate the trade and replace it with the three Cs of Christianity, commerce and civilisation. It was Kirk who issued the Sultan with an ultimatum to close the slave market. And when Susi and Chuma brought Livingstone's body back from Chitambo, Kirk was there to receive it, and carry it back to triumphant burial in Westminster Abbey.

So many spirits to be found, then, in Burton's arabesque of disorderly lanes. But how remote they now seemed. Zanzibar's old buildings suffered a fate common in rundown but historic places discovered by tourism:

structures not terminally dilapidated were being hastily done up and turned into hotels. Kirk's consulate had become the headquarters of a state corporation. The Beit el-Ajab, or House of Wonders, the first palace of the sultans, was occupied by the ruling party.

The ghosts of a later era lingered in another crumbling pile. Africa House Hotel used to be the English Club, a Zanzibari mansion in traditional style. A pair of cannons at the door led to a broad staircase from which a moth-eaten buffalo head glowered down and which led to a balcony overlooking the sea. Forty years earlier, men in khaki and white duck loitered here over clinking glasses as the sun set. The sight was just as spectacular now and by late afternoon the balcony was congested with tourists. As the pyrotechnics of a sunburst unfolded and the Indian Ocean turned from gold to black, the crowd fell silent. It was as Wolfgang Dourado said: the British always had a good eye for the best sites.

'I COULD TAKE you on the motorcycle,' Canon David said brightly.

It was not an option I had considered. Canon David, as his congregants called him, was the vicar of Zanzibar, a missionary priest from Wiltshire in his mid-seventies who had some difficulty ascending to the pulpit. The question of how I might get to the village of the freed slaves had not entailed being his passenger on two wheels.

The machine was Chinese-made and as noisy as a new year firework show in Shanghai. Canon David manoeuvred it into position like a maribou stork caught astride a fence. Climbing on to the pillion, I realised that neither of us had a helmet. The first test was infiltrating the traffic on Creek Road. *Matatu* taxis, scooters and buses flew in either direction. We lurched out, Canon David sounding his hooter in admonition. Astonishingly, as if realising that he was not to be trifled with, the traffic parted. As we proceeded, he waved airily about him while steering with one hand and providing a running commentary over his shoulder. 'Old cricket ground,' he shouted, pointing towards an overgrown maidan set about with orange-blooming spithoedea trees. 'State house – used to be the governor's residence.' Groves of mango trees and coconut palms flashed past until our hectic pace slowed at the village of Mbweni. Canon David dropped me and wobbled jauntily off on his rounds. I walked down a path to St John's.

At first it seemed too English a scene for pathos: a small country church, more appropriate to a parish in the shires. But the red roof was corrugated iron, the square bell tower had been weathered to grey-black and the wooden door was carved in the florid Zanzibari style. The churchyard was a sunbaked square of dirt surrounded by a jungle of palm trees. Here Caroline Thackeray and her ladies were buried.

The venture had begun with all the absolute certainty and high-mindedness of the Victorian church. In 1871, the Universities' Mission to Central Africa, the body formed in response to Livingstone's appeal, bought thirty acres of land from the Sultan, five miles or so from the town. It was a tranquil spot, set against the background of a milky opal sea. There was an air of the retreat about the place and both the Sultan and Kirk maintained country residences here. The first freed slaves were brought to Mbweni in February 1874. Bishop Edward Steere wrote thankfully: 'We begin our village with seven men and fifteen women.'

This new colony grew rapidly as Royal Navy vessels continued to trawl the coastal waters for illicit slavers and frequently intercepted dhows bound for Muscat. Two years later Steere baptised eight couples, Mbweni's first converts. An even more ambitious project was in hand. Soon afterwards he set off for the Yao country, 400 miles inland, with a party of thirty-one men, twenty-one women and two children, to restore those plucked by the slavers from Africa to their own. Meanwhile, Caroline Thackeray, East Africa's first woman missionary, arrived as a teacher at Mbweni's school.

Caroline was a cousin of the author, William Makepeace Thackeray, and one of those indomitable spinsters of Empire who, with level gaze and firm chin, set out for corners of the world of which they had no comprehension, if not blithely, then at least with conviction. She found the makings of a model community. Steere recorded Mbweni's progress, 'a village free and independent, the houses all numbered on little plates of tin in green paint, and the shop stands at the cross-roads'. Soon he was expressing appreciation for Caroline's success at 'making the adults and the girls into real Christians'.

She stayed for the rest of her life and by the time she died was the grand dame of the British community, a formidable figure who, though she might have inspired little love, had yet found a purpose and her place in the world. She was steely to the last, even her grave in the parched patch at St John's betraying no hint of emotion: 'For 48 years a member of the UMCA. Died Jan 30, 1926.' Beside her are two young assistants whose deaths from fever are recorded even more dispassionately: 'Alice Marion Gay, Fell asleep, January 19, 1894' and 'Eleanor Mary Barnett, Jan. 8, 1856 – May 16, 1893.'

A short way off, the crumbling walls of the school told their own tale of ruin: a stone stairway overgrown by weeds; stucco cracked and peeling from walls sloping drunkenly askew; passageways to classrooms now open to the sky and piled high with rubble. All that high endeavour, hope and self-sacrifice come to this – a picturesque ruin at the edge of the Indian Ocean, a dilapidated church and three lonely graves.

I dismissed these melancholy thoughts. After all, the fact that the colony had dispersed indicated that Caroline and her ladies had succeeded in equipping the slaves' descendants for reintegration into the world. That, surely, was no small legacy. In fact, it was only later, when I came across the accounts by Steere's successor, Frank Weston, that the full extent of Mbweni's failure became apparent.

Weston arrived in 1908, a very different character from his predecessor. Where Steere was imperious, Weston was diffident. While Steere offered authoritarian leadership, Weston sought to involve Africans in decision-making. It was not long before old hands, and most notably Caroline, were comparing the new bishop unfavourably with Steere. The truth is that Weston was an unusually far-sighted and astute man and had quickly comprehended Mbweni's real problem. The place looked charming with its well-kept roads, coconut plantations and neat houses; but the forcefulness of the mission leadership, far from equipping its dependants to live beyond its boundaries, had institutionalised them. Left to their own devices, they lacked initiative and motivation. Moreover, proselytising had made little impact. Far from being Christians, most of Mbweni's inhabitants had reverted to the practice of witchcraft.

Weston tried to confront the challenge. When a woman was accused of leading a devil-worshipping cult of ghouls who dug up the bodies of Christians to eat them, he arranged to have one of her supposed victims exhumed. The body, a child's, was found intact. Weston put it on show to demonstrate the woman's innocence. The villagers were unconvinced. Weston himself had cast a spell over the body to restore it, they said. The failure was heart-breaking. 'Of all workers, none, I think, need so much sympathy as those who work at Mbweni,' he wrote.

Though painful, the lesson was valuable. The settlement had been an artificial creation and there could be no real community where there were no elders, no social traditions and no sense of common origin. Unusually for a missionary, Weston recognised that for Africans to benefit from European influence, rather than be damaged by it, the institutions of tribe, family and custom needed to be nurtured, not destroyed. But his was a lonely voice and it was, in any event, too late for Mbweni.

I walked back past the church, up the dirt road and at the end found a wooden kiosk. A few men stood around with soft drinks. They paused to greet the *mzungu*, curious, friendly. I motioned down the road. Did anyone go to the church any more? They shook their heads. 'People here are Muslims,' said one.

It was a pretty irony: the slave masters' faith had endured better than that of their liberators.

I ASKED MY new friend Denis about witchcraft. He nodded enthusiastically. 'We have many witches,' he said. 'Like Pepo Bawa.'

Pepo Bawa was a creature of Pemba, an island twenty-five miles north of Zanzibar and a place even more notorious than Mbweni as a nest of the black arts. Sorcerers from all over central Africa visited Pemba to refine their skills, while the victims of their spells came to be exorcised. Cannibalism, as a form of demonic ritual, persisted; babies were sometimes killed because they cut their top teeth before the bottom ones and were therefore thought to be possessed. It was not only Africans who feared the doings on Pemba. As recently as the 1950s, the Universities Mission to Central Africa published a cautionary booklet by Eleanor Voules, who lived for twenty-five years on the island, in which she related dispassionately accounts of possession and power which she believed to be authentically demonic. When I mentioned Pemba to Canon David, he all but shuddered. 'A dreadful influence,' he muttered.

The origins of Pepo Bawa, like accounts of its manifestations, had many versions. According to the most common, however, it was a demon which had taken the form of a fruit bat and tormented the people of Pemba until a powerful spirit medium cast it out and Pepo Bawa crossed the sea to Zanzibar. For years the island had been afflicted. Sometimes the demon was an invisible presence, a malign force which terrorised individuals. Often its victims, both men and women, reported being seized in an embrace and then sexually violated. In some instances, entire neighbourhoods had been reduced to hysteria and although Pepo Bawa had not been active for some months now, and was thought to have moved to the mainland, Denis said most people expected it to return.

We were sitting on the balcony of the Africa House. Denis intrigued me, for although he evidently had no doubts about Pepo Bawa's existence, he evinced none of the fear which he described with such relish. 'That is because I am a Christian,' he said proudly. He looked round. 'But you can speak to my friend.' And he called out to another youth.

The young man walked over smiling. Denis motioned to me. 'Tell him about when Pepo Bawa came to you,' he said. The smile was dashed, and it appeared to me that the young man's face actually went from a healthy shiny brown to grey. He shook his head sickly. We offered him a drink but he was clearly shaken and soon left.

Demons apart, Zanzibar appeared to be in something of a spiritual ferment. Christians and Muslims were engaged in a battle for souls and an assertive new breed of missionary had arrived on the island. At St Monica's, I encountered Frank, a blazing-eyed evangelist from Kent who declared that if only Christians realised the *power* they had within them, the Gospel would sweep the world. Among his acolytes was a tall Swahili youth of striking presence who had recently been baptised and christened Zephaniah. Born into a Muslim family, Zephaniah had become an outcast, forced to take sanctuary at the cathedral.

Denis interpreted: 'He says he will stay in Zanzibar to make converts. But there is danger. He has been stoned.'

'Stoned?'

'Four times. When preaching. But the Bible tells us this is not a new thing.'

Between Denis and Frank, there was no lack of fervour to see Zephaniah achieve martyrdom. Only Canon David appeared to regard the competition for converts with misgivings. David Bartlett and his wife, Marion, were missionaries of the old school with more than ninety years in Africa between them, he as priest, she as a surgeon. A frail, shy woman also well into her seventies, Marion's contribution to African well-being was in fact the more tangible. When polio was still a dreaded disease, she had been the only surgeon in the bush performing a relatively simple operation to release contracted leg tendons in children. Many Tanzanians were only able to walk because of the skills of this small, unassuming woman. Yet with their simple devotion and faith, the Bartletts had become almost anachronisms.

They had retired once, to the West Riding of Yorkshire, until receiving an appeal to return for one last spell of service in Africa. 'The people were ever so nice,' Marion said. 'But one hated the supermarkets.'

I TOOK MY leave of Zanzibar seated on the balcony of the Sultan's palace, cooled by a breeze coming off the harbour below. It was called the People's Palace now, a monument to the revolution, but few among the masses appeared interested in coming to gaze on the decadence of the past. There were more ghosts than visitors and that afternoon I had the place, in all its mournful tawdriness, to myself.

In 1964, as the revolutionaries stormed through the alleys of Stone Town, the last of the Omani sultans, the amiable Khalifa II, fled to his yacht out in the bay and escaped to Mombasa, and thence to exile in Bournemouth. The sultans had long since ceded their authority to Britain and, since the declaration of a protectorate over Zanzibar in 1890, had withdrawn to the shadows to enjoy the grace and favour of imperial servitude. They welcomed the pomp bestowed by an avuncular colonial regime, presenting themselves on ceremonial occasions in robes encrusted with CBEs, KCMGs and even, in the case of Khalifa, a GCMG, as well as lesser gewgaws and Omani daggers. Year had succeeded year in what a biographer of another contemporary monarch, George V, described as 'benign verisimilitude'.

Most spirited of the lot was not a sultan, but a princess. Salme, a sister of Sultan Bargash, eloped with the local German agent and lived the rest of her life in Jena as his wife with the name Emily Ruete, bearing him numerous offspring. She died in 1924, having written poignantly about her double life. Her apartment aside, the mood of the palace was glum. One of Bargash's favourite objects, a large grandfather clock, tolled ponderously beside a life-size oil painting of Sultan Hamid KCMG. The furniture was ornate, heavy, the antithesis of the Arab design virtues of lightness and simplicity. Most depressing of all were the Sultan's living quarters, where a fine writing desk and chest stood beside a formica wardrobe and a cheap black dressing-table with chipped and peeling lacquer. Here the unmanned monarchs lay abed at night, listening to the Indian Ocean lapping among the dhows, all power and vigour gone.

The balcony, at least, was a grander theatre of Zanzibar's decay. A polished blue sea slid away to three small islands glittering green and white. Down at the waterside palm trees brushed the whitewashed fortifications of the palace and the road curled past the honeyed walls of the Beit el-Ajab. For a moment it was possible to imagine the great *jehazi* down from Arabia, the clamour in the harbour as they were loaded with cloves and ivory, the whisper of the south-west monsoons; and to recall the words of James Elroy Flecker . . .

> *I have seen old ships sail like swans asleep*
> *Beyond the village which men still call Tyre . . .*

2. The Coast

BAGAMOYO, THEY CALLED IT, which in Swahili means 'lay down your heart'. The town, a dishevelled ruin of slow loveliness, lies at the beginning of the 800-mile Arab trade route to the Great Lakes. This was the terminus from which caravans set out for the interior, and where the returning journey ended before the crossing to Zanzibar. Lay down your heart, said the grateful porters, returned to family and home after months, years, away in the perilous interior. But the words might as easily have been spoken by the millions who passed here in chains, pausing perhaps to look back for the last time on their native land before the voyage into bondage.

A whitewashed plaque marked the place where the Nile quest began in earnest: 'On 25 June 1857 Burton and Speke set out from near this site on their expedition to Lake Tanganyika.' Having been brought across from Zanzibar in the Sultan's corvette *Artemise*, with the consul Hamerton who came to bid them farewell, the Nile explorers haggled in the bazaar of Bagamoyo to find porters before a party of 132 set out on the march westwards into the fearful green void. Twenty-one months were to elapse before Burton and Speke saw the sea again, and by that time the seeds of a famous enmity, and a celebrated geographical feud, had been sowed.

The plaque was among the better preserved of Bagamoyo's structures. A dirt road carved through a town composed of buildings similar to those of Zanzibar, but whereas the island's flourishing tourist industry had led to a good deal of restoration, Bagamoyo was a forgotten backwater, overgrown with weeds and lichen. The avenues of spithoedea trees planted during colonial times held the crumbling town in an embrace of green foliage and flaming orange blossom. Among the old houses left standing, the carved doors were splintered and awry and the great latticed balconies sagged like drunks.

Most of these derelict hulks were not even inhabited. In its heyday Bagamoyo's population had numbered about 5,000, including the Indian trader Sewa Haji, who built an empire on supplying the caravans and endowed Bagamoyo with fine buildings like the Customs House. There followed the Germans who built the fortress and Liku House, the old administration block. Now the Indians and Germans were gone and their old quarters were abandoned. Such profligacy is rare in Africa where squatters are apt to take up neglected property but here the Swahili folk preferred their own rudimentary huts.

I walked down the dirt road, grandly named India Street, to Liku House. It was another picturesque ruin, whitewash streaked with green mould, the shuttered windows hanging, broken and skewed, from their moorings. There was no plaque, but there could have been for Liku had a piquant place in the footnotes of imperial history. In December 1889, Henry Stanley – who had come a long way since finding Livingstone thirteen years before – emerged at Bagamoyo from the interior with a new prize. Emin Pasha was a protégé of General Gordon who made him governor of Equatoria in southern Sudan. After Gordon's murder in Khartoum in 1885 during the Mahdist uprising, a campaign was raised to rescue his gallant lieutenant, cut off in the south. Nothing would do but that this enterprise should be led by Stanley, whose implacable resolve had earned him the African sobriquet, Bula Matari, or 'Smasher of Rocks'.

In fact, Emin had no great need of rescue and was reluctant to leave. He was, indeed, one of nature's ditherers; a slight, scholarly figure in glasses and fez, he could never decide whether he was Turkish or Egyptian, though he was actually born Eduard Schnitzer, a German Jew. Stanley, however, was not a man to be denied, still less after a hellish forced march through the Ituri rain-forest of the Congo in which he had lost two-thirds of his men to disease and desertion. So, after months of wriggling, Emin consented to leave and was finally brought to Bagamoyo as the last and most costly of the journalist/explorer's great scoops. Crossing Africa from west to east had taken almost three years and cost more than 200 lives.

Once in Bagamoyo, at Liku House, a celebratory banquet was held in an upstairs room. After years of privation, there was to be no stinting and a German chef produced a feast of seafood, roasts and champagne. In the streets below, the Zanzibari porters held their own revels with drumming and dancing. Emin, having decided at last that he was pleased to have been rescued, gave a speech of thanks. Then he disappeared from the room. Some time later he was found lying outside in a pool of blood. Always short-sighted, he had fallen from the balcony in the dark and now, it appeared, was critically injured with a fractured skull.

Emin recovered in due course and promptly returned to the African interior, this time as an agent of the Kaiser, only to have his throat cut by Arab traders. It was a bleakly appropriate end for a man hailed in his lifetime as a mystic and an enigma but whose life in truth was more black farce than riddle. Beside the ruin of Liku House, a giant spithoedea tree shrouded the spot where he fell. The banquet room was silent and bare.

The German fortress had stood the test of time better. In the courtyard four young men sat around listlessly. Even my feeble attempt at Swahili was enough to establish that they were not locals but, it turned out, visiting Zambians. 'We are staying in this place,' said one, gesturing at the deserted fortress.

I commiserated. It was in better shape than most places in Bagamoyo but not much and now, on a weekend, there seemed little in town to divert four young men. They nodded in mournful agreement.

'We are here on a United Nations course,' the same man explained. 'We have come to learn about preserving our historic buildings.'

Was it my imagination, or did I detect a hint of mockery here? I had spent some time in Zambia and had never thought of it as having a great deal to preserve.

'You mean like the museum at Livingstone?'

'Ah, you know our country. No, not Livingstone, Lusaka.'

'State House,' said another of them. They giggled.

I had not been wrong. Here, indeed, was irony.

'The Pamodzi,' put in a third, in a reference to the capital's top hotel, a bit of modern grotesquerie. They nudged each other and chortled. This was a routine.

'Cairo Road' – Lusaka's grossly rundown main thoroughfare. They hooted.

'The bus station' – perhaps the most blighted on the continent. They roared.

'And ... and ...' the first picked up the thread again, 'and we are learning about preserving this heritage ...' he struggled to control himself, '... in Bagamoyo.'

They shrieked.

We compared dates, but they were still to be in Bagamoyo when I expected to reach Lusaka. It was a big disappointment. I had not met ironic Zambians before.

I started back for town to catch the bus for Dar es Salaam, still savouring the encounter. The truth is, I had been feeling a bit apprehensive. The guidebook had prepared me for trouble in Bagamoyo. '[There is] a real possibility of being violently mugged,' it said. 'This can happen at any time of the night or day and your assailants will usually be armed with machetes which they won't hesitate to use even if you don't resist.'

Just when I was thinking my anxiety had been misplaced, there was a terrific thud to one side, as if from a rock falling from a great height. This was not far from the case. A coconut weighing perhaps 10 lb had dropped from the top of a palm tree and landed just a few feet away. If it had hit me, my skull would have been crushed. This was not as remote a possibility as it might have seemed. I had once read an intriguing item of trivia about some tropical paradise where the highest incidence of accidental death was due to falling coconuts.

Suddenly, an urchin was flying across my path towards the fallen object, an expression of fixed intent on his face. Too late. A young woman on the other side of the road was already swooping. She collected up her prize, chirruping delightedly, and bore it off. The urchin grimaced, then noticed me watching and grinned.

There was no bus station, just a clearing beside a few wooden stalls selling soft drinks and chicken stew with rice, and a thatch shelter where travellers waited until the bus turned up. After that the driver waited until the bus was full. I had boarded promptly to get a seat, then waited sweating for almost an hour while the bus slowly filled up. It was my first lesson. To avoid being stifled even before the bus departed, the trick was to board at the last moment that seats were still available.

At least I had a seat. The bus was full when we left town; by the time we were a few miles down the road the interior resembled Groucho Marx's cabin in *A Night at the Opera*. The aisle was so tightly packed that standing passengers were forced by pressure from the centre to lie on top of those on the seats. To round off the discomfort, the road was abominable. Once the fifty-mile stretch from Bagamoyo to Dar had been under tarmac, but that had long since dissolved and not a trace of bitumen was now left. The dirt surface was gouged by deep rents, forcing the driver to proceed as though ferrying a cargo of precious china. Even so, there was no avoiding all of the troughs, and our crawling progress was punctuated by a series of sickening bangs which shuddered through the length of the bus like rolling thunder. At a speed averaging a little under 20 mph, this seething, broiling caravan of misery crashed down the trail forged by traders and explorers.

My breezy optimism evaporated again. I had barely set out on a journey of some 8,000 miles and, if the next 7,995 were anything like as bad as this, I could not imagine how I was going to last the course. I had to acknowledge to myself that my spell as a foreign correspondent in Africa more than ten years earlier had not done much to prepare me for this. As a tribe, journalists in Africa dwell amid the sweetest landscapes, live off the finest pasture and know all the best watering holes while making fleeting forays – on expenses and usually in packs – into what they like to call the Heart of Darkness in order to tell the rest of the world what a hellhole Africa really is. This time I would be staying in cheap guest-houses, travelling by bus and *matatu*, the ubiquitous minibus transport of the masses, and eating at roadside kiosks. There was nothing original or intrepid about this; thousands of young travellers did it every year and took the discomforts in their stride. But the thought occurred now that a backpacker entering his fiftieth year was a rather pitiful and ludicrous figure.

The bus had been lurching along for some time when I noticed that among the standing passengers pressing up against me was a child, a girl aged about four. She was out on her feet, slipping into sleep and kept upright only by the press of bodies. Her mother was a few layers of body away. Almost without thinking, I collected the child in my arms and lifted her into my lap. She barely looked at me before falling asleep.

It would have been unthinkable in my own country. For more than an hour the girl slumbered, oblivious of me and the tortuous progress of the bus. I was left to reflect on a curious pleasure; the pride of being accepted by a child, and to realise that I had not enjoyed such a degree of physical contact with one since my teenage son and daughter were that age. Every now and then I was forced to adjust my position, insofar as the human pressure allowed, to avoid cramp. The child would wake, look around for a moment, and go straight back to sleep.

Eventually we reached the outskirts of Dar es Salaam and bodies started to drain away from the bus. Before they got off, the mother looked at me, smiled and said a thank you: *'Asante sana.'* The child hopped off without a backward glance.

THE HOTEL WAS near the bus station but it served no beer so I set out into the night to find a bar. Down an alley I came to a dimly lit shebeen where a woman dispensed drinks from behind a metal grille. I took a seat on a plastic chair outside. The Safari lager came, icy and foaming, and I sat sipping quietly on my own until a ragged cripple with a deformed foot, vaulting himself along on a pole up the alley, stopped beside me.

'My friend . . .' he began, and I waited for the inevitable gambit, the entreating eyes, the extended hand. Then I looked up and saw that his face was alight with excitement.

'My friend, let me buy you a beer,' he said. And he sat down and shuffled through a wad of banknotes. I did a rapid calculation that there was roughly $22 in the hands of a cripple in a dingy quarter of one of the world's poorest cities.

I thanked him but said I had not finished my own beer yet. We were joined by a man named Jackson who said he was a fish trader, down among the rusting hulks beached in the port. The cripple introduced himself as Joseph, bought beers for himself and Jackson and ordered skewered meat to be brought from a nearby stall.

The place bustled with the camaraderie of workers winding down at the end of a week. They were labourers, *matatu* operators, street traders and perhaps the odd pickpocket. The shebeen owner moved among the tables, replenishing empty beer glasses. Word of Joseph's hospitality spread and soon others were drawing up seats to enjoy it. Most drank from the bottle or in a glass, but one sipped fastidiously at his Safari from a straw; insects, centipedes and even small snakes sometimes turned up in beer bottles.

I wondered how Joseph had come by his windfall. Breezily he dismissed the question as though such were an everyday occurrence. Conversation continued but I was unable to get any more out of him before, beer and food consumed, he got up with his pole and vaulted back down the alley into the dark.

Jackson said: 'Don't worry. Everyone around here knows him.'

So where *did* the money come from?

'He is a gambler. He begs some money, then he comes down to the port to play dice. Sometimes he has very good luck, and you will see him like now and he wants to buy for everyone. Then another time he will lose and you hear him say' – here he dropped into a theatrically feeble voice – ' "Please my friend, help me, I have nothing." '

'And people help him?'

'Oh yes. When he has plenty, he gives, when he has nothing, we give.'

I bought a round myself and left, walking down a teeming street to find an eating-house. By the time they brought the rice with a watery bowl of chicken curry I knew I had picked the wrong place but it was too late to leave. The wall of sound thudding from the music system was nothing new; Swahili pop poured out of ghetto blasters on every corner, garish and cheerful like the streets themselves. In the eating-house, though, the sound came from a CD system. Either the disc or the player was faulty and the music would get through just five bars before skipping back and repeating the same five-bar phrase.

Like any Englishman, I waited in confident expectation for someone to change the track. No one did. The waiters went about their business, the owner sat at his table filling out bills, the diners appeared oblivious. After five minutes I was grinding my teeth. After ten minutes I started humming in an attempt to set up a rival sound world in my head as a distraction. It was hopeless. I gave up and measured the duration of the five bars: just under five seconds. Each minute, the phrase was repeated roughly twelve times.

The other customers seemed heedless of it, their attention fixed on the business of eating. Either their thoughts were in a place where the noise could not reach them, or apathy gave them a kind of protective resilience. In any event, here was evidence of an awesome capacity for detachment that I would do well to mark.

Then the thought came to me: this was the test. Many petty irritations lay ahead, crowded buses, frontier queues, street hassles, experiences more challenging than mere noise. For enduring in Africa, however, this was a starter: one had to be able to pass the Five-Bar Test. When I left half an hour later the same five bars were still playing.

ALLY SYKES WAS an unlikely name for a Zulu and Dar es Salaam an unusual place to find one of Shaka's people. Ally was one of the most prosperous businessmen in Dar, kept a house on Hampstead Heath and had educated his numerous children at British public schools. Yet he had been a leading light in the founding of Nyerere's socialist Tanu party.

It was all quite simple, he explained. His grandfather, Sykes Mbowane, came from Zululand, having adopted the name Sykes from an English employer. The Germans recruited Sykes Mbowane in 1888 as part of a mercenary Zulu force to drive the Arabs from the coastal area around Bagamoyo and, after the job was done, he stayed on. His son duly took a German name, Kleist, during the period of the Kaiser's rule, and fought with General von Lettow Vorbeck's *Schutztruppe*, which led the British East Africa Expeditionary Force such a merry dance from 1914 to 1918.

After the war, Germany lost its colonies and the territory fell under a British mandate, so the family dropped the name Kleist and reverted to Sykes. And when the Second World War broke out, Ally volunteered for the King's Africa Rifles. Thus, while the father fought against the Crown, the son fought for it, seeing action in Burma and ending the war as a staff sergeant, the highest rank attainable by an African.

'I can tell you, if there had been no war, there would have been no *uhuru*,' he said. 'When I joined up, we thought the whites were gods and the Asians were demigods. Then we got to Asia, and we saw there was poverty – more poverty than in Africa. We mixed with the white soldiers. We saw them get drunk like us, and go out looking for girls. In Bombay we were waiting to go home and I said, ''Hey, these Indians are talking about independence. Why not us?'' That was even before Nyerere got involved.'

He had an unremarkable office in a typically rundown block of Dar. The floor was carpetless, paint peeled from the walls and the only decor consisted of school and university certificates of Ally's children. Even at the age of seventy-two he was a broad, powerful man with a great hoary head, an African version of Anthony Quinn. When he laughed, which he did easily and frequently, his mouth opened like a walrus's. There was something unnerving about him though, a lurking ferocity.

Why, I asked, had Nyerere's socialism failed?

'We Africans are much more capitalist than Europeans. I told Nyerere. I said, "You know yourself that no African will be respected unless he has a farm and cattle."'

So why then had Africa failed to develop under capitalism?

'The problem is the Asians. They corrupt everything. They are here to milk the blacks.' Suddenly there was real venom in the genial countenance. 'They must go, by force if necessary.' He spat it out.

Like Idi Amin did in Uganda?

'Amin's mistake was he did not replace the Asians with intelligent Africans.'

But now Museveni had invited the Asians back and Uganda was booming.

'You can't trust them. They will always keep to themselves. Take the British Legion clubs here or in Kenya. You will find blacks and whites drinking together. But Asians do not have Africans at their clubs. The Asian is like that. He thinks differently to us.'

The last time I had heard racism expressed as virulently was in South Africa. Now here was this old monster, a regular at the British Legion and a lion of the diplomatic circuit, fêted as a jovial cove with good connections and a deliciously indiscreet line in gossip. If any demur was raised about his attitude to Asians, it was dismissed as an eccentric quirk, Ally's little *thing*.

What about the differences between black and white, I asked.

'That's another question. We have a similar understanding, we can talk straight,' he said. He winked conspiratorially. 'And we can share a joke.'

THE OLD SLAVERS' route continued to define the way to the interior. When Burton and Speke left the coast, the track swung south-west out of Bagamoyo towards the Uluguru mountains, then turned north-west, through the wilderness of the Wagogo country towards the Arab stockade at Tabora before proceeding directly west across the Malagarasi river to the Inland Sea. Forty-seven years later, the Ost Afrikanische Eisenbahn Gesellschaft was formed, to build a railway that would trace the explorers' footsteps. To this day it is the only land link from the coast to Lake Tanganyika.

The Germans were late to start African railroads. The Uganda Railway, the British line from Mombasa to the lake region, had been in operation for four years before the first track was laid from Dar es Salaam towards Ujiji in 1905. The terrain was, if anything, more difficult – albeit without the complication of man-eating lions which plagued the British around Tsavo – but the Germans' work rate was exemplary. Tabora, 530 miles away, was reached in 1912, two years ahead of schedule, and the lake in 1914. The first locomotive completed the 795-mile run from Dar just seven months before the outbreak of war.

In colonial times the journey took thirty-nine hours. The buffet car was well-stocked, compartments offered sleeping accommodation and, as I had heard from a friend who used to be a district commissioner near Kigoma, the journey was regarded as a pleasant prelude or coda to home leave. Now, according to travellers' reports, there was no certainty of food or drink and even less about the time of arrival.

In the late afternoon passengers and friends milled around carriage windows in a colourful riot involving the wrestling of suitcases and bulky packages through tight openings. Most of the passengers wore their best outfits, as though for a festival. One family boarding a third-class carriage was especially resplendent: the father, a tall, angular young man, wore a tropical suit of Graham Greene era and vintage and an emerald green tie, his wife a dazzling African print outfit; she carried a baby on her back in a vivid swaddling cloth of red, green and orange squares; their son, about four, wore a turquoise jump suit in which his little torso was sweating like a yam cooked in a banana leaf. I saw them again after they had spent two nights in third class; their clothing was a bit dishevelled but their dignity was intact and their appearance remained somehow radiant.

The train pulled out precisely on time at 5 p.m. I had a 1915 map of Dar es Salaam which showed the town limits ending in a grove of coconut palms about 500 yards down the track. Now the train ran through mile after mile of shanty suburbs, each with a dustbowl football ground at its centre surrounded by breeze-block homes under rusting corrugated iron roofs. Late on a weekend afternoon, the touchlines were packed but the passing of the train, an event which occurred a mere four times a week, was sufficient for a game to come to a temporary halt while crowd and players turned to wave.

When Burton and Speke set out in June 1857 their objective was not so much 'the coy sources of the White Nile', as Burton put it, as ascertaining the limits of the 'Sea of Ujiji', the vast inland lake known only by repute from Arab travellers. The two men had made one previous journey together, a brief and disastrous foray to Somaliland, but at this stage there was no hint of the tragedy ahead. Burton, the dazzling polymath, soldier, swordsman, linguist, ethnographer and eroticist, was unquestionably the leader. Speke, a rather inarticulate man with a seemingly placid nature, worshipped him like an elder brother.

They were equipped on a heroic scale. In addition to their food and camping requirements, the 130 porters carried books, medicines, tools, cases of brandy, muskets, cutlasses, medicines and scientific instruments including two chronometers, two prismatic compasses, two sextants, a sundial, rain guage, barometer and pedometer, all of which had been lost or stolen long before they reached Lake Tanganyika. Among their miscellanea were two dozen penknives, two thousand fishing hooks, seven canisters of snuff, arsenical paste for specimens and one Union Jack. But neither man had brought adequate clothing and by the end both were reduced to rags stitched together from blankets.

Little navigation was required as the caravan followed trails running from one village to the next and occasionally encountered parties coming the other way with ivory or slaves, but the prevailing mood among the porters was fear of the unfamiliar: stories circulated about hostile tribes who were unerring shots with poisoned arrows; of rhinoceroses able to kill hundreds of men in a single charge; and of armies of elephant which fell upon camps at night. Partly as a result, the expedition was to be plagued by desertion. Burton claimed that over the two years of the journey, every man attempted to desert, including Sidi Bombay, who was in charge of the bearers and was beginning his own considerable career in African exploration.

Of even greater concern was the explorers' susceptibility to sickness and disease. They had barely left the coast before suffering their first bouts of the malaria that was to afflict them almost constantly. Sunstroke prostrated them. Their legs swelled and their eyes became infected; at various stages both suffered blindness. When ill they initially rode on mules but as the animals were whittled away by tsetse fly they had to be carried in hammocks slung on poles between porters. They were tormented by mosquitoes, scorpions, ulcers, insomnia and flesh-eating ants. One night, Speke awoke to find a beetle burrowing into his ear 'like a rabbit at a hole' and in trying to extricate it with a knife succeeded only in perforating his eardrum, which became agonisingly infected.

The coastal belt extended for about ninety miles inland across the hardest country they would encounter, a combination of swamp and jungle 'monotonous to the eye and palling to the imagination', as Burton put it, a steaming miasma from which an odour of sulphur arose and where 'the traveller might fancy a corpse to be hidden behind every bush'. Marching from dawn until late morning, when they made camp and spent the rest of the day writing up their notes and journals, it took them four weeks to clear the coastal belt and reach the Uluguru mountains. Once the high ground was attained the going became easier. By then, however, a problem more intractable than any of the others was emerging.

No two less suitable companions for such a journey could be imagined. Speke's outward affability concealed a burning ambition and a growing resentment of the older man's condescending manner. It did not help that he had little interest in their surroundings besides hunting. 'Nothing could surpass these plains for dull sameness, the people are the same, everywhere in fact the country is one vast senseless map of sameness,' he wrote in a fit of depression.

Burton, opinionated and domineering, was absorbed by everything. He learnt Swahili and took notes on geology, zoology and botany. He remarked on the quality of the local *cannabis indica* – 'a fine large species' – while demonstrating his breadth of acquaintance with the subject whether 'the *bang* of Persia, the *bhang* of India, the *benj* of Arabia, the *fasukh* of northern and the *dakha* of southern Africa'. Above all, he immersed himself in the study of ethnography and here the contrast with his companion was perhaps most acute.

Burton believed, like virtually all of his contemporaries, that Africans were inferior to Europeans. But, as his biographer, Fawn Brodie, has written, he was unlike most in seeking a scientific explanation for racial differences. He attributed African torpor to the effects of climate and disease, and 'degradation' to the slave trade. Witchcraft, he believed, was the source of a debilitating 'fear which ignores love'. He did a good deal to promote the notion of black men as sexual athletes but did not simply take at face value the envious whisperings about penis size and staying power; he claimed to have measured a Somali 'who, when quiescent, numbered nearly six inches', and to have evidence that Africans could prolong intercourse for an hour, yet be 'capable of performing twice during the night'.

Speke simply believed in African inferiority because of the biblical curse on the sons of Ham, a notion that Burton dismissed as 'beastly humbug'.

Brodie summed it up eloquently: 'Burton was like a sponge, Speke a stone. For Burton the natives were an intoxicant and a passion. Even when repelled he observed and recorded with a minuteness Speke found incomprehensible. Perhaps he sensed too that Burton held his own solid British virtues in contempt and found him to be not only a dull fellow but an intolerable prig. If so it was Africa first of all that came between them.'

Central Line, Tanzania: Thursday, 13 March

LUNCH IN THE dining-car is a pleasant surprise, served by an engaging moon-faced young man whose tie-pin said that his name is Love. He brought a large pitcher of water and a basin to the table and I was about to make a fool of myself when he indicated that it was not for drinking, but washing. Remarkably the beer was still cold and the usual chicken and rice came with a fiery chilli sauce. Even the overhead fan worked.

Briefly the train stopped at a small station where the woman at the next table, one of an exotic trio of prostitutes from Burundi, started to bargain noisily with a youngster outside selling three live chickens. The usual ritual was played out. She lifted one of the birds through the window before proclaiming it inferior and disdainfully handing it back. Before the ritual could reach its proper climax, however, the whistle went for the train's departure. Suddenly she was up, demanding to know what the youth's best price was. But now it was his turn to be offhand and as the train jolted into motion she sat down in a furious sulk.

Gaggles of urchins descend on the train at every station with coconuts, fruit and corn cooked over wood but their salesmanship is perfunctory and well before departure they have returned to their game of soccer beside the track. One which I observed today involved a goal of two sticks topped off with plaited palm fronds and a ball made from a chunk of foam rubber sewn into a cotton bag. The boys soared and darted for this object like performing seals, delighted to have an audience before which to display their skills. Sir Richard Turnbull, the last governor of Tanganyika, said that Britain had brought only two things of lasting value to the country; the English language and football. Both have endured.

The Jeremiahs are confounded. This is rail travel as it ought to be: unhurried and comfortable in a basic sort of way, and there is every sign that we will get to Kigoma in the morning. I felt a brief pang of guilt about travelling first class; what would Wilfred [Thesiger] say? But at $32 for a journey covering 800 miles and saving two nights in a hotel there can be no questions about value for money and there will be discomforts enough without looking for them. I shall go second class on the next leg.

Farahahi is an ideal companion in a small compartment, a police detective heading back to his post in Kigoma from leave and discretion itself, deflecting my questions about the nature and scale of crime in the lake region with polite vagueness. Like all the Tanzanians I have met, he is beautifully mannered, interested but never intrusive. Last night he showed me how to wedge the length of wood provided in the compartment against the window to prevent thieves breaking in. Cat burglars are said to prowl the roofs of carriages at night in search of open windows through which to swing, although the agility and daring required for such a career defy belief.

Overnight we left behind the palms and swamps of the coastal plain and the sun came up today on the African savannah with which I have been familiar since childhood. It is hard to fathom how so empty a landscape can still hold one in its power. The only features to rise above the scrub and thorn bush that stretches from horizon to horizon are the baobab trees, frozen as if in alarm like giant scarecrows.

This route was followed by generations of Nyamwezi, the indefatigable tribe of porters employed by the explorers and traders. Harry Johnstone remarked: 'What other race would be content to trudge twenty miles a day with a burden of 60 lb and be regaled on nothing but maize and beans?'; and their skills were so valued that the Germans prevented their movement to British territory. But we are now passing through the land of the Wagogo, Tanzania's least envied people. Looking out on this void, one is struck by the absence of opportunity for improvement or escape. The odd settlement consists of a few mud and thatch huts of a type unchanged for centuries, a mournful looking cow and a straggly maize patch. No road reaches here, no enterprise, only the train which passes four times a week. What hope does this bring to the naked child squatting in the dust, or the teenage girl in rags, barely out of childhood herself but already with a baby on her breast? No more than did the caravan of the explorers passing by this very way 140 years ago.

My greatest discomfort is that the ice in the zinc tub behind the bar has all melted, and the beer is now warm.

3. The Inland Sea

Ujiji, Lake Tanganyika: Saturday, 15 March

THE INLAND SEA WAS slow to reveal itself. Although no more than a few hundred yards away, the longest freshwater lake in the world, 420 miles from north to south and covering almost 14,000 square miles, was quite invisible.

I stood at the top of the village where the *matatu* dropped me from Kigoma, looking round for some indication of the direction in which it lay. A faded wooden sign painted 'memorial' was the only clue. A rutted dirt path sloped down through an avenue of palms and mud-and-pole huts from which children chirruped like crickets, '*Mzungu*, hello *mzungu*.' Finally, out of the black-green foliage of a mango tree, an iridescent shard emerged.

In Burton's case the disclosure was so gradual that he was initially dismayed. His first glimpse of the Sea of Ujiji was a streak of light that suggested little more than a pond and he cursed his folly for having endured such hardships over the eight-month march for so poor a prize. Then, advancing a few yards, 'the whole scene burst upon my view, filling me with admiration, wonder and delight. Forgetting toils, dangers and the doubtfulness of return, I felt willing to endure double what I had endured.'

This coyness of the lake to show itself is part of its allure. Since arriving in Kigoma yesterday I have come to it from different points and there seems always to be a moment of revelation. Moreover, like all natural features with the power to enchant, its mood shifts constantly. At dawn today it was a tranquil sheet of colourless glass. Later it turned ugly and brown under a heavy sky and choppy little waves broke on the beach. Yesterday at sunset I sat transfixed at the water's edge as the sun fell away towards the rumpled blue mountains of Zaire in the west, then dropped over the edge, drawing the two elements of air and water together into a single blazing arc of copper.

It was not just the spell of the place that convinced Burton he had solved the riddle of the Nile, but logic. The mountains visible on the western side are about forty miles away, while to north and south the waters run away seemingly without end. In their explorations of the lake by boat, the explorers reached neither extremity. Even so, it was clear that the Sea of Ujiji, or Tanganyika as it was known by the lacustrine peoples, was the largest freshwater lake yet known outside North America. This *had* to be the fountain of the Nile.

The mango tree through which I first glimpsed the lake also concealed the memorial. Fourteen years after Burton and Speke became the first white men to reach Lake Tanganyika, a second encounter took place. Livingstone and Stanley were here for different purposes, the missionary having been drawn into searching for the still-unresolved source of the Nile, the journalist for a scoop. If African exploration can be said to have had a symbolic nexus, it is surely here at Ujiji.

The memorial to two Englishmen is better kept than most modern state buildings in Tanzania, as if by a secret and capricious hand dedicated to maintaining relics of a forgotten past. A concrete path lined by canna lilies rises to a mound set against the backdrop of a vast mango tree and surrounded by blossoming trees and shrubs – pink and white frangipani, purple bougainvillea and scarlet poinsettia. The monument, erected by the colonial administration, is an ugly thing, a cairn of stone blocks engraved with an outline of Africa superimposed by a cross; a bronze plaque, donated by the Royal Geographical Society, reads: 'Under the mango tree which then stood here Henry M. Stanley met David Livingstone 10 November 1871'.

Ujiji had been founded by the Arabs as a slave-trading centre around 1840. Its reputation was dreadful. Livingstone, who had learnt to rub along with the slavers when necessary, detested the place. 'This is a den of the worst kind of slave traders,' he wrote. 'Those who I met at Urungu and Itawa were gentlemen traders. The Ujiji slavers, like the Kilwa and the Portuguese, are the vilest of the vile.'

At the water's edge a dozen or so fishing craft lurched on the crest of small waves. They were handsome and substantial vessels, low and broad in the beam, high at the prow. Similar craft landed here to disgorge slaves in Livingstone's day, having crossed from the other side of the lake where Tippu Tib maintained the raiding outpost of his empire. Now the boats are bringing across a new human cargo from the distant blue mountains of Zaire to the west. Refugees – albeit refugees able to afford the $15 a head in hard currency demanded by boatmen – are fleeing civil war. African armies are rightly notorious for their handling of civilian populations and there is no sign that Laurent Kabila's rebel guerrillas are any better than the norm. Even on the boats the refugees are not out of danger. There are stories of engines failing and overloaded boats foundering on the lake with the loss of anything up to eighty lives.

The beach settlement was a seething little place with a hard edge. Among

the huts made from plaited palm fronds were the suspicious faces of a
community dependent upon illicit or surreptitious trafficking. For the first
time I have sensed some of that brittleness of the African trouble zone. It
is felt in a place where the easy laughter is suddenly not heard, it shows in
stony eyes and hard appraising looks, and it coalesces around groups in
which one figure, with the cool contemptuous lip of the strong man, stands
out.

KIGOMA LAY JUST up the lake from Ujiji. Like most colonial towns, it was
located a decent distance from the native settlement. These days though,
Ujiji and Kigoma are consorts and *matatus* constantly ply the ten-mile run
over the hills.

The *matatu* is the transport system of the African masses, and an agent
of almost revolutionary change. Where a generation ago peasants were tied
to the land from birth to death, the coming of cheap mobility – in the form
of networks of Japanese minibuses criss-crossing the continent, leaping
borders – has altered the demographic shape of Africa. It has also made
Africa's roads the most dangerous in the world. I was to travel a good deal
by *matatu* but my appreciation of their convenience and reliability as a
means of travel was always tempered by apprehension. And at times I was
frightened almost to death.

My first experience that morning had been nasty and brutish, if mercifully
short. Setting out from Kigoma, I had looked over the white vans jostling
with one another on the red earth like termites. Each had a legend stencilled
on the windscreen, a sort of mantra to attract passengers. I was not taken
with either Bongo Wagon or Sugar Baby. Dear Mama was too wistful and
One Lord King too pious. Big Boss and Top Squad were slightly ominous
while No Time to Waste and Over The Top ruled themselves out. In the end
I opted for the neutral-sounding Mwanga, named after an early Bagandan
monarch.

It was a bad choice. The driver was a hatchet-faced cowboy in white
shoes and sharp T-shirt determined to pass anything that moved, despite
the poor state of a road that obliged oncoming traffic to veer into the middle
to avoid pot-holes. His taste in taped music was execrable too, the worst
sort of 'yo-bitch-who-ya-callin-muthafucka' American rap. Although I was
in a privileged front seat position, insulated from the seething mound of
bodies in the back, it was an unpleasant journey.

Matatu stands are places where the stratification of African society is
immediately visible. Here boys become men and men become demigods,

with power not only over mobility but life and death itself. As befits members of a dangerous profession, the drivers are swaggering dudes, their conductors street-wise youths handling fistfuls of banknotes as coolly as any Las Vegas high-roller. In this hierarchy, passengers are only one step up from the vendors who hustle drinks or fruit and dream of becoming conductors.

As ever though, status is a deceptive thing. The most powerful figure in this chain, the *matatu* owner, is not even visible. Most drivers lease their vehicles and pay out a large chunk of their takings before dividing any profits on an agreed basis with their conductors. Each has a role in maximising the potential of their partnership – the conductor to squeeze as many bodies into the available space and the driver to cover the route as rapidly as possible. The twin imperatives of crowding and speed are what make *matatus* so perilous.

I decided to return to Kigoma by Cobra Line, for despite the menacing legend the driver had a sympathetic face. It was pleasing to find my instinct vindicated: he had better road manners and his tapes were reggae and Zairean electric; and I realised, as I nestled between a large lady's bosom and the spare wheel, that the discomfort of the back had its compensations. You felt a lot less vulnerable. Africans tend to opt for the front seat if given a choice, while the few whites I met who used *matatus* went for the back. Not that there is much difference; in high-speed crashes there are few survivors.

I FOUND THE hotel in Kigoma with the help of a lady I met along the way. Armed only with a sketch map, I had been tramping down a muddy Lumumba Street for about twenty minutes and was beginning to think I had lost my way when she appeared from behind a tree.

Did she know the way to the Lake Hotel? In reply she asked if I spoke Swahili.

'*Nafurahi sana kukuona*' I said. This was my standard conversational gambit and means roughly, I am very pleased to make your acquaintance.

Up to now this had been greeted with hoots and guffaws of derision, but now it produced a crow of delight and a high five. She pointed the way to the hotel and in English invited me, entirely without archness, to her club in the evening. 'Cold beer, fish and chips, dancing . . .' Clearly, my accent was improving.

The Lake Tanganyika Beach Hotel was a relic of colonial times, rather frayed but clean and a travellers' delight. Its appeal had nothing to do with nostalgia: there was no faded sign pointing to the Ladies' Powder Room, as at the African House Hotel in Zanzibar, or the Dornford Yates novels in a glass-fronted bookcase at the Outspan Hotel in the Kenya Highlands. What the Lake Tanganyika Beach offered was courtesy and a view overlooking the lake that one might happily contemplate in the hour of death. The English convention that breakfast is not complete without an egg endures, and here, under a thatch umbrella, I feasted beside the lake every morning on an omelette and fresh fruit.

Courtesy was the feature of Tanzania which, I confess, had surprised me the most. My only previous attempt to visit the country had not been encouraging. Travelling on the Tazara railway with my wife in 1976, we were set upon by immigration officials, abused, arrested, marched off the train under armed guard and sent packing back to Zambia on no more than the suspicion that we might recently have passed through South Africa. The fact that we had done so did not reconcile me to the treatment we received.

Power and Africa appear uncongenial companions. Too often the meek and affable young man has been transformed by the possession of a Kalashnikov into an unstable brute, the earnest graduate by some minor bureaucratic office into a vindictive pedant, the new leader assuming office with the promise of reform into yet another egregious autocrat. Yet now it was not only the grace of the humble which was touching, but the politeness, and an even rarer quality, kindness, of officials: the railway clerk going out of his way to find me a place on a packed train, the policeman taking pains to see me to my destination after being asked for directions. These services were all the more unexpected for being offered without any hope of reward.

Kigoma was a leafy and attractive little place with a single tarmac road curling up the hill towards Ujiji, lined with mango trees distinctive for the density of their foliage and fleshy leaves of a green so dark that the tree sometimes appeared black. The town was a combination of rusty native shanties and ponderous Germanic architecture, the yellowing railway station built to last until Doomsday and the whitewashed pile of the Kaiserhof on the hill which remained the headquarters of the local administration. Kigoma was comfortable with this ambiguity. A few streets had been renamed to reflect the era of independence but the changes were not wholesale, and imperialists had been left to co-exist with revolutionaries and nationalist heroes, Burton with Lumumba, Stanley with Nyerere.

This tolerance was reflected in Kigoma's attitude towards the refugees, not just those from Zaire, but the hundreds of thousands who had fled the holocausts of Rwanda and Burundi. Whereas the mood in Ujiji was edgy because of the refugee traffic, here the migrants were being left to improvise new lives. By night they found shelter at one of three United Nations camps. By day they emerged to trade. Private enterprise was flourishing by the roadside – a Burundian man barbering a customer on a wooden stool, a woman whose two children played under a mango tree while she roasted maize cobs over charcoal, a youth at a shoeshine stall bearing the legend 'Customer is the KING!'

The most striking thing about the refugees was the matter-of-fact way they went about their affairs. These were not the faces one associated with the images of African crises, haunted and dislocated casualties, enduring but helpless. The elderly woman and her daughter, calling out a greeting as they walked gracefully by with little bundles of possessions balanced on their heads, did not look like victims.

They had been walking for two weeks. When the ethnic killings started near their home in southern Burundi they wrapped a few essentials in bright cloths and turned away from the *shamba* where they lived by cultivating *matoke*, the plantain which is the staple of these parts. Living under open skies and by their wits, they walked south-east towards the Tanzania border. As Tutsis, they avoided Hutu settlements when it was possible, although in one place it had been a Hutu woman who gave them food when their few grubby banknotes, hoarded and wrapped in an even grubbier handkerchief, ran short. They also avoided the men in uniform whose behaviour could never be predicted. Nearing the border, they simply walked off into the bush – which in these parts is very thick, and dramatically beautiful – and crossed into Tanzania without even knowing it. They had probably covered 160 miles since setting out, and now were about to present themselves at the local office of the United Nations High Commissioner for Refugees.

A local UN worker told me the flow of Burundian refugees had slowed but there were still around 170,000 in the district. Now it was Zaireans who were arriving at the rate of about 1,500 a day and this influx of a further 90,000 from across the lake had strained local patience as well as aid resources. The Burundians were thought of as placid folk, amenable to administration, but the Zaireans had a reputation for being difficult.

'It's as if they believe we owe them,' the UN worker, an Australian, said. 'I mean, of course we're here to help. But we had a riot at a Zairean camp the other day because there was a hold-up in food supplies. They can be awkward bastards.'

He paused. 'Weird too,' he went on. 'There's been talk about witchcraft at one of the holding centres for weeks. A few days ago an old couple arrived on their own. One of our people saw them going down to the water supply. The next thing a mob attacks them, starts stoning them. By the time our people got there they were dead. Everyone was standing around yammering that these were the witches who had come to poison the water supply.'

He was a gawky young engineer just three months out of Melbourne. He shook his head. 'Weird,' he said again.

I STARTED UP the hill to find the grave of a missionary failure. It was a good sweaty climb to the little Anglican church, but before reaching it I was hailed by an elderly gent with white whiskers in a dark three-piece suit.

'Are you going to pray up there?' he asked. I said what I was really looking for was the missionaries' graves.

'There are no graves up there,' he said emphatically.

'Where are the missionary graves, then?'

'Well,' he said, swaying, 'we have many graves. Over there' – sweeping a hand towards the hill opposite – 'we have Christian graves, Muslim graves, all sort of graves.'

I laughed. 'I am sorry,' he said, swaying again, 'I am a little drinked. Come, and we will look together for the graves of your missionaries.'

We finally found them on the hill opposite, at the end of a track. Bushes and shrubs grew restlessly across the little plot and billowed around the entrance, two stone pillars on which mould sharpened the blackened outline of a crucifix. Amid the turmoil of grass and weeds were two or three mounds. The headstones were gone and the resting place of John Boden Thomson was unmarked. This was all that remained of the London Missionary Society's expedition to central Africa in 1878.

Like so many of his calling, Thomson was a Scot, but he grew up knowing none of the wretchedness in which the young Livingstone was forged. Indeed, childhood indulgence made him a bit of a prig. In 1870 he was assigned to his first missionary posting, among the Matabele people of central Africa.

A new mood was on the rise in Britain. That year the writer and philosopher John Ruskin delivered a lecture at the Sheldonian Theatre in Oxford that inflamed a generation. 'Here is what England must do or perish,' Ruskin said. 'She must found colonies as fast and as far as she is able, formed of her most energetic and worthy men; seizing every piece of fruitful waste ground she can set her foot on . . . If we can get men, for little pay, to cast themselves against cannon-mouths for love of England, we may find men also who will plough and sow for her, who will behave kindly and righteously for her, and who will bring up their children to love her.'

Thomson was not the best example of the new generation and his first mission was an utter failure. His companions, a melancholy Yorkshireman named William Sykes and Thomas Morgan Thomas, a manic-depressive Welshmen, were ill-suited, and the Matabele were a warlike folk forbidden by their king, Lobengula, to follow the Gospel. After a demoralising encounter with the king Thomson wrote: 'He told me that God had given the Bible to the white man, but as He had not given it to the black man also, it was clear He did not mean the black man to have it.'

After five despairing years among the Matabele, Thomson's heart lifted at the receipt of orders to join an expedition to plant a new mission at Lake Tanganyika. The objective was nothing less than a living monument to the society's most revered son, Livingstone, in the place with which his name was synonymous, Ujiji. Thomson sailed for Zanzibar to join the expedition leader, Roger Price.

Price was no stranger to disaster in Africa. In 1859 he and a missionary named Holloway Helmore led their families, four adults and five children in all, 500 miles through the Kalahari desert to the source of the Zambezi where, one by one, they started to die. The last to go were Price's daughter and wife, who was so emaciated that in places her bones had broken through the skin. Only Price and two of the children reached safety.

After this harrowing experience, Price may not have been well suited to lead a new expedition. He and Thomson were at odds even before they started away from the coast, in July 1877. This time it was the pack animals which died one by one, bogged down in swamps. The expedition had not yet cleared the coastal belt when the last wagon had to be abandoned and the missionaries started to suffer bouts of fever. At this stage Price, haunted by memories and intimations of catastrophe, recognised that the project was inherently flawed and announced he was returning to advise the directors that a mission could be set up at Ujiji only after supply stations had been established along the route. Now he and Thomson quarrelled openly. The party divided, three other members carrying on with Thomson. They were still 600 miles from Ujiji.

Fever afflicted them all. Thomson was also haemorrhaging internally and had to be supported as they limped along. But his tongue had lost none of its sharpness, especially towards the younger brethren, who came to dread their leader's disapproval. As the party stumbled agonisingly towards Ujiji, Thomson became increasingly isolated from his companions, and their peril. He wrote to the directors in a shaking hand: 'Please do not let Mrs Thomson know I have been so ill. It would only make her anxious for nothing.'

On a day in late August, when the weather was fine and mild, he received his reward with the sight of the inland sea. For a few days he rallied. 'I cannot tell you how pleased we were to get here,' he wrote to the directors. 'We have found a most healthy-looking site for our station close on Kigoma Bay. It is the highest hill here.' Soon afterwards he suffered an apoplectic attack. His companions nursed him for a week, immersing his body in water to bring down the raging temperature. Then he died. He was thirty-seven and in eight years had failed to make a single convert.

Although Price's judgement had been amply vindicated, the directors were looking for scapegoats rather than explanations and he was disgraced. Now Joseph Mullens, the society's foreign secretary, determined to find out for himself just what it was that made central Africa so uncongenial to missionary activity. A month after setting out from Zanzibar, he died of fever.

After that the society abandoned Ujiji. In a flash of unusual candour, an official report noted that this 'painfully fascinating story stands as a striking example of how great missionary enterprises ought not to be attempted'.

THE LITTLE ANGLICAN church stood on a spur of the hill identified by Thomson, across the valley from his grave. I had intended to pause just for a moment but a service was in progress and a sidesman who spotted me bustled up and shepherded me to a pew.

The crude whitewashed walls, unadorned by images or symbols, were surmounted by wooden rafters and a roof of corrugated iron which radiated eddies of heat down on the congregation. Relief came with a light air wafting in through large glassless windows that looked out to the lake. Even so, I was soon sweating profusely. We were tightly bunched on the pews, 350 people or so, and I was pressed up against a corpulent man.

I was in a reverie when he nudged me. 'You must go up,' he said.

'What?'

'You must go up. The minister wants you to introduce yourself to everyone.'

From the back, I walked up the aisle, aware of the buzz at the appearance of a *mzungu* which trailed me like a slipstream. Grinning foolishly, I was enfolded in the arms of the minister at the lectern. 'Now you tell us about yourself,' he said firmly. 'I will translate.'

I did it as best I could. I said I was from a town named Windsor, near London, that I brought greetings from Anglicans in Britain. I told them a little about my journey, I said I loved their country and thanked them for their hospitality. At the end I said: *'Nafurahi sana kukuona.'* This went down very well and I returned to my seat amid applause and shining faces.

The rest of the service occupied almost two hours. An animated pastor, who somewhat resembled Archbishop Desmond Tutu, gave an extended sermon in sonorous tones; a youth group improvised a piece of theatre that I was unable to follow but which induced a general state of hilarity; the singing was lovely.

At the door the minister embraced me again. 'Come back, Stephen,' he said.

I was halfway down the hill before it suddenly struck me that I had missed an opportunity. What I should have said was that the *Quini Ingrezi* (Queen Elizabeth), also lived in Windsor and, if she had known I was going to speak to an Anglican congregation in Africa, she would have wanted me to pass on her greetings. It might have sounded twee, but I know they would have loved it.

AFTER A FEW days by the water I could imagine how painful it must have been for the explorers to drag themselves away from the lake and start back into that fearful void, back into the inferno described by the most indefatigable of them all, Henry Stanley:

> . . . the torrid heat, the miasma exhaled from the soil, the giant cane-grass suffocating the wayfarer, the rabid fury of the native guarding every entry and exit, the unspeakable misery of life, the utter absence of every comfort, the bitterness which each day heaps upon the poor white man's head, and the little – too little – promise of success one feels on entering it.

Each evening at the hotel I took a table beneath a thatch umbrella on the grass leading down to the edge of the lake. It was the day's reward, the dried sweat and crusted grime showered off and a cold Safari at hand, looking across that miraculous stretch of water at the fireworks of sunset. One evening a malachite kingfisher, a dazzling creature the size of a large, stubby thumb, preened himself on a reed. He took off, and at a height of about thirty feet above the water poised, a beak almost as long as his body pointing down like a tiny harpoon, body arched and frozen, wings a blur, before plunging like a stone into the water with a surprising splash. For an instant he disappeared entirely, then burst through the surface again with a fish, a filament of silver seemingly impaled on a needle. It was the most exquisite and perfect act of hunting I had ever seen.

Later, poring over a map, the majesty of the place became even more clear. The world's longest lake was also the deepest after Lake Baikal, a great cleft in Africa's surface. Imagine standing on the edge of an escarpment running 200 miles in either direction and falling away almost vertically to a depth of a mile and the dimensions may become more clear. The grandeur does not stop with Tanganyika. The map shows a great chain of lakes. Starting with Lake Malawi, another awesome gash 350 miles in length with fjord-like depth, the chain swings in a curve up through Tanganyika and curls back through lakes Kivu, Edward and Albert. This vast semi-circular fissure in the earth's crust, almost 2,000 miles in length, is now largely forgotten as the western branch of the Great Rift Valley. That term has come to mean the eastern rift, which breaks away at the top of Lake Malawi and turns north-east through Tanzania, passes through the middle of Kenya, rises into the Ethiopian Highlands, plunges into the Danakil Depression and runs up the length of the Red Sea all the way to the Lebanon.

There is, however, a symbolic as well as geographic wholeness to the two rifts. Joined at Lake Malawi in the south and Lake Turkana in the north, they enfold in a great oval a bed of territory that might be likened in shape and function to a womb in Africa's body. For here, at Olduvai Gorge and along the banks of Turkana, were made the discoveries of the Leakey family, culminating in the fossils of *Homo erectus* and *Homo habilis*, that have certified this as the cradle of mankind. Burton, infatuated as he was by Lake Tanganyika, was closer to the mark than he realised when he wrote of 'this African Eden'.

Burton and Speke were at Ujiji for three months. While Burton interrogated the inhabitants, Speke bartered for the use of vessels to explore the lake. Now, once only, came the chance of a discovery that would have forestalled years of feuding and geographic controversy. They set off in canoes to find the river at the lake's northern tip. From chiefs and traders they received contradictory reports: some said the river flowed into the lake, some that it flowed out. The point was fundamental: if it flowed in, the river could not be the Nile, and the lake could not be its source. The balance of the reports favoured that alternative, but the issue was destined to remain unresolved. When only a few days from the northern mouth their boatmen refused to go further, for fear of cannibals. Both men were thoroughly done in and one suspects they did not protest much. In any event, they arrived back in Ujiji after a month on the lake, no more certain on this critical question than when they set out.

In May 1858 Burton gazed back at the lake for the last time. 'The charm of the scenery was perhaps enhanced by the reflection that I might never look upon it again,' he wrote. In later years he could still claim the satisfaction of being the first European to see the inland sea, but by then the memory was tainted by knowledge that what he had discovered was the source not of the Nile, but the Congo.'

Tabora: Wednesday, 17 March

THE TRAIN FROM Kigoma got in at 6 a.m. The little second-class compartment was packed and stuffy, heaving during the night with bodies, snoring, grunting, muttering. In the thin light of dawn I wrestled the rucksack from the train and walked the half-mile or so to the first hotel. An omelette and lady-finger bananas restored the spirit.

In town I met Jemaal, a tall and willowy young man with a battered Toyota for hire. Like most folk here, he was a Nyamwezi, the Bantu people who were the Arabs' most formidable rivals for control of the trade route. During the mid-nineteenth century, these were badlands, and the Nyamwezi chief, Mirambo, built an empire on porterage, trade and war. I like the description in my history volume of Mirambo's army of mercenaries, the dreaded *ruga-ruga*: 'Distinctive with red cloak, feather head-dress, ivory and copper ornaments, they are somewhat reminiscent of the predatory companies of the European Hundred Years' War, attaching themselves to whichever leader held out most hope of plunder.'

Jemaal evidently had hopes of plunder, too, and was saddened to discover that I was a scrawny prize. But pickings are leaner on the old trade route these days and eventually we settled on a price for the round-trip to Kazeh.

Once a crossroads, Tabora is now more a dead end, isolated by the collapse of Tanzania's road system. The tarmac broke up as soon as we left town. After about five miles the road trailed off into a track, gouged and rent by stormwaters, that would have challenged a Land Rover. Jemaal, his face set in a rictus of determination, forged gamely on, the Toyota bucking and grinding, until with a shudder and a bang we came to a halt, a rear wheel sunk in a trench.

I was beginning to have my doubts. The Toyota was not just stuck, it was steaming and looked fit to explode. I feared that Jemaal might decide on reflection that his fee had been insufficient or, worse still, discover damage to the car, turn nasty and summon the local *ruga-ruga* to secure adequate compensation.

'I could walk from here,' I suggested.

He would not hear of it. Gesturing towards a couple of wide-eyed and naked children who had appeared from a thatch hut, he shot out an order. One scurried away and came back with a *badza*, a short-handled hoe. Jemaal started to hack away at the sides of the trench while ordering us to collect rocks and stones. Within half an hour we had built a bridge under the wheel, and the Toyota rolled free. Jemaal grinned triumphantly and I felt ashamed at my faint-heartedness. Rather more gingerly now, we sailed on.

It was Evelyn Waugh, in his dazzling little travel diary, *A Tourist in Africa*, who observed 'wherever you find old mango trees in East Africa, you are on the Arab slave-tracks'. I knew we had reached Kazeh when large green-black shapes billowed above the maize fields.

Even Burton, who rejoiced in its Arab inhabitants, never made great claims for the place. There was nothing, he wrote, that could properly be called a town; rather it was a 'scattered collection of oblong houses with central courts, garden plots, storerooms and outhouses for the slaves'. Only one of these Zanzibari dwellings survived amid the *shambas* and huts of the little settlement, although it was in remarkably good condition and had been kept as a museum. The Toyota's arrival was an occasion of astonishment then delight to the curator who had been weeks without a visitor and was slumbering on a chair beside the carved wooden door.

All the explorers seem to have stayed here, Livingstone and Stanley for a spell during which their friendship acquired a closeness that neither was able to achieve with anyone else. Burton lingered, too. Here, perhaps in the courtyard with the mango tree, he renewed his acquaintance with the Arab, Snay bin Amir, delighted to be back with 'the open-handed hospitality and the hearty good-will of this truly noble race' and contrasting it with 'the niggardness of the savage and selfish African'. The indulgence was to cost him dear. For now Speke was galvanised. From the slavers, the white men had heard of a second lake, even larger than Tanganyika, lying to the north. Speke, bored by the company of both Arab and African and tired of being patronised by Burton, decided to go in search of it.

Tomorrow I will take the train following in his trail.

4. The Nyanza

THE OVERNIGHT TRAIN TO Mwanza, seething with passengers in sweaty, hot darkness, brought back memories of long-ago railway journeys in India. Fleeing a swarming compartment, I set out in search of refreshment. In the dining-car an overhead light spread a thin ochre smear on the grimy walls. A few men sat around drinking warm beer. Two figures caught my eye.

One was a peasant woman with her head deep in a book. It came as a shock to realise that she was the first person I had seen reading since setting out. She wore a ragged skirt, a grubby T-shirt bearing the legend 'The Dark Secret' and had her hair tied up in a cheap purple scarf. Her book was entitled *Chinese Literature*. On the back cover was written *The Women's Trilogy*.

The second figure was an Asian in his thirties with a moustache and glassy smile who was drinking with a group of Africans. He noticed me and brought his beer over. He was a coffee trader, a wheeler and dealer in a notoriously sharp business, but had been cutting deals of various sorts all his life. He had made big money in the 'good years' under Mobutu in Zaire and had interests in Canada and Australia, where he had scraped under the immigration wire – 'it's hard to get in, but even harder for them to get you out'. He was tough, shrewd, sleek and cosmopolitan, an artist in the game of survival.

He asked where I was going next. Across Lake Victoria by ferry, I said. His face lit up with a look of demented glee. 'My wife was on the *Bukoba*,' he said, and sat grinning wildly at me.

I was stunned. Nine months earlier the grossly overloaded ferry *Bukoba* had been approaching her berth in Mwanza when she capsized. Well over 700 people were on the boat, which had a capacity of 430, and only those on the upper levels managed to scramble into the water. Many more could have been saved but rescue workers, who heard shouts and banging from those trapped in the air lock, drilled into the hull. As the air giving the *Bukoba* buoyancy rushed out, she sank like a stone. Only fifty-three survivors were picked up. Perhaps 700 people died, including a Ugandan businessman on whose body was found $27,000 in cash; the great majority were still entombed in the wreck at a depth of about ninety feet.

I must have looked horrified and muttered an apology. The man was obviously a maniac, perhaps demented by grief. His face was still flushed with mad excitement.

'No, no, you don't understand,' he said. 'She escaped.'

As he related it, he had always known the *Bukoba* was ill-fated. 'Even when it was empty it stood so,' he said, indicating a list to one side. 'I have worked in ships and I knew that was a bad one. I said to my wife, "If you are on that ship look out, and if anything happens, don't fight the water. You can't fight the water." When it happened, when the boat went over, she remembered. She just let herself go, and the water pulled her out. She could not swim, but she remembered, "don't fight the water." So she floated, and they rescued her.'

He was an Ismaili Muslim, one of a community living around Lake Victoria. I had thought him an unattractive, mercenary fellow. Yet he was typical of the outsider, grafted on to Africa by colonialism, who had endured and persevered as we, the Anglo-Saxons and Celts, had failed to do.

This fact was starting to affect my hopes for the journey. Since leaving Daudi Ricardo in Dar es Salaam, I had encountered not a single white who might be categorised as 'staying on'. That was not entirely unexpected. The flow of settlers to Tanganyika had been restricted under the British mandate and confined to two main farming areas, the Southern Highlands, where Daudi had his ranch, and the Arusha–Moshi region in the north; even there virtually no white farmers remained as they had lost their land in Nyerere's disastrous nationalisation of agriculture. Old age had carried off all but the last of a handful of diehards.

Nevertheless, it was a sobering thought that the nation which had once taken such pride in its imperial legacy had left so little of itself behind. A colonial census of Tanganyika in the 1950s recorded a white population of 18,000. In England I had met a number of them, former colonial servants whose task had been to prepare one of the Empire's most neglected territories for independence, and had been struck by their high-mindedness, their dedication and their genuine love for the country. All continued to wish Tanzania well, many maintained ties of friendship, some were active benefactors. Yet none had stayed on. It was as if their love of Africa had survived because of, rather than despite, their distance from it.

Here, on the other hand, was the descendant of one of the 80,000 Asians recorded by the census. They had consolidated and prospered. My companion had his bolt-hole in Australia to flee to if there should be an anti-Asian purge here. In the meantime, he was part of Africa, living from day to day, adapting for survival, disdaining complacency, mixing easily with blacks but totally without sentiment.

'One day they may send us out,' he said matter-of-factly as he moved off to rejoin the African drinkers. 'Sometimes they hate us, sometimes not. It comes and goes.'

THE FEATURELESS, GREEN landscape passing outside the train window had hardly changed in a thousand miles. I was reading *Nostromo* when Conrad's description of a hard peasant landscape in South America brought me upright with its echoes from 'a great land of plain and mountain and people, suffering and mute, waiting for the future in a pathetic immobility of patience'.

So it continued on the route that Speke followed north of Kazeh. Still, he made comparatively rapid progress and had covered about 200 miles in two weeks when a transformation came upon the landscape, hinting at the imminence of discovery. From the plains emerged at first hills, dotted with granite boulders. Then the hills closed in, rising on either side of a valley while the boulders multiplied, piling in chaotic profusion on top of one another but creating strangely logical formations – a great turmoil of grey shapes on which, here and there, improbably balanced, stood a single column of granite. As the train threaded its way down through this grotesque and capricious avenue, the Nyanza came slowly into view, a steely blue plate stretching away under a leaden sky.

From the moment he saw it, Speke was convinced: this and not Tanganyika was the goal of the quest. Standing on a hill near the modern town of Mwanza, he surveyed his prize and decided to name it Victoria in honour of his sovereign. He had no doubt, he wrote, 'that the lake at my feet gave birth to that interesting river, the source of which has been the subject of so much speculation. This is a far more extensive lake than the Tanganyika, so broad that you could not see across it, and so long that nobody knew its length.'

Speke's conviction was stronger than his reasoning. While it was true that nobody knew the Nyanza's size, the same could be said of Lake Tanganyika which, it turned out, was almost twice as long. He stayed at the Nyanza just three days, not long enough for even the rudimentary survey that he and Burton had carried out at Tanganyika. When he returned to Kazeh and declared that he had solved the Nile riddle, without advancing any evidence other than that of his eyes, Burton was dumbfounded; his dull lieutenant had suddenly become a deadly rival. In the furious debate that ensued after the explorers returned to London, each took up his position on the basis of prejudice, Speke because he had found the Nyanza, Burton because he had not.

Speke did not live to see the truth of his conviction verified. A year after their return, by which time he and Burton were bitter foes, Speke went back to Africa, this time with his own obedient deputy, James Grant. In an epic three-year journey they penetrated to the Nyanza and passed up the western shore to Buganda and the court of the Kabaka Mutesa; from there, Speke alone proceeded to the rapids at the northern outlet of the Nyanza where the White Nile took its rise, before rejoining Grant and continuing their march up the Nile to Cairo, cabling ahead 'the Nile is settled'.

But it was not, and now geographers divided into Burton and Speke factions. Livingstone, back from his own African explorations, joined the Burton camp. A public debate, almost in the nature of a gladiatorial contest, was arranged at the British Association in Bath for September 1864. It never took place. Out hunting on the eve of their confrontation, Speke discharged his shotgun into his chest and died within minutes.

Accident or suicide, it was never resolved. Burton hinted at the latter, aware that the suggestion of Speke having lost his nerve strengthened his own case. All the more bitter then must the truth have tasted fourteen years later when Stanley finally resolved the issue in Speke's favour. It was the most painful lesson of Burton's life. The prize had been within his grasp but he had failed to go the extra mile. In a poem reflecting on the tragedy of their venture, he acknowledged privately: 'I did but half.' To Speke – plodding, unattractive, repressed Anglo-Saxon Speke – belonged the glory.

Moreover, because he was the first European to visit Buganda, the most organised state yet to be encountered by the explorers, he became the bridge between Britain and East Africa.

FOR ALL THE grandeur of the approach to the lake, the site of Speke's discovery had evolved into a seedy, unappealing place. Mwanza is Tanzania's second largest town, comfortably poised to profit by commerce with Uganda and Kenya and the hundreds of islands on the lake, yet it exuded an air of defeat. I spent a morning walking the town, the sad and barren streets, the broken clocktower, and decided it was not a place to linger. Even the traders were forlorn; the fruit piled up in little pyramids was flaccid and the dull flesh of bog-eyed Nile perch, laid out in rusty wheelbarrows, broiled gently in the sun.

The granite pile of the Bismarck Rocks, rising near the water's edge, were as solid as the old Iron Chancellor himself. Another lakeside landmark had endured less well. The flowering shrubs and lawns of the Botanical Gardens – 'those inescapable amenities of the British Empire', as Jan Morris called them – had long since been consumed by more robust species. But here at least a small flame of spirit flickered. Into the vacuum had moved a woman of majestic proportions and enterprise.

She told me her name was Victoria, the combined legacy of being born by the lake and having a father who served in the King's Africa Rifles. A cheerful as well as ample sight in a gay rayon dress, she nevertheless had the focused gaze of the born commander. She was waging war on rampant papyrus and supervising a clean-up of botanical corpses that might have been bohenia and crocosmia. Three or four subordinates leapt to her orders.

Off to one side their campaign was starting to show gains. Victoria confirmed that the paddies at the lake edge were rice. Individual plants, flowers and vegetables, were being cultivated in plastic bags. She pointed to a thriving tomato crop. 'Very popular with the people,' she said. 'Veeery popular.' Her eyes flared in emphasising the point and she trilled it like the climax of a Bellini aria.

Clearly this venture was a relic of Nyerere's socialism, *ujamaa* co-operative farming in action. The soil was of excellent quality and water was abundant, so now, instead of providing a gracious setting for the leisure of a colonial elite, the gardens were supplying the needs of the masses. I asked Victoria if the gardens were the responsibility of the ruling party or some public body like the Mwanza council.

She looked blank. 'The party?' Then she shrugged. 'There is no party here. This is good land. We are using it. That is all.'

But what about the money, I asked. Surely under *ujamaa* the enterprise was regulated by the party.

'The money is for me,' Victoria said crisply.

AS WELL AS being a woman, Victoria was successful and a Sukuma. I hoped the combination would not prove malignant in her case, as it had been for so many before.

The Sukuma are the people of the southern lake region. They had a strongly developed chiefly system and a tradition of closely knit communities, a cohesiveness no doubt bolstered by a comparative blessing of resources, including fish from the lake. They were self-sufficient, having proved resistant to Christianity and Islam and suspicious of outside authority, whether colonial or post-colonial. Like most Bantu peoples, they retained their belief that witchcraft, *bulogi*, can be held responsible for almost any

trouble. The concept of good fortune or bad had no validity. That a hardwork-
ing grower might have his crop wiped out by a hailstorm while his lazy
neighbour was unaffected could be put down not to the caprice of nature,
but an intervention from the spirit world. The most likely source of harm
was thought to be the magic of an enemy employing sorcerers. In turn,
those who felt themselves afflicted would consult a diviner, or *nfumu*, to
identify the source. The *nfumu* could provide a charm or remedy but in
unresponsive cases dealing with witches became the business of elders who
considered allegations and meted out punishments, ranging from verbal
warnings and fines to ostracism. In rare and serious cases, witches could
be clubbed to death. The chief was the ultimate arbiter in all such matters.

Under the British, the chiefs were left in charge of grassroots administration. A great deal has been written, much of it critical, about this system
known as Indirect Rule, promoted by Lord Lugard in East and West Africa.
It was certainly not adopted for idealistic motives, but rather as a cost saving
method by which a handful of white officials could exercise a degree of
control over a vast domain. But while it is true to say that it did little to
prepare the great mass of Africans for the modern world, it did at least keep
the traditional social fabric intact during the colonial cataclysm.

At the same time, Indirect Rule set up a tension between the chiefs and
the new intelligentsia produced by colonial education, who constituted the
first wave of nationalist leaders. Tribal leadership became tainted with the
brush of collaboration. One of the first acts of the Nyerere government after
independence was to abolish the chiefs and vest their authority in party
officials. When I spoke to him, Daudi Ricardo, a party man himself,
described this social revolution as 'the biggest mistake we ever made'.

Whether there was a direct connection between social dislocation and
the mass killing of witches among the Sukuma cannot be said with certainty,
but both began in the early 1960s. What is clear is that once the killings
started they acquired a ferocious momentum of their own. In early reports
of witch-killing among the Sukuma it was noted that in Mwanza district,
mobs of men had taken to dealing with accused witches – usually women
– by chasing them and beating them to death with freshly cut branches. But
it was not until the 1970s that the practice became widespread. By then a
new factor was aggravating social disruption – the forced relocation under
Nyerere's *ujamaa* policy of entire communities into model villages. The
trauma was felt everywhere but particularly among those whose cultural
values were deepest, notably the Sukuma.

It would start with a whispering campaign, usually instigated by an envious or malicious neighbour. A woman with a good crop of sorghum or cotton was a typical target. In communities already suffering confusion, it did not take long for hysteria to take hold. As the killings spread so the ways of witch-slayers became more sophisticated. Instead of being hunted down by mobs, the supposed sorcerer would be hacked to death with a machete by a paid killer, part of whose fee was spent on his own ritual cleansing afterwards. Far from being outcasts, these hired assassins were a focus of public gratitude as, for a while at least, the demons of anxiety and panic that had gripped the community were laid to rest.

By the mid-1970s witch-killing in Sukumaland was serious enough for the government to intervene. Hundreds of suspects were rounded up, and for a while the killings tailed off. Then twelve people died of beatings in custody. Four policemen were convicted and jailed. Government ministers were dismissed and the operation was called off. Here was proof to the Sukuma that even the government feared the witches. The witch-killings resumed and were soon worse than ever, intensifying through the 1980s.

Government statistics show that some 4,518 people were killed in incidents related to witchcraft in Tanzania's thirteen regions between 1970 and 1988. Of these, 2,946 occurred among the Sukuma. Although Tanzania's largest tribe, they are still less than 12 per cent of the population in an ethnically diverse country of 120 or so language groups. Yet they have been responsible for 65 per cent of all witch-killings. While the belief in witches is no less pervasive in other regions, suspects were generally dealt with by more traditional and lenient methods. In Kigoma district, there had been fewer than twenty witch-killings, in the regions of Mtwara to the south and Morogoro west of Dar es Salaam, just one each. In Mwanza, there had been 1,924. Of those, 1,365 were women.

Academic studies have been written on why witch-killing became pathological among the Sukuma. A Tanzanian anthropologist, Simeon Masaki, concluded that it was a direct consequence of a clash between a state strategy of modernisation and a peasantry with its roots embedded in tradition – in effect, that social dislocation opened the way to a descent into mass hysteria.

MY FRIEND Randal Sadleir had a few stories about witchcraft. He was a district commissioner in Handeni where the chief was Salim Mhapi, a doughty old warrior who had been decorated for bravery as a member of von Lettow Vorbeck's *Schutztruppe*. In 1953 the chief fell ill. A missionary doctor was called in but could find nothing wrong with him.

Randal went to see him. 'I have been bewitched,' the chief said. Nothing could shift him from this conviction, and he soon died.

After the funeral, mourners were returning in a lorry which overturned. A number of people were killed, including Randal's messenger. Deeply distressed himself, he returned the body of the young man to his distraught family. They were adamant that the accident was a result of the original curse on Chief Mhapi.

Two years later Randal was in Dar es Salaam and was invited to meet the rising star of the African nationalist movement, a young teacher named Julius Nyerere. They drank brandy at the Cosy Café and Randal was impressed. Nyerere, a chief's son but a devout Roman Catholic, had recently returned from Edinburgh University trailing laurels. He was witty and culti-vated. Somehow the subject of witchcraft came up.

'I said that in the rural areas where I had served we came across a good deal of it. I felt a bit of a fool talking to this brilliant chap about witches, and said quickly that I was sure it didn't happen among educated people in Dar. He looked at me shrewdly and said in his high-pitched voice: "Randal, I can tell you – the most important thing in the lives of people in Dar is witchcraft."'

THE AMERICAN MISSIONARIES were taking stock of the Sukumaland ministry. We were seated in a comfortable old colonial house outside Mwanza but the prognosis was bleak.

'I'm pissed off at Satan – I'm pissed off as hell. You see, I know it's not fake. This is real demonology.' They murmured in agreement. The speaker was Dale, a pilot and Vietnam veteran. He looked like an ageing hippie, with long locks and beard, cowboy boots and thin legs encased in denims, but his experience was of a medieval world. He was a pastor, his wife a nurse, on the islands of the lake.

I had met them after booking my passage on the ship crossing the lake that night. My instinct was to flee from evangelicals but they had shamed me by their hospitality and as Dale spoke I was drawn in to the dark, outlandish, compelling world he described.

'The islands have always been a refuge for outcasts, criminals and fug-itives. Mainlanders are frightened of the lake, they believe demons collect over the water, and they do everything they can to avoid it. The islanders say "*Vita uya bara*" – which kind of means that the mainland is at war with them.'

There were about sixty inhabited islands in the Tanzanian sector, forested and jagged outcrops of ironstone rising hundreds of feet from the lake, in two main archipelagos. A few of the bigger ones, such as Ukerewe, were served by ferries and some form of administration, but most existed entirely beyond the pale. Anyone, no matter how heinous their past, would be accepted, provided they submitted to the culture of the island. Each was a kind of independent pariah state.

No one knew the numbers living out in the lake but Dale said they had been growing rapidly. Freed criminals had always been drawn by the absence of formal constraints. In recent years people fleeing accusations of witchcraft and refugees from Rwanda and Burundi had followed. Now outcast Aids sufferers were joining the migration. The upshot was a social laboratory in which all the ills of the mainland were stimulated to grow in hothouse conditions. Dale conjured up a place of terrible dread. Aids levels were 25 per cent higher than the mainland and growing. New schools of witchcraft were being spawned and he was frequently accosted by individuals showing all the signs of possession.

'These things have always been there but it's worse now and for one reason – Aids. Once Western medicine could solve the problems. This time we don't have an answer. We're not Superman any more. Aids has sent people back to the witchdoctors.'

It was at this point that Dale launched his outburst against Satan. After a while he went on. 'You know our biggest mistake? We have failed to address the Africans' innermost fear – that terrible, daily fear of being bewitched.'

'I agree,' chimed in Andrew, a young Englishman. 'We have taken centuries of our gospel benefits for granted. We have our nice cosy security and we don't talk about sorcery any more. The people are embarrassed to raise it with us, so the whole thing is swept under the carpet.' It was time, they agreed, to confront the threat. 'We've got to say, "we understand your fears, we know there is evil out there, and we are going to stand by you and see you through this."'

For all their earnest determination, I wondered whether they were not sometimes tempted to give it all up.

'I can't,' said Dale.

I had noticed that he walked with a limp. A few months earlier he had fallen off his motorcycle. The accident was quite minor but his leg was broken and complications set in. He spent months in hospital and nearly lost the leg.

'I can't go,' he said again. 'The people believe the accident happened because I've been bewitched by someone in our village. If I leave it means that power is stronger. I've got to stay to show we can take on the powers of darkness and win.'

It sounded like a life sentence. For a moment I thought I detected a hint of fear as if, isolated as they were here, witchcraft was more real a threat than any of them was prepared to admit. For me, it was time to sail. They said a prayer for my safe journey, for which I was grateful, and I left them to their demons.

THE MV *VICTORIA* was a proper ship. She had wooden decks off which shuttered doors led to neat little cabins, companionways, a single round funnel, and a rail at the stern over which you could watch the foam being churned up by her screws. She was a product of the Yarrow shipyards and was launched in 1959 when colonials might spend a week sailing around the lake, calling at ports in Kenya, Uganda and Tanganyika while being well fed and marvelling from the afterdeck over a sundowner on the magnificence of this imperial domain. I settled into a seat at the bar with *Nostromo*, a cold Safari and a sense of deep contentment.

Impressive though they were, simple dimensions did bare justice to the Nyanza. Roughly rectangular, it was 230 miles at its longest point from north to south and 160 miles in breadth. Its area of 25,285 square miles could contain Wales three and a half times. More than size though, it exuded an elemental power.

Environmentally, it was a mess. Once an evolutionary biologist's dream, with a range of hundreds of tiny perch-like fish called haplochromine cichlids that offered a unique laboratory for the study of Darwinian theory because they were descended from a common ancestor, the lake had been infested by alien flora and fauna to pernicious effect. Nile perch, *Lates niloticus*, a large, voracious species, was introduced in the 1950s to stimulate fishing but had caused ecological disaster. The cichlids, potentially more significant for evolutionary studies than the finches of the Galapagos, had been severely reduced in numbers.

Another invader, the water hyacinth, had spread across the lake like an oil slick from a breached tanker. This floating mass of weed, *Eichhornia crassipes*, appeared in the Nile swamps of Sudan in the 1950s but only reached the lake thirty years later. Since then it had become a plague to those dependent upon the lake for their living, obstructing fishermen, choking ports and disrupting the generation of hydro-electric power.

For the dugout fishermen who had worked these waters for millennia, the Nyanza was the giver and taker of life. Its appearance of calm immensity was deceptive, as storms came blowing out of the darkness with terrifying suddenness and force. Their world was described by John Roscoe, one of the earliest and finest of the missionary anthropologists, who crossed the lake by this same route a number of times in the 1890s. The journey by canoe then took around two weeks, paddlers hugging the shore to evade storms and landing on uninhabited islands at night to avoid attack by raiders. Hippopotamus and crocodile were other hazards, and Roscoe noted quite a few men who had lost limbs on the lake.

Canoes travelled in groups for twelve hours at a stretch, one of the paddlers roasting a meal of plantains for his fellows. Although expert canoeists, few men were able swimmers and to be caught in a storm was usually fatal. Roscoe related an occasion . . .

> when a storm burst upon us with such suddenness that, before we could reach the land, the waves were lashed up into mountains of water so high that even when standing up in the canoe, it was impossible to see land over them. The men began to cry 'We are dead men,' and to drop their paddles. I picked up a paddle and ran along the canoe, slapping each man on the shoulders and calling out *'Vuga'* (paddle). The men responded with alacrity and began to gain in confidence with their exertions. In half an hour we had reached a creek. The water was boiling and lashing itself into a fury and had it not been for the ready help of the natives from the shore, we should have sunk in the surf. The natives shook us by the hand as we landed and congratulated us on our escape, as though we were their relatives. It was most refreshing to find people so interested in our welfare.

The bar of the *Victoria* was a fine place to reflect that this enigmatic, primitive body of water was the fountain of civilisation's greatest river. It was dark when I finished my Safari and walked down the deck to the wooden rail at the stern. Looking out over the black lake, I suddenly felt as though I really was at the very heart of the continent, where life was flowing out through riverine arteries into an organic body, and I rejoiced at my own adventure.

5. The Enclave

Lake Hotel, Bukoba: Friday, 21 March

ANOTHER LAKE HOTEL, ANOTHER decrepit old colonial hangout, but here dilapidation is on the grand scale. I arrived at about seven yesterday morning, having trudged a mile or so from the port, and at first thought the place had been abandoned. Everything was shut, panes of glass were missing from doors and windows and of guests or staff there was no sign at all. I unslung the rucksack, sat down on the verandah and dozed off. After an hour a man in his underpants appeared on the lawn with a toothbrush and set about his toilet at the tap.

The hotel lies at what must have been the social hub in colonial days. It looks out towards that glittering lake across what was the Gymkhana Club, now a blackened concrete shell with a fading Pepsi sign painted on the side, and the golf course. Walking this afternoon among the scrub and sand dunes, I could find no trace of the course save for what appears to have been an elevated green set between palm trees; around it are indentations that might once have been bunkers. Off to one side is the remains of the telegraph tower which kept the local German garrison in touch with Berlin and which was destroyed in 1915 during one of the few British successes in the East Africa campaign. In an overgrown glade near the hotel lies a small European cemetery, but its occupants predate the war: there are a few Italians and a Portuguese or two as well as German soldiers like Wilhelm Muller, a sergeant who died here in 1909 at the age of twenty-three.

I got back from my walk yesterday evening to find the verandah crowded and a party going on in the tiny bar. This used to be the men's snug and there are still touches of an English pub, like the fox hunting print over the fireplace. There was nothing complacent about the drinking, however. I fell in with a languid fellow who was doing fearful damage to the only bottle of Scotch on the shelves. It turned out that he was a pilot from Uganda. I was alarmed to hear the drone of his aircraft taking off on a run to Dar early this morning.

Tanzania must have Africa's noisiest birdlife. In Kigoma it was crows, chorusing in a state of constant outrage. Here the hadeda ibis sets up a clamour well before dawn. It has a harsh bray astonishingly penetrating for so small a creature, but which fades away into an unearthly and heart-rending cry, like a woman or a child sobbing inconsolably. A strange animal. It made me think of the family and the months of separation ahead, and for a while I felt deeply lonely. I took out the photographs but looking at them caused an almost physical pain, and I quickly put them away.

Then there was a bang on the door and a cry of 'Welcome'. When I went out there was a steaming pail of hot water.

The only decoration in the breakfast room is a notice with the worst bit of doggerel I can recall:

> *Always remember to forget the things that made you sad,*
> *But never forget to remember the things that made you glad.*

The food is almost bad enough to make me sad. Tilapia, which I remember as a delicious fish, seems unobtainable. Nile perch can sometimes be had but is coarse and muddy. Neither goat nor beef, much in evidence in the countryside, ever seems to turn up on a plate. I never want to see chicken and rice again. As ever, though, the service is gracious.

BUKOBA EPITOMISED ALL that was worst in colonialism. Not worst in a brutal, Maxim-gun way, nor even perhaps the sneering, contemptuous sense, but as it reflected the ignorance and greed that gripped the European powers during the later stages of the 'Scramble', when Africa was carved up with set squares and compasses without thought to the viability, let alone the ethnic composition, of the territories being created. Far more damaging than the physical abuse suffered by Africans at the hands of the odd individual sadist was the system which created the borders of modern Africa. Bukoba is a case in point.

The people here are the Haya, descendants of the kingdoms which evolved west and north of Lake Victoria and which so impressed European travellers with the state of their development. Buganda was the most power-ful of these kingdoms when Speke arrived in 1862, but others had flourished at other times – Ankole, Toro, Bunyoro and Karagwe, the kingdom of the Haya. For long it was believed that the kingdoms had been founded by a superior race of pastoral folk from the Ethiopian highlands, probably of Nilotic origin. More recent evidence suggested that they were western Bantu, having emanated from one of the greatest and most successful of all migratory movements, which started in the Niger–Congo region around the time of Christ. By the fourteenth century a series of petty states had developed into prosperous monarchies familiar with pomp and ritual. The kings ruled through sub-chiefs but their authority was total and unquestioned.

Although they frequently warred with one another over cattle, they were isolated from the holocaust of slavery going on around them and flourished in a sort of regional cocoon. The Haya, although militarily weak, were able agriculturalists and produced a fine robusta coffee. Their king, Rumanika, was a vast, amiable man with a fondness for fat wives; members of his harem were force-fed until they resembled young hippopotamuses. One woman measured by Speke had a bust of 52 inches and a thigh of 31 inches.

By the time of Rumanika's death, Britain and Germany were rivals in East Africa. Since Speke's time, the British had been predominant north of the lake, in Buganda, while the Germans had been taking an increasing interest in the territory to the south. As the scramble gained momentum, Germany, through the energetic and genuinely brutal agency of a self-proclaimed *Übermensch* named Carl Peters, started to occupy the terrain from the coast to Tabora.

In all the manoeuvrings of the scramble thus far, the area of modern Kenya had remained unexplored, largely because of the fearsome reputation of the warlike Maasai barring the way, but in 1882 the Royal Geographical Society commissioned Joseph Thomson to lead an expedition to the lake via Mount Kenya. Thomson returned with details that started to fill in the blanks on the map, and became the first of a string of visitors to rhapsodise about the nobility of the Maasai.

In the first of two pacts, London and Berlin agreed in November 1886 to divide the region between them. A straight line was drawn on the map from the coast running north-west to Lake Victoria, with a blip around Mount Kilimanjaro, to define their spheres of interest. With this stroke, which was to mark the frontier between Tanganyika and Kenya, the nomadic Maasai were destined to have their wanderings curtailed. Four years later, in a second agreement, the two powers drew another straight line west of the lake at a latitude of one degree south, which became the boundary between Tanganyika and Uganda. The Haya were caught south of the line, cut off from their cultural kin in Uganda, bound in destiny instead to ethnic groups with whom they had little in common, and so remote from the centre of power in the new German colony that they might almost have been on another continent.

Independence only increased Bukoba's isolation. In Uganda it would have been another matter, but in Tanzania it was marooned, like an appendix at the extremity of the territory. The only tarmac road dissolved six miles from town. The distance to the capital was not that great by African standards – about 1,100 miles – but by road it was an expedition liable to take up to a week and quite impossible during the rainy season. The only practical route was as I had come, by ferry and train. The Ugandan capital, Kampala, on the other hand, was a mere 200 miles distant and, atrocious though the road was, reachable in a day. Bukoba was on the very margins of a marginalised state.

What was also remarkable was that, although bypassed by development, the Haya had been at the leading edge of national life. One of the smaller of Tanzania's 102 tribal groups, they produced at one stage half of its top civil servants and a high proportion of its successful businessmen. Within the Colonial Service, the Haya were highly regarded. One old district officer of my acquaintance thought them 'a very superior kind of folk'.

Now, a new era in the alienation of the Haya had begun. Uganda, having put the dreadful Amin and Obote periods well and truly behind it, was prospering. Disillusioned by the failures of Tanzania's leadership, it was said that many Haya were looking wistfully north for reunion with their ethnic kin. Such hopes have invariably been doomed in Africa, often bloodily so, but I wanted to hear from local leaders what they made of this colonial legacy.

HE LIVED ON a *shamba* at Itahwa, a village five miles from Bukoba. The plot was 10 acres on which he grew *matoke*. Orange bougainvillea burst across the entrance to the bungalow which was tiny. The interior was sparsely immaculate: some local basketwork, a family portrait. It was an unusual residence for a senior public servant in a state where holders of office are more renowned for lining their pockets than serving their public. Not the least perverse thing about Gosbert Rutabanzibwa was his integrity.

He answered the door, a white-haired, patrician figure buried in a dark duffel coat although it was still summer. 'Ah, is it Mr Taylor?' he asked. It was six months since I had written to introduce myself. 'So sorry not to have got back to you.' He patted his stomach and grimaced. 'My health . . . not good.'

He was, in fact, dying. For more than an hour he held forth, acerbic, wry, and avuncular; he was generous as well as critical about the British legacy, devastating about Tanzania's mistakes, and ultimately at a loss to explain a world from which he would soon depart without a great deal of regret.

He was a child of the 1920s when Bukoba consisted of a small fort and a few European business houses beside the lake. The only whites with whom Africans had any regular contact then were the handful of Lutheran missionaries who ran a clinic and a junior school. Like most young Africans, Gosbert reached out hungrily for education and the opportunity of self-improvement. The nearest high school was a two-day journey away, at Tabora. He still had a photograph of his teacher, an elderly, bearded Dutch monk. Discipline was firm but there was no beating. There was no need. The missionaries were demigods.

In 1943, two Tabora schoolfriends were among just four young men from the whole territory of Tanganyika to win the privilege for which every pupil prayed. A place at Makerere university in Kampala then conferred a status in African society that no contemporary award can begin to approach. At that point, Gosbert and his friend Julius Nyerere joined the demigods.

I wanted to hear about Makerere. Since its inception in 1922 as East Africa's sole institute of higher education, it had been both a social and political hothouse and an ideological battleground. From the start it was regarded with suspicion by settlers alarmed to see those they knew only as naked and picturesque tribals assuming European clothes and aspirations. Even progressive educationalists worried about 'forcing the pace', and about students 'losing touch with their own people'. (In the 1940s an English lecturer got into hot water for prescribing Tom Paine's *Rights of Man* as a text.) Under its best known principal, Bernard de Bunsen, it attained full university status and, staffed after the war by Christian socialist educators, produced a generation of post-colonial African leaders – Nyerere, Milton Obote, Tom Mboya, and ministers, diplomats and academics beyond number. De Bunsen's claim that the East African states 'could hardly have won or sustained their independence' without Makerere was extravagant, but not entirely without justification. Even Idi Amin gave it a twisted form of recognition: in his fear and hatred of intellectuals, he brought about its destruction.

Gosbert's memories of the Makerere of the 1940s were of the way it equipped his generation for citizenship. The political emphasis came after the war, when he and Nyerere met up again in London. 'We used to go to pubs and talk about how we should rule ourselves.' He chuckled. 'That's when we started causing trouble.' Even then though, Gosbert was involved in grassroots activism rather than nationalist politics. He studied the co-operative movement in Britain and was involved with George Kahama in creating the Bukoba coffee co-operative, which did selfless and valuable work helping peasant growers.

Where, I asked, had Britain failed? He spread his hands. 'Schools,' he said. 'We never had enough schools. When the British left, only seventy of us were graduates. The crucial time for development was before the war. But Britain had her eyes elsewhere. So after the war the people said: ''Why are they here? Either they are indifferent to us, or they are here to exploit us.'''

After independence, Gosbert went abroad as Nyerere's ambassador. His years in Delhi. Ottawa and, finally, Washington were happy. Despite his socialist policies, the urbane Nyerere was widely admired. 'We were very good boys then,' Gosbert said with a hint of irony. But when he returned home in the mid-1970s, the country was much changed. Nyerere's socialism, *ujamaa*, intruded into every sphere of life. It had brought improvements in healthcare and schooling but at the same time a failure in commerce and industry, and a catastrophic decline in agriculture and public utilities. Most concerning to Gosbert was what it had done to his beloved co-operative.

'Our movement had become politicised. The people were no longer able to elect their leaders, everything had to be vetted by the party.' He grimaced and shook his head in disgust. 'The crooks were in the house. Small people were being cheated. They were poor and there was nobody to look after them. These crooks were thieving them every way.'

His wife, a small serene woman, served juice crushed from sugar cane.

I asked about corruption. In reply, he started to talk about his health. I was momentarily bewildered, then recalled the deep-rooted aversion in Africa to coming directly to the point on sensitive matters.

His stomach was the problem, he explained. His wife chipped in. 'It makes noises like before the rain starts,' she said, imitating the sound of thunder.

He sighed. The local doctors were not to be trusted – 'I don't know what their qualifications are,' he said darkly – but he also hated the idea of flying to Dar – 'all those plane crashes'.

'He reads *Reader's Digest* and finds things to worry about,' she said.

'Well, I suppose if it's my ticket, it's my ticket.' He mulled this thought over before trying a new idiom. 'If I kick the bucket, I kick the bucket.' He chuckled, then mused sadly. 'Some of the children couldn't come, of course.' Three of their six children lived abroad.

'It's been much better recently,' she soothed.

In pride of place on the mantelpiece was a vast card which had arrived on his seventy-fifth birthday. Inside were individual inscriptions 'To Dad' and affectionate tributes.

'You must miss them,' I ventured. 'Don't you wish they would come back to Tanzania?'

His look was piercing. 'You asked about corruption. How can I ask them to come back – from Britain, from America? No, I can't really recommend that they come home, not with the way we conduct ourselves now. Not when they will find themselves below someone with lesser qualifications just because he is favoured.'

'Not everything is so bad,' she said.

'Ha,' he burst out. 'It's hopeless . . . lies . . . incompetence. Look at this road' – he pointed outside – 'the colonialists built the road, and we can't even maintain it. We have water cuts here, and the lake is just a few miles away. How can that be? This is what we ask ourselves.' He was coming to the boil. 'I can't even get a phone. I went to them, I said "I need to be able to speak to my children." You know what they said? "One million shillings." They wanted me to pay a bribe of one million shillings. I worked for my country and now I must pay a bribe to get a telephone. Ha.'

He sighed and sat back. 'Ah, Steve,' he said after a while, at once the old diplomat again. 'I'm sorry about your letter. I must have mislaid it. You must give my best wishes to Trevor' – an old district officer, now living in Uxbridge – 'you know, he is my best friend.'

He went on: 'We can't blame anyone. Britain had to look after the best interests of her own people and she still did a good job in nursing her colonies. We like the British, although I think maybe you have forgotten us. Yes, either you have forgotten us or we have been bad boys.'

Before I left he wanted to show me one of his prized possessions, a photograph of himself with Nyerere in Makerere days. His wife came back with the album, but when he turned to the page it was gone. He looked mystified, then it dawned that it had been taken by one of the children as a trophy. 'They have smuggled my pictures,' he murmured.

I left him among his plantains, a crusty anachronism, an aristocrat in humble surroundings. Soon afterwards his stomach pains were diagnosed as cancer and within a few months he was dead.

I WALKED BACK along the ruins of the tarmac road that wound down off the hill to Bukoba. The land was all primary colours, the red of the soil, the green of the *matoke*, but the lake in the background was etched in the soft glitter of gems, the emerald of a solitary island among waters of the palest aquamarine.

Along the way I came across a policeman in a clean white uniform and a peaked cap. He smiled benignly and asked if I was enjoying my day. 'Oh, yes,' I assured him. 'That's fine,' he said. 'Cheerio.' Further down the road, two children passed by, eyes cast down, murmuring in unison, 'Good afternoon'.

I had been in Bukoba only a few days and found myself thinking of my British acquaintance, the one who had thought the Haya 'a superior folk'. There was undoubtedly a serenity about life in this little enclave that suggested isolation from the centre of power might not be an altogether bad thing. Dealings between individuals were marked by what could only be called graciousness. Children were respectful to adults as a matter of course. The Haya women were renowned for their beauty, sensuality and independence, but these were less noticeable than their dignity. The men were almost courtly.

I recognised that I was falling prey to a familiar affliction. Most Europeans with experience of Africa have a kind of chosen people, an ethnic group with whom they identify, however vicariously, and imbue with virtues they find lacking in Africans as a whole. At its most basic, this works at a picturesque, coffee-table book level which celebrates, for example, the nobility of the Maasai or other nomads. Not far off is the visceral response to the savage grandeur of African tradition, of heroic deeds in war, naked burnished bodies locked in mortal combat with red-coated soldiers. As I recalled from studying the Zulus in South Africa, it was not uncommon to find belligerent, pot-bellied whites of racist views who became almost misty-eyed about the warrior past of 'our Zulu people'. This kind of tribalism was often based on self-interest. In the final days of Rhodesia, whites tried to reach an accommodation with the Ndebele, a Zulu-speaking people who also have a military tradition, as a bulwark against the more politicised Shona. An identical pattern was repeated during the death throes of apartheid, when the white Right threw in its lot with Zulus whose conservatism they saw as a counter to the more militant Xhosa.

Lone colonial officials were susceptible to a more romantic form of tribalism. In preparation for work in Africa, they studied anthropology and law at the London School of Economics, Swahili at the School of Oriental and African Studies, and finished up with a course on colonial administration under the formidable Margery Perham at Oxford. Then they headed off into the bush to an up-country station. They came, as Elspeth Huxley put it, 'wearing their prestige like a cloak, or a suit of armour', and were treated accordingly. Detached from the fetters of class and precedence, living alone in what were frequently surroundings of ethereal beauty, and among an unsophisticated and uninhibited people for whom they were responsible, young men from backgrounds as diverse as Kent and Cheshire often found themselves drawn to a world which would inspire and nourish the most powerful feelings of belonging and loyalty they would ever know.

Remarkably few conformed to the blimpish figures of fiction. Randal Sadleir remembered 'there were some bigots, but the whole ethos both in Tanganyika and Uganda was against it. There were not many whites, and we had none of that powerful aristocratic clique of Kenya, so there was no white party and no bastion of white supremacy like the Rift Valley Club and the Muthaiga Club. A good DC, it was always said, was someone who worked 60 per cent for his people and 40 per cent for his king. You simply did your best for them because they were *your* people. Out of this there developed a profoundly strong affection. You might even call it love. It's an atavistic thing. You had the privilege of feeling needed.'

This bonding brought out all the intensely tribalistic instincts of the British. The fondness for the Haya of my acquaintance who had served in Bukoba was matched by another from Moshi for the Chagga. They were merely two among the many officials in Tanganyika who regarded the Haya and Chagga as the people most quick and adaptable to development. Evelyn Waugh, repeating the prevailing wisdom during his visit in 1957, called the Chagga 'the most prosperous and intelligent of the native peoples of East Africa'.

Such ready ethnic categorisation these days sounds facile, even racist, for if there be superior folk it follows that there must be inferiors as well. I recalled the timeless lethargy of those isolated villages along the Central Line, the land of the Wagogo, and the notes of an early missionary who found them 'peaceful but apathetic . . . resistant to attempts to educate them'. Yet, guiltily or not, I felt bound to accept certain ethnic distinctions myself. The old cliché that tribal identities were constructions of colonialism had been good enough when, as a young man in South Africa, there seemed no alternative explanation other than the downright racist. But now I felt obliged to look further, to acknowledge that there was diversity and seek an explanation as to why some societies had developed in power and complexity and others not. Hardest of all perhaps was the most basic question: why had sub-Saharan Africa failed to develop the wheel or the plough, let alone gunpowder or writing?

A scientist named Jared Diamond had advanced a theory of cultural evolution which chimed strongly with what I instinctively felt to be true. This was that the fate of peoples had been ordained by a geographical lottery. When mankind migrated across the face of the Earth tens of thousands of years ago, he took up habitat in an environment that determined the destiny of his descendants. Europe and Asia, blessed by all five of the main domesticated herbivores and indigenous plant life suitable for cultivation, were winners in the lottery. Africa, Australia and, to a lesser extent, the Americas, were the losers, their indigenous populations isolated from the development race, vulnerable to conquest and in some cases destined for extinction.

The argument in the case of Africa was compelling. While the east and south of the continent provide the earliest and most continuous record of human evolution, the region was singularly hostile to man, with poor soils and fickle rainfall. All it possessed in abundance were inimical wildlife and disease. It followed that ideology was based on fertility and social cohesiveness was concentrated on defence rather than conquest. Moreover, because of its isolation, millennia passed without the kind of outside influences that, for example, China gave to Europe. Indeed, an African staple, maize, had been introduced by the Portuguese less than 500 years ago. In a luminous phrase, Jared Diamond summed up the absence of docile indigenous animals in Africa as the reason why 'rhino-mounted Bantu shock troops never overthrew the Roman Empire'; for while some African animals may have been periodically tamed – Hannibal's elephants, for example – none has ever been successfully domesticated.

Diamond's theory seemed even to make some sense of the homely tribalism of my colonial friends. It happened that both the 'superior' Haya and Chagga people inhabited comparatively good land and that both were producers of coffee – another recently imported crop – which had associations of prosperity and status. Little could be done, on the other hand, with the poor soil of central Tanzania, as the sad and tattered maize patches of the Wagogo testified.

These were random and unfocused thoughts among my baggage, but they formed the basis of a pattern to which I hoped to add during my journey. On one point I had become convinced. Africa's condition as the dysfunctional child of the globe was not permanent. Her resourcefulness and humanity had endured. As the Africanist historian, John Iliffe, had written, her people were frontiersmen who had colonised an especially hostile region of the world on behalf of the human race: that was why they deserved admiration and careful study. Their time would come.

THE DAY BEFORE leaving Bukoba I went for a last walk along the road that wound among the palms and low-slung German bungalows, up the hill from which a Lutheran church with a spire of corrugated iron overlooked the lake. Normally it was a tranquil azure but now a hazy, forbidding cloud was rising from the surface and hanging there like a dust storm.

Turning away, I started down the hill but soon noticed that the air was alive with flying insects. I flicked a few away from my face but, instead of dispersing, they grew more numerous. Within minutes they had enveloped the entire landscape, countless billions of silently swarming creatures, infesting the air like a noxious gas. I waded through the haze towards town, mouth clamped tightly shut, eyes slitted to prevent intrusion by the flies. Instead they invaded ears and nose. It was pointless to wave one's arms; the creatures just seemed to come on in thicker waves. Along the road I came across one or two other walkers, heads down like figures in a blizzard.

The flies did not bite or sting but the infestation was unnerving. There was something of an Old Testament plague about it, and I was pleased to reach town and find sanctuary at an Asian trader's store. Others were sheltering already, looking out on streets darkened by the pestilential swarm. I could gather only that the flies were called *shami* and that they incubated just beneath the surface of the lake, then hatched and swept inland in waves that infested Bukoba for anything between two hours and two days.

This time the blight was short-lived. The swarms thinned, then suddenly were gone and when we emerged into the late afternoon sunlight it was to the shrieking of ibises. The *shami* appeared to have brought out the rest of the local birdlife in all its profusion and walking down to the lake I came across a dozen species, including a grey heron which allowed me to get within 20 yards before it rose majestically with one languid motion of its wings, and a row of pied kingfishers hunched on a telephone line like hooded inquisitors.

A black tide lapped at the beach; the creatures, their brief lifespan exhausted, had returned to their source to die. The numbers were unimaginable. Just as they had filled the air in their countless billions, so they now lay deep and black on the lake or dried in crusting piles on the sand.

A few youths splashed naked and boisterous in the water. There was something especially aesthetically pleasing about these well-made bodies, so statuesque and luminous. And it occurred to me that every time I reached out for the modern in Africa, I was brought back to the elemental. The outside world had touched this place but left no lasting mark. The German houses could crumble, the erratic utilities could fail entirely, and not much would change. Outsiders thought of Africa as the most fragile continent, but a case could just as well be made that it was the most resilient. In the primeval lay its strength.

On my way back to the hotel I passed a housing block where a woman was watering tomato plants, pouring the contents of a bucket into a rudimentary sprinkler, a tin can with holes punched in the bottom. I did not immediately take it all in. Only an hour later, taking a shower myself, did it suddenly register that there was no piped water to a residential area, less than 500 yards from one of the largest bodies of fresh water in the world.

EMIN PASHA FOUNDED Bukoba in 1890, soon after his 'rescue' by Stanley and two years before renegade Arabs cut his throat somewhere in the Congo rain-forest. But the place was always a backwater and when George Bayone's father, Raoul, arrived from Italy twenty years later there were still only a handful of European residents.

George was Bukoba's last link with its colonial past, his German friend Paul Lomberg having died recently in his big stone bungalow at the bottom of the hill. After George's father came out, Bukoba flourished briefly with the discovery of tin, and he built an office of mud bricks, which was to become the Lake Hotel, and took up with the daughter of a local chief. George, the product of their union, was born in 1920.

We sipped Safaris on the hotel verandah. Although he had lived all his life in Africa, he spoke English like the owner of a little trattoria in Fulham. 'Always we were on the wrong side,' he said resignedly. 'In the first war, this was German and Italy was on the British side. Then, in the second war, this was British and Italy was on the German side.'

Raoul was interned by the Germans in 1914 and spent most of the war at a camp near Tabora. In 1939 the British decided he was too old to be a threat but now George, who had an Italian passport, was arrested. Still in his teens, he was shipped to South Africa and spent five years at the Koffiefontein camp for Afrikaner Nazis and German internees, then another two years in somewhat easier conditions outside Salisbury in Rhodesia.

He shrugged. 'It wasn't too bad. There was enough to eat.' But he had been robbed of his youth. By the time he got back to Bukoba he was twenty-seven. The hotel had been sold to a Goanese named Machado, an ex-steward on the lake steamers; when he went bankrupt it was taken over by a Jewish refugee from Germany named Lomberg. George went prospecting in the bush for nickel and the hotel passed in time to his friend, Lomberg's son, Paul. After independence it was nationalised but George and Paul still used to come down in the evening for a beer in the garden among the cyprus trees. Now only George was left.

On this, my last evening in Tanzania, the place became for a while a theatre of the magically surreal. There was George, sipping his drink in the place built by his father seventy years ago, surrounded by old Haya cronies. An Englishman named Rod who ran a fishing business told me about an island off Bukoba which was being turned into a sanctuary for chimpanzees maddened by their existence in European zoos; for a moment I felt overwhelmed by a sense that I was living in William Boyd's wonderful parable of simians and humans, *Brazzaville Beach*.

As the drinking continued, the night started to take on a slightly hallucinogenic quality. A sombre young oriental introduced himself as Chan Shik Min, a Korean missionary. He began a long story about how he had built a church on one of the islands, then became convulsed with mirth as he described how it had immediately fallen down. He laughed even harder as he told of his move to another island where he was robbed by one of his converts.

For a moment he looked grave. 'This is the stony ground Christ spoke of,' he said. 'For them we are just money machines.' Then he began to talk about Aids which started him laughing again. After a while I noticed he was weeping. 'I have lost so many friends,' he said.

By the time I got to the snug bar, I was drunk too. The Ugandan pilot, Godfrey, had flown back with a Tanzanian coffee trader, a sumptuous figure in a gilt-embroidered shirt, wreathed in gold rings. They were looking blearily at a snowstorm on television. Through the blizzard it was just possible to make out some African drummers.

'Oh God no,' said Godfrey. 'Heart of bloody Africa again. Why are there never any Western shows?'

THE *MATATU* DRIVER was the spitting image of Robert Mugabe but had none of the Zimbabwean autocrat's frostiness. He beamed. The Uganda border was just fifty miles away, no problem, there I would pick up a lift to Masaka, no problem. Kampala, same day, no problem.

But there was a problem. I had dragged my pack up to the Bukoba *matatu* park at dawn with a fearful hangover and this was the most crowded vehicle I had ever seen. It was a model designed to carry nine people in comfort and which I subsequently found to be licensed for fourteen in Uganda. At one stage, we were kneaded, layered and moulded to the interior of this particular vehicle in a dough made up of twenty-six adults and children.

The road was atrocious but after covering ten miles in the first hour I was sure it was not just the crevices and gorges that slowed our progress.

Bob Mugabe, chatting and smiling breezily up front, favoured the wrong side of the road and chugged along serenely in second gear, oblivious of drivers overtaking on the inside, hooting and gesticulating.

I was better off than most, having no one actually on top of me, but was still flattened like a wildflower in the pages of an encyclopaedia and, when Bob stopped to let off one passenger and take on three more, I extricated myself to allow some blood back into my legs. There was the odd chuckle of sympathy at this for it is well known that *mzungus* are hopelessly soft. But as I was levered back into place I found myself being looked at in accusing fashion by an adolescent boy on the seat facing me. His face said it all: poor, weak *mzungu*.

'What your matter?' he demanded.

I made a helpless sort of gesture with my free hand. 'I am a bit old.'

'You not old,' he said firmly.

'Well, quite old.'

He shook his head. 'Lazy,' he pronounced.

'What?'

'You lazy.'

'You cheeky.'

His elder brother was beside him. 'Ha. Yes,' he snorted in agreement.

For at least another hour the blood supply in my right leg was cut off by a tourniquet consisting of two knees, one on either side of my calf. I had both cramp and pins and needles. Somehow, the *muntu* in me kept the *mzungu* from asking for another stop.

We got to the Uganda border at lunchtime, having covered the fifty miles from Bukoba at an average speed of less than 14 mph. Bob Mugabe seemed delighted and shook hands with us all as we got out.

6. The Hills

Namirembe Guest-house, Kampala: Tuesday, 25 March

THE GUEST-HOUSE IS ATTACHED to the cathedral on Namirembe hill and the rooms are a bit like monks' cells, spotlessly austere with just a narrow bed, desk and wardrobe. Tonight, as most nights, there is a power cut so a single candle completes the monastic effect. This is appropriate. After today's journey, it is right that I should be contemplating mortality.

The border was easier than expected. Memories of my arrest the last time I tried to visit Uganda were still clear and accounted for a slight apprehension, but immigration formalities could not have been simpler. I hitched a couple of lifts and with just 150 miles to Kampala picked up a *matatu*.

The driver was too fast from the start. I told myself it was always so, yin and yang, one moment crawling along with Bob Mugabe, the next flying with this young tearaway, but the truth is the *matatu* culture is quite different in Uganda. Roads are better, vehicles less crowded. The ride is more comfortable and more perilous. The driver steered with one arm, the other dangling insouciantly out of the window, exchanging gestures in an elaborate fraternal code with oncoming *matatu* drivers.

I tried to keep my mind on the surroundings. We passed through Masaka, the streets and buildings still showing the scars of the 1979 war when Nyerere finally lost patience with Idi Amin and drove him from power. The aftermath proved far more baleful than the war itself: Nyerere's troops, returning home down this road, carried a virus into Tanzania that swept through East and southern Africa like a bush fire in the dry season. I remember Zimbabwe in the early 1980s when it came to our notice that heterosexual Africans were dying at a terrifying rate of a condition thought until then to afflict only drug addicts and homosexuals. Masaka is still a crossroads for Aids. Trucks converge from Zaire, Rwanda, Burundi and Tanzania, and drivers stop for the bars, the lights and the girls. Despite the roadside booths which sell condoms – four for 100/- (about 7p) – the Aids rate here is the same as in Bukoba, an estimated 60 per cent, which is to say the highest in the world. It was an eerie feeling to look around at my fifteen or so fellow passengers and reflect that between five and ten of them were probably living dead. I recalled hearing about a European traveller involved in a minor *matatu* collision. He received only cuts from broken glass but his blood mingled with that of another passenger and he caught the virus.

These doleful thoughts were interrupted by a shriek of brakes. We had pulled out to overtake a second *matatu* and were now tearing headlong at a third, oncoming, less than 40 yards away. Wheels locked, the hurtling van started to slide. The oncoming vehicle was also on the slide, towards us. It had to hit. We veered in, right beside the passengers in the *matatu* alongside who were gazing bemusedly in at me. My heart seemed to stop. Hopelessly out of control, the three vans glided past each other without quite touching at any single point and we slithered to a stop.

In the sudden silence I could hear someone shouting. I recognised the voice as my own, screaming abuse at the driver. He looked coolly round, then threw the *matatu* into gear and drove on without a word. Nobody else had reacted. I felt foolish, but was still trembling and inwardly raging. Were they all mad? How could they be so regardless of having their lives jeopardised by a boy drunk on speed and power? We Europeans do all in our power to keep death at bay even when the purpose of life itself has been lost; our fear of death rises in inverse proportion to our capacity to delay it. But that is the defect of a society whose motivation comes from recognising the sanctity of life. At this point I was having one of those moments when one wonders if Africans recognise any such sanctity. The Western belief that we can control our destinies may be deluded but here acceptance of mortality goes deeper than mere fortitude. Aids may even have compounded the African tendency to fatalism. People die in legions because men still decline to use condoms; a doctor told me the other day that he now thought it better not to tell patients when they tested positive because they just die more quickly.

Rested in my little cell, I can see the experience as salutary. Travelling in Tanzania was safe and trouble-free. Uganda's familiarity with sudden death is an admonition to be more on my guard.

WHILE IN KAMPALA I was hoping to meet King Ronnie. Or, more correctly, the Ssabataka, Ronald Muwenda Mutebi II, the thirty-ninth Kabaka of Buganda, ruling head of Africa's oldest monarchy.

Ronnie was something of an enigma. After his father was forced into exile, he had grown up in Britain, attended Eton and spent a year or so at Cambridge without obtaining any qualification. Then he dropped out of sight. There were stories, perhaps apocryphal, that he had earned his living as a gas fitter in Reading and as a double-glazing salesman, before returning to his native home in triumph to be crowned in 1993. I had written to

King Ronnie's office, explaining the purpose of my journey, and received a delightful reply from Godfrey Kavuma, the First Deputy Katikiro, that the subject 'greatly interests His Majesty, who would very much like to meet you when you come to Kampala'.

On arriving, I telephoned Mr Kavuma. It turned out that the Kabaka had just flown to London on private business. He was expected back in about a week. In the meantime, I set out to explore the old capital of Buganda.

Kampala was a turmoil of lush greenery, rich, red soil and tumbling buildings. Guidebooks described it as a city of seven hills. This sounded suspiciously like literary licence to draw a spurious comparison with Rome and a quick inspection from the balcony at Namirembe suggested that Kampala indeed had rather more than seven hills. In any event, a better comparison could be made with Calcutta, another place of somewhat saturnine beauty, familiar with disaster and tragedy, by nature artistic and temperamental, yet indomitable as well, with a gift for life and laughter.

Mengo, site of the Kabaka's palace for more than a century, was historically the most important of the hills. It was here that Protestant missionaries were permitted to build their church. Namirembe cathedral occupies the highest point, with a view grand and serene over the city from the lovely little cemetery. I spent days walking the hills but always came back here for quiet and reflection. Under the coconut palms were the lichen-encrusted graves of Alexander Mackay, the first missionary, and Hannington, the first Bishop of Equatoria, murdered on the orders of Ronnie's great-grandfather Mwanga. Over there were a pair of marble crosses with fresh wreaths over the remains of Albert and Katherine Cook, who founded the hospital on the other side of the hill; Albert's inscription reads 'a tribute from H.H. the Kabaka, chiefs and people. A true friend of Uganda.'

Uganda was always special to the British. From the time of Speke's arrival, there was a love affair with the place that encompassed the whole spectrum of personalities involved in the colonial experience. From the selfless devotion of the Cooks, to the twisted love of loners and misfits like Bob Astles, Idi Amin's adviser, the British association with Uganda touched depths of intimacy and passion that were not achieved with any other colony besides India. That was what made the ghastly spectacle which followed independence so horribly gripping. When a baffled Neanderthal went on the rampage it was not just old-timers who wept for the violation of paradise, but Africa's well-wishers everywhere who saw the eclipse of its most cultivated state. Terrible though those years were, the country then proceeded to suffer even more dreadfully under a mild-looking graduate, Milton Obote, who proclaimed the Common Man's Charter and slaughtered his fellow citizens in still greater numbers than had the brute Amin.

There were still plenty of reminders of those days. Walking down the hill from Mengo into town, I passed what must once have been Kampala's smartest residential district. The fact that Uganda's Asians had lived here invested these ruins and shells with pathos. Stucco was peeling from gables, verandahs were piled with debris. Most of the homes were occupied by squatters but the finest of them, a mansion set among palms, was a pillaged wreck. Coming into town, I reached Luwum Street, renamed for Uganda's last martyr, the murdered Archbishop. Here, too, the scars were still fresh. Pavements were torn up and I picked a way through puddles and piles of waste washed up by a storm. A man in his thirties squatted there. He seemed all head, an animated face on top of a body that melted into the ground. Four other ruined humans from the era of horrors clustered in the middle of Kampala Road, waiting for a break in the traffic, before crawling or scraping their way to the other side.

But there was regeneration as well. New buildings were going up and the *matatu* park on Luwum Street was the liveliest and best regulated civic amenity I had seen so far. Stand-up hawkers touted the most fantastic panoply of cheap and garish wares. At night the area revealed a new layer of life. As the shops closed, the unlicensed traders emerged like burrowing creatures of the dark. Ragged but meticulous, they set out their wares on boxes and blankets, side by side. Because there was no street lighting, each stall was lit by candles and walking among the tiny flickering lights and the press of bodies was like being caught up in a religious festival. Not much trade seemed to be transacted, but the mood was optimistic and there was something extremely moving about this spectacle of fringe dwellers enduring with humour and spirit.

I liked to walk in Kampala at night because the dark brought the rare sensation of complete anonymity. In daylight, I immediately became a *mzungu* again. All the same, I could recall nowhere else where the traveller was so unpestered. I had last encountered a tout in Zanzibar and the sole scrounger I met in Uganda was an elderly gent in a battered suit who wandered up to me in the botanical gardens at Entebbe and said: 'I'm hard up.'

One might even have forgotten the past, but for the maribous. They were everywhere, the hideous great carrion-eating storks, hunched on trees and buildings, silent and sinister like phantoms. Then the images came back: of the naked men sprawled across one another in the basement at Nakasero, their skulls oddly misshapen because they had been forced to beat one another to death with hammers. Or the bodies piled thick and bloated against the dam at Owen Falls.

PETER BEWES WAS living in Kampala again, in a small upstairs flat; he was a medical specialist in what was known as 'appropriate technology'. This amounted to teaching rural paramedics how to perform life-saving operations with whatever equipment was to hand – for example, undertaking a skin graft on a child suffering burns using a safety razor.

On the morning in 1971 when Dr Bewes heard that Idi Amin, commander of the armed forces, had ousted Milton Obote in a coup, he knew he would be needed. He set off for the hospital on a bicycle with a stethoscope around his neck and wearing a crash helmet. 'I thought the odder I looked, the less likely I was to be interfered with,' he said. He found a tank parked at the hospital gate. 'Obviously with a coup on our hands we were going to need blood, so I told the tank commander to drive to the blood bank. He trundled off and duly came back with the blood. Even in a coup, you could always find someone helpful in Uganda.'

Peter, a slight, almost birdlike man, was Kenyan-born but at that stage had been a surgeon at Mulago hospital in Kampala for three years. As it turned out, there was no great need for his skills that day. One incident, though, gave a foretaste of what was to come.

'An army major had been brought in a few days earlier with some minor problem. As soon as he heard that the coup had been led by Amin, he dressed himself in women's clothing and went to hide in a women's ward. A squad of soldiers came in. They found him and took him out into the hospital grounds and bayoneted him on the spot.'

Later there came the sound of drumming and cheering from the city. 'The radio was on and they announced that political prisoners had been freed. Then people started coming in, other doctors, and they were saying things like "I know the new man, met him at a party. Pretty basic sort of a chap, but very pro-British." I started to think perhaps the bayoneting was an aberration. Then three days later I was asked to go out to a barracks. There were about a hundred men. They had been beaten but the main thing was they all shared a particular wound, a puncturing at the top of the scalp. It might have been some macabre ritual. Then a captain came in and told me to leave. They were never heard of again. I think it was at that point I realised the country was in for a dreadful time.'

*   *   *

THE MARIBOUS COULD probably have been seen that day in February 1977 when a group of journalists arrived from Nairobi after receiving a call from Amin's pet white man, Bob Astles. About 5,000 people were gathered outside the Nile Hotel. Laid out on the pavement was a small arsenal of guns. Off to one side stood Archbishop Janani Luwum and seven bishops, all in clerical garb. 'We didn't realise it at the time, but they were under arrest,' remembered one of the journalists, Charles Harrison.

A few individuals were pulled out of the crowd. Publicly they confessed that they had smuggled the guns to the Archbishop's residence at Namirembe. A colonel in the security bureau then read out details of what was patently a trumped-up plot. Harrison's shorthand notes relate that the colonel claimed Muslims were to be 'slaughtered like chickens'. The plot had been set up 'through people who cannot be suspected, like Janani Luwum'. This harangue went on for about an hour. Finally, General Mustafa Adrisi, the army chief of staff, addressed the throng. 'What is to be done with them?' he cried, gesturing at the clergymen.

'Kill them,' roared the crowd. 'Kill them today.'

Luwum, still standing across the road, shook his head.

Astles had been silently hovering all this while. Now he shepherded Harrison and the other newsmen into the hotel. Amin was waiting. He told them: 'I am going to tell the people to control their temper. Everyone will be properly charged.'

That night Harrison flew back to Nairobi and filed his story. The next day Astles phoned. 'You won't believe this,' he said, 'but Archbishop Luwum has died in a car crash.'

MOST OF THE Englishmen who lived through those mad, dangerous years had moved on. Denis Hills, the lecturer sentenced to death by Amin for describing him as a village tyrant, knocked around Africa for a few more years before retiring to Brixton. After his master's fall, Astles spent six years in prison before being acquitted of murder. Of all those whose destinies had been bound up with Africa, Astles had seemed the most likely to stay but he was now living in a tree-lined avenue in Wimbledon.

One who had stayed was an elderly exile who I will refer to here as Ron. An opaque figure, he was regarded by those who remembered him as 'a bit of a bum' with a flair for tall stories. But he was one of perhaps six old-timers left from the 7,000-strong British community at the time of Amin's coup. Ron had been pals with Astles and became a wealthy man in the Amin years, when shortages left the way open to opportunism and

profiteering. Now in his seventies, he was broke again and doing odd jobs
at a casino for pin money. These facts may have had something to do with
his elusiveness. Three times he failed to turn up for our meetings.

Once I ran him to ground at the City Bar. He was corpulent, with the
florid cheeks and easygoing manner of Englishmen who have lived long in
the sun. We ordered Nile beers and he was soon lying fluently about his
experiences in the war and against the Mau Mau. The outline was typical
enough. He came to Africa in 1946 and, after a few years doing not much
in Ethiopia and Kenya, washed up in paradise, the Queen Elizabeth Park
at the foot of the Ruwenzoris in western Uganda. He had a fishing business
while his wife, Lily, ran the local hotel. Twenty years passed in a happy
haze of pink gins and spectacular sunsets.

Then came Amin. The hotel, owned by Asians, was seized and Ron and
Lily moved to Kampala. There he met Astles.

'He was an odd fish, but I liked him and he was good to me. He got on
well with Africans. He had access to Obote, and of course with Amin he
was like *that*. We had a problem with my daughter once. She was picked
up by some security goons, so I phoned Bob and he got her out within the
hour.'

Astles had long been a shadowy figure in the English community. He
came to Uganda after the war and appeared to find in it a homeland of the
heart. An outsider, he loathed the white colonial establishment, despite
carrying himself in a military manner and sporting a handlebar moustache.
He kept pet chimpanzees at a house overlooking the lake at Entebbe and
wove extraordinary fantasies around his past life. Most whites viewed him
with profound dislike and suspicion, but he mixed easily with Africans. He
married a Mugandan woman and made a friend of the prime minister,
Milton Obote, who elevated him from a roadworks foreman to head of the
broadcasting corporation.

It was easy to see why Ron had so taken to him. After Amin's coup,
both men really prospered; Astles was a sort of unofficial court jester,
assuming the rank of major to Amin's field marshal and acting as his
go-between with the British community; Ron was Astles's crony, with the
privileges that went with it.

Other whites, although still sacrosanct, started leaving in waves, unnerved
by the disappearances going on around them and Amin's increasingly bizarre
behaviour. In the aftermath of the Hills affair and the Asians' expulsion,
Britain cut off diplomatic relations.

'After that we were down to about a dozen Brits in Kampala. One day we all got a summons to meet Amin at the Nile Hotel. He said "Your high commissioner is gone. I will be your high commissioner. I will look after you." We were taken out to Cape Town View, Amin's home on the lake, and got absolutely squiffy. That's when Astles got the wheeze for the White Man's Burden.'

A few days later the picture appeared in newspapers around the world: four white men staggering along under the weight of a sedan chair in which reposed a beaming Amin, complete with decorations, among them the CBE he had just awarded himself, chortling that it stood for Conqueror of the British Empire. The photograph was taken at night and off to one side can be seen the ghostly figure of Astles, applauding the spectacle.

'You didn't mess with Idi,' Ron said by way of explanation. 'I liked him. Keep him happy and you could have plenty of laughs. But if you crossed him or got into politics, now that was very dangerous stuff.'

Bob Scanlon, one of the carriers in the photograph, had no interest in politics but he sold electrical equipment to the army that turned out to be defective. Like Dora Bloch, Amin's only other white victim, he vanished. 'Nice bloke, bit naïve,' Ron said cryptically. 'Had a wife who used to say "'ello Ron, 'ow's yer piles?" Last I heard she was in Blackpool.'

When the economy collapsed, Amin launched a new financial policy which he said was 'to see that all Ugandans are very rich in future'. Ron, on the other hand, had become very rich in the meantime. He was evasive when I asked him how he came by the wealth to send his children to school in Britain. 'Odds and ends,' he murmured. 'I made a lot and spent a lot.' Others I spoke to suggested that he had not been above skulduggery. His connections had given him access to foreign currency and he cornered a market in imported foods from Kenya as well as being favoured with tasks by Amin. Astles was in even deeper. He set up an anti-smuggling unit to prevent goods being shipped across the lake under cover of darkness. There were tales of murky doings, of smugglers being shot out of hand.

'The worst time was Obote's comeback – from 1980 to 1985,' Ron went on. 'I don't get frightened easily but that was bloody dangerous. No security at all, just goons with guns. We didn't go out for days on end. Then Museveni came in. It's been okay ever since.'

He sipped the last of a Nile beer. 'It won't last, of course. The Baganda are making trouble. They're a greedy, disputatious bunch.'

Did he plan to stay? He shrugged. 'I'm seventy-seven. What else can I do?'

I wanted to hear more but he had tired of questions. We agreed to meet

a few days later at the British Club, a bar which sold cut-price drinks in
the bowels of the high commission for two hours every evening. It was a
dismal, cavernous place with a thin, milky light. Four expats were at the
bar engaged in desultory slander. A frail old girl in leggings weaved over
and said she was Ron's wife, Lily. 'He couldn't come. A meeting came up
suddenly.' She was tipsy.

We sat nursing drinks. I asked about her own experiences, but no sooner
had she started a story than she lost the thread of it and trailed off. She
seemed to know the expats but they ignored her with studied contempt.

I spoke to Ron once more on the phone. 'Sorry about that, but we could
have a drink tonight,' he said. He never showed up.

AT MENGO HOSPITAL a young nurse looked baffled when I asked where I
might find Gwen Whittaker. A matron passing by looked shocked. 'Do you
mean you don't know Auntie Gwen?' she scolded. In a little chalet as neat
as a cottage in her native Wiltshire, Gwen was living in the hospital grounds,
'waiting to go to heaven'. She was a large woman, almost blind and virtually
confined to a vast armchair. She had nursed in Africa for forty years and
seen the miseries of the Congo and Burundi as well as Uganda, but Amin's
fall ushered in what, for her, was the worst time of all. 'Amin killed a lot
of prominent people, but he never set his army on to the population as a
whole.'

The army, recruited from Amin's Kakwa tribe and other Nubian Muslims,
had been comparatively disciplined. When Milton Obote returned in 1980
the soldiery was purged and replaced from his Langi and other northern
people. They were untrained and, worse, unpaid. Those off whom they were
left to scavenge were their old ethnic foes, the Baganda. The Luwero triangle,
an area north-west of Kampala, became the killing fields of Uganda. 'You
would go out and in what had been crop beds you would find bones and
skulls,' Gwen said. 'You couldn't go into the countryside without being
physically sick.'

Even then there was a privilege to being white, which made Gwen
valuable. 'At the hospital it was believed that Obote had told his people not
to harm whites. So, of course, if the African staff needed to go somewhere
dangerous they would ask me to go along. If a white was there, the others
were protected. We would get to these roadblocks of Obote's special force.
Horrible men. Dark glasses and bazookas, that's what I remember of them.
But when we were stopped I'd greet them, "Aha, you are doing a good
job. How's your wife and family?" That sort of thing. And I'd give them

books, usually the New Testament, which they would take very happily.'

We were served tea and cakes by Gwen's help, Wilberforce Luaga, a member of a prominent Baganda family whose father had been tied to a tree and bayoneted.

'At the root, it's tribalism. You just can't get rid of it. We played our part, of course. They say the British favoured the Baganda, and they did. Most of my friends are Baganda. They have great qualities, but they are not a very honest people, and they are not much liked. What the end of it all is, I don't know.'

THE RELATIONSHIP WAS always based on a degree of equality. Alone among Britain's colonial possessions, Uganda was founded on an agreement negotiated rather than imposed on the inhabitants. This was partly due to the fact that by 1900 the practice of colonial agents who got chiefs to sign away their territories by putting an 'X' on a blank pro forma had become less acceptable. In addition, though, it is clear that from the outset Englishmen thought the Baganda a cut above other African peoples.

Speke – dull, stuck-up old Speke – started it. He had been on the march for more than a year when he arrived at the palace of the Bagandan monarch, Mutesa, in February 1862. 'It was a magnificent sight,' he wrote. 'A whole hill was covered with gigantic huts, such as I had never seen in Africa before.'

More surprises awaited him: the monarchy was centuries old and Mutesa's court was extremely grand; ordinary Bagandans were confident, well-dressed, and fond of joking. While Mutesa exercised a godlike authority, ordering executions as a matter of routine, Speke was struck by the fact that there was nothing cringing or servile about his subjects. Indeed, Speke found it necessary to upbraid some of them for their 'impudence', but they charmed some of the priggishness out of him and he seems to have enjoyed chaffing and flirting with the women who called daily at his camp. 'They smoked my tobacco, chewed my coffee, drank my *pombe* [beer], and used to amuse me with queer stories of their native land,' he wrote. When he was given directions by Mutesa to the spot where the White Nile coursed northwards from the Nyanza, the king sent him on his way with a magnificent gift, sixty cows, fourteen goats, butter, coffee, tobacco and bark cloth for trading.

Speke raised the possibility of a Christian mission to Buganda in his *Journal of the Discovery of the Source of the Nile*, but it was Mutesa's next white visitor, Henry Stanley, who took up the idea. 'I am perfectly convinced there is no more desirable locality in Africa than Uganda. I admire the people immensely; they are cleanly, they are most intelligent, they are always decent. They are full of the traditions of their country, and they are just the material where one would expect Africans to become good Christians.'

For once evangelical optimism was to be vindicated. Stanley's appeal was heard by Alexander Mackay, who arrived at the Mengo palace of the Kabaka in 1878 and proclaimed it 'out of sight the finest part of Africa I have seen'.

By now the French had received similar reports, and within a few months three Catholic missionaries had followed Mackay to Mengo. Mutesa was quick to sense the rivalry between these teachers who proclaimed the same message yet clearly detested one another; his interest was in playing one off against the other to obtain firearms. Yet although the Baganda were baffled by disputes over the niceties of gospel interpretation – 'Every white man has a different religion,' one Muganda complained – both Protestantism and Catholicism gained adherents. After the death of the masterful Mutesa in 1885, and the succession of his weak and unstable son, Mwanga, the strains began to show.

A purge of Christians at court was likely to have come sooner or later, but the trigger appears to have been the refusal of a converted page to submit to being sodomised by the Kabaka and his chancellor, the Katikiro. Buggery, introduced by Arab traders, was preferred by Mwanga to the favours of the harem. Under the influence of the page, Charles Lwanga, other boys at court started to resist the practice. Matters came to a head in June 1886, when thirteen Catholic and eleven Protestant boys were burned alive on a mass funeral pyre south of Mengo. Missionaries hailed reports that the converts had gone to their deaths singing. At last, after decades of failure and disappointment, Africa had her martyrs.

Having identified the Baganda as a superior people, it was but a matter of time before the British started to turn them into gentlemen as well as Christians. In 1902, the new Katikiro, Apolo Kagwa, was among a delegation to be invited to Britain. Apolo, who was later knighted, visited Windsor, declaring it 'the finest place in England' probably because he thought it similar to Mengo. 'There is no noise and it is on a hill,' he wrote.

The public school system sealed the bond between the British and Bagandan ruling classes. King's College, Buddo, founded in 1906, was the Eton of East Africa, the alma mater of every scion of the tribal aristocracy. A new generation adopted English nicknames and learnt from masters like

Freddie Crittenden to enjoy Thackeray and P. G. Wodehouse. Among them was Sir Edward Mutesa II, the thirty-eighth Kabaka, or King Freddie as he was fraternally known in London clubland.

The British view of the Baganda chimed comfortably with that of Bagandans themselves, but hardly with the other regional kingdoms – Ankole, Toro and Bunyoro – which also saw themselves as a cut above other neighbouring tribes. While Buganda was the largest and probably the most sophisticated state absorbed into the Ugandan Protectorate, the belief rapidly gained currency among other ethnic groups that the Baganda had been favoured and were getting above themselves. But if the protectorate agreement fostered ethnicity, it did at least defend indigenous rights and institutions. By 1914 Uganda was prospering and pressure grew for land to be made available for white settlement, as it had in neighbouring Kenya. Bagandan resistance and the efforts of white officials such as Governor Sir Hesketh Bell ensured that the agreement was honoured. Uganda never did become another 'White Man's Country'.

FROM NAMIREMBE IT was a short walk down to the royal enclosure at Mengo. Without being challenged, one could advance beyond the perimeter fence and look up to a giant statue of King Freddie's father, Daudi Chwa. Beyond it lay the Lukiko, the parliament, and facing it about half a mile away on a mossy ridge opposite, the Lubiri, the palace. The architecture was in the manner of Sir Herbert Baker, a whitewashed fusion of Raj and imperial styles. The gardens bristled with palms, enclosed within bands of hedge, illuminated by flowering shrubs.

How King Freddie must have pined for it, as he lay dying in a miserable Bermondsey bedsitter with a black and white television and a two-bar heater. He was no stranger to banishment. But his first spell in exile, in 1953 during a strained spell with the British over political reform, was as Her Majesty's guest and, as he elegantly put it, 'while we were at official loggerheads with the British, it seemed almost a duty to spend their money'. He was put up at the Savoy until he got rooms in Eaton Place, the Duke of Hamilton invited him to stay in Scotland, and he was able to compare notes over oysters at the Ritz with another African exile, Seretse Khama of Bechuanaland.

Freddie had no illusions about his hosts. 'The British have a disconcerting habit of greeting you warmly, going out of their way to assure you of their friendship and then disappearing, which baffled me,' he wrote. But he knew that sooner or later he would be allowed to go home. When he was, it was to a tumultuous welcome from the Baganda and the status of a national hero. On independence, he was installed as Uganda's first titular president by Obote's government. The two men represented opposite poles in African society. Freddie was the epitome of the traditional leader. Obote, as well as being a Langi from the north, was a nationalist, one of an emergent class who had no place in the traditional tribal system but found an outlet for their ambitions and grievances in African politics. In that social and ethnic polarity, the root of so much African misery, lay the seeds of Uganda's ruin.

In May 1966, the army, under its commander, General Idi Amin, surrounded the palace on Mengo and opened fire indiscriminately. The *Daily Express* proclaimed 'King Freddie is Dead'. In fact, he had been spirited away, but his second exile was to be endured in very different style. The Wilson government decided it would not be in the interests of relations with Obote to help Freddie and, contrary to general practice, he had made no provision for a rainy day with a Swiss bank account.

He went downhill quickly. One friend lent him a small flat in Bermondsey but although the slight, diffident-looking figure never lost his courtesy and elegance he turned to drink. In November 1969, aged forty-five, the Lion of Buganda was found sprawled on the floor of the flat. Although it appeared that he had died of alcoholism, the Baganda were convinced he had been poisoned on Obote's orders.

A year later Nemesis overtook his foe. While Obote was in Singapore at the Commonwealth summit, Amin seized power.

7. The River

Namasagali, Victoria Nile: Monday, 31 March

Dawn AT THE SOURCE of the Nile. So magical is the phrase that it repeats itself in my mind again and again. So timeless is the scene that it might be as the earliest travellers saw it. Having come by their route, this feels like an arrival.

Dawn at the source of the Nile, and as the light comes up the river stretches a mile across to the west, as flat as a silver sheet. Only gliding clumps of water hyacinth hint at movement. A fish eagle is frozen to the top of an acacia tree. Figures stir among the *shambas* along the bank and women wander down to a thatch lean-to at the water's edge where the fishermen land. Fires flicker and as sleep is shrugged off there is a murmer of conversation and the clatter of large blackened kettles being set to boil. The fish eagle cries.

From off to one side dugout canoes start to appear, rippling the silver surface, each paddled or poled by four or five men. The women go to meet them and help bring in the nets. The catch looks small.

Namasagali lies about thirty miles north of the spot where the White Nile takes its rise on Lake Victoria. From this flatland savannah, it courses north to Lake Kyoga and on through the swamps of Equatoria, carrying life and civilisation into the deserts of Sudan and Egypt before debouching into the Mediterranean. It is the mightiest of the world's rivers, 4,160 miles long, compared with the 4,050 of the Amazon and the 3,965 of the Yangtze. It is almost twice the length of the Mississippi and Europe's longest, the Volga. My own favourites, the Zambezi and the Ganges, are striplings at 1,650 and 1,560.

But the Nile is so much more than mere dimensions. When Speke came upon just such a scene as this in 1862, he found the answer to a riddle which Herodotus had sought five centuries before the birth of Christ, and which eluded expeditions dispatched by Alexander, Julius Caesar and Nero. As he had spent more than five years and suffered unimaginable privations on his quest, it would be gratifying to record that he was able to savour his triumph. Sadly, while Burton, Stanley, and even Baker, wrote passionately upon reaching their own personal grails, Speke, as always, had difficulty finding the right words.

'Here at last I stood on the brink of the Nile,' he wrote. 'Most beautiful was the scene, nothing could surpass it.'

A HAND-PAINTED SIGN outside the bungalow read 'Camelot'. From within came the thin bleat of an electric organ and the strains of the great Easter hymn, Handel's *Judas Maccabaeus*. At a knock on the door to a verandah enclosed in mesh it ceased. Then came the sound of footsteps and humming as the door opened.

'You're the chap who wrote to me,' said Father Damian Grimes.

Africa was home to many remarkable schools, from bush institutes performing miracles with the barest resources, to uninhibitedly elitist models of British public schools, like Uganda's Buddo and Malawi's Kamuzu Academy. Namasagali College was as singular as any of them. It was founded amid the wreckage of a Nile transport system destroyed by floods in 1961. Namasagali, which means 'I have greeted the train', was the lowest navigable point on the Nile and a railhead for trade goods brought down by steamer from Lake Kyoga. From here they would be taken to join the main line of the Uganda Railway at Jinja for onward shipment to Nairobi and the coast. Then came the floods. The Nile rose nine feet, swamping siding, installations and homes. Namasagali was abandoned and over the next five years buried by elephant grass, until the local authority acquired the site and asked the Mill Hill Fathers, a small Catholic order in north London, to set up a school.

Thirty years on, the order was long gone, the government subsidy had ceased and the school, which had nearly closed any number of times, was bankrupt. Staff were frequently unpaid. But Father Grimes was still headmaster, a gimlet-eyed martinet who kept his wallowing ship afloat with a blend of cajoling, extortion, figure-shuffling and sheer force of character.

I never did summon the nerve to ask his age, but I would have put him at about seventy. A slight, owlish-looking Yorkshireman with a fondness for Latin phrases and incandescent waistcoats, he was not to everyone's liking. Kampala newspapers occasionally ran critical stories about the rigour of discipline at Namasagali; and a BBC television crew had produced a documentary on the school which cast Father Grimes as a faintly ridiculous figure, a Catholic traditionalist trying to turn African children into upperclass English boys and girls by teaching them to eat with knife and fork. It struck me as he showed me to a room, however, that the fact he was willing to put up yet another potential critic bespoke a certain degree of candour.

He took me on a tour. The setting evoked a recurring sense of wonderment: we were in a primeval landscape of grass huts and grinding poverty, thirty miles from the most rudimentary town, among a string of white bungalows with enclosed wire mesh verandahs at the edge of the Nile. And yet, among the mimosa and yellow-blossoming marcania, this was still discernibly a school, with dormitories, classrooms and playing fields, and pupils making their way purposefully to class, chorusing 'Morning Father' as they passed. But what really distinguished the place was the personality of the headmaster.

'We have helped a number of wild youngsters settle down with methods that are no longer politically correct,' he said as we walked. 'This has given us a reputation for rescuing hard cases. *Refugem pecatorem.*' Almost without pause he launched himself at a lad hastening by: 'You there, boy, why are you not in class?' A muttered explanation followed about a delay at the toilet block. 'That's no excuse. Report to the prefects at first break.'

I was beginning to hear discomforting echoes of my own former headmaster in Johannesburg, a silver-haired Glaswegian of the Marist order with all the love squeezed out of him by the harshness of his upbringing; Brother Anthony could cast dread with a glance and chill the blood with the iciness of his smile.

Near the office, four pupils were standing beside a tree. It was explained that they had been 'arrested' by prefects for offences such as running to class or not speaking English.

'Not speaking English?'

'I insist that English must be spoken at all times. If we allow youngsters to use their own languages, they very quickly start forming ethnic cliques. Besides, they must learn English if they are to use textbooks and it is a tool they will never lose if they should find careers in government or business.' This was true. Swahili had never become the lingua franca of Uganda as it had of Tanzania and Kenya. However, it was the use of the cane at Namasagali to enforce this policy that had attracted the attention of the press.

We reached his office and sat down. So how did he react to the criticism?

He fixed me with a stony stare from behind bottle-thick glasses and I quaked inwardly as the ghost of Brother Anthony took shape on the other side of a desk again. 'I look at it this way. Uganda is a country ruled by envy. You can liken it to a bucket of crabs. Each of the crabs has the ability to get out. But as soon as it looks as though one is about to make it, the others pull it back in. I see it as my role here to help individuals get out of the bucket.'

So he saw Africans as inferior? 'Far from it. England had its feudal age. Here we are not out of that culture yet. On top of that, the family is still the basic unit. Loyalty to family and, after that to clan and tribe, over-rides all other obligations. So when a man is in a position of authority, his first responsibility is to do something for his family. As the abstract notion of service does not exist, we have a classic recipe for corruption.'

I recalled the routine deployment of the cane at my old school, and challenged him to justify its use. 'The cane is used very casually at Ugandan schools. If we cane here it is only after the culprit has passed through a series of disciplinary procedures which includes an appeal system. We have been singled out in the press, but I suspect that is something of a colonial hangover, the fact that I am a white man. Frankly, that level of criticism bothers me not at all. Nobody disputes the excellence of our pupils.'

Set free to roam, I had to acknowledge that the youngsters to whom I spoke had a confidence and poise I had not come across anywhere else so far. The girls in particular had a directness and a freedom from self-consciousness that was immediately striking. I had noted before the feminin-ity of African girls; this was quite different, a clear sense of individual personalities ordering their own lives. The school had a court system admin-istered by pupils; while the head boy and head girl had roles in this authority, the supreme disciplinary figure, the chief justice, was always a girl.

The ghost of Brother Anthony was starting to dematerialise. The monks of my schooldays had feared women. For all his rigid orthodoxy, Father Grimes evidently liked them, recognised their qualities and encouraged them.

BESIDE THE RIVER where the steamers once came stood the rusty hulk of a steam crane with a plate stamped 'Taylor & Hubbard, Leicester, 1925'. Here a gang of boys offered to take me boating on the Nile. Monavi was the leader, a bold-faced lad of about eighteen. 'We'll take Hope and Charity, chaps,' he cried. Whooping and crowing, a couple of boys raced off to get paddles.

Hope and Charity turned out to be two of Namasagali's flotilla of three wooden dugouts and we were soon heading downriver towards Lake Vic-toria. Monkeys sported in the papyrus on the bank. Suddenly I was reminded that hippopotamuses kill more people in Africa every year than anything besides road accidents.

Monavi was reassuring. 'We have had no hippo here for more than ten years.' He grinned. 'Plenty of crocs, though.' He called over to Hope. 'Race you to the rocks, guys.'

Three paddlers, one on either side and one at the rear, pulled strongly. Between the banter and a snatch of boating song, young muscles strained for ascendancy. Perhaps it was the youthful exuberance, the public school chaff, but I could close my eyes and almost imagine I was among Eton boys rowing on the Thames.

Hope narrowly eclipsed Charity. We spent some time resting at the rocks. A dugout with fishermen appeared and passed close by without a word being spoken between the groups. Silent encounters were rare in these parts and again I was reminded of Eton, and the muted suspicion and hostility across the street between college boys and local youths.

FATHER GRIMES SEEMED less forbidding out of school and over a dining-table sprinkled with a few home comforts – Worcester sauce, cornflakes – I asked about his feelings for women.

'We had women teachers from Britain here in the 1970s and they taught me a lot about the needs of girl pupils. It fitted with my ideas about extra-curricular activities. When we started things like drama, dance and debating, the girls came into their own. There have been problems. The locals are very opposed to the way we teach our girls to stand up and argue. You may hear people say they can tell a Namasagali girl. The implication is that she is licentious. The fact is that she is liberated.'

Thanks to its remoteness, Namasagali was spared the worst of the Amin and Obote years, but Father Grimes still had to acquire some of the arts of African survival. His relations with Amin, indeed, had once been quite cordial thanks to a shared passion for boxing. In the old days, the priest was in charge of amateur boxing in Uganda, and supervised the boxing section of the African Games held in Kampala, at which Amin was invited to present the medals. As the ceremony approached, it became clear that the tyrant, whose mercurial moods were matched only by his fondness for gaudy trinkets, had set his heart on a medal for himself. The trouble was, the only spare was a bronze, which would have certainly offended the self-styled Champion of All Africa. Overnight, Father Grimes daubed it gold with model aircraft paint, and a beaming Amin received it without a second glance.

More serious was the time in the final days before Obote's fall when a band of his soldiers came into the district and started terrorising it. Reports reached Father Grimes that girl pupils had been harassed, and he went to see the commander. 'A right bastard,' he said, rolling the phrase around with all the vehemence that a Wakefield accent could produce. 'I asked him what his men were playing at. He didn't say anything, just took one of these automatic rifle things and fired a burst around my feet. I was stunned but also outraged. "What do you think you are doing?" I said. "Put that thing down, right now."'

For once the imperious tone failed. The sergeant's eyes narrowed, he raised the rifle and pointed it at Father Grimes's head. 'He said, "I am going to shoot you" – very cold, he was. I think he would have, but then his men were between us. Some were holding him back, others were saying, "You go now, Father, please." Well, I can tell you, I went.'

The next morning I tried to wriggle out of an undertaking, given after a couple of beers, to hold a journalism tutorial for students on a media studies course. Father Grimes delivered a stern lecture about people who availed themselves of Namasagali's hospitality without giving anything back. Conscience conquered churlishness, but I was relieved to discover that my student group numbered just three, all of them girls.

We set chairs out in sight of the Nile. Brenda was dutiful, writing everything down in a notebook under the heading 'Tips'; Sharon was a bright spark, vivacious and pert; Linda was the cool-eyed sceptic who sensibly took down very little of what I said. They were in their late teens, outgoing modern girls who were not yet born when Amin was in power, products of the rebirth of hope under Museveni. They had, moreover, seen the rise of a free press. Throughout East Africa newspapers were flexing their muscles as never before, but nowhere more so than in Kampala where a natural love of debate, combined with a tolerant regime, had stimulated a rash of new publications. Most successful of these was the *Monitor*, a pugnacious independent. The three girls took the *Monitor* as their ideal. For the rest of an hour they talked animatedly about democracy and the role of the media in political opposition. I imagined that a similar group from my children's schools would have held forth with similar conviction, but could not be sure of it.

I told Father Grimes that my tutorial had added nothing to their knowledge. He tried to look patient. 'Yes, but by speaking to them as someone from *The Times*, you validate what they are doing,' he said.

I was to meet one other woman before leaving Namasagali. Ann Namiiro was a former pupil who had gone on to Makerere, then returned as the college's registrar. She was a typical Namasagali product – bright, fresh, forthright. At one point I speculated that Father Grimes must be near retirement. 'He is, and it really worries me to think about it,' she said. 'I would feel more reassured if I knew he was to be replaced by another European.'

I was taken aback. Why not an African? 'An African would not maintain standards. We have seen it before, Africans are not firm on discipline. Favouritism creeps in, morale goes. And Africans will always argue with each other.'

But this was Uganda, thirty years after independence; whites were gone and schools like any other institution, surely, had to be run by Africans. 'I am not impressed by Africans as teachers. At Makerere we had lecturers who looked for sexual favours from us girl students. I despised them.'

It was a troubling talk. While living in Africa I had confronted the endlessly repeated platitudes of white racism. Now there was the stirring of a black voice that not only admitted the failure of independent Africa, but expressed it in racial terms. But what made it really troubling was that I suspected Ann was right.

Namirembe Guest-house: Thursday, 3 April

RETURNING TO KAMPALA feels a bit like coming home. The hills are now familiar so I find my way easily around the city and at the guest-house there is a cheering welcome from the improbably named maids, Teddy, who serves breakfast, and Alan, who cleans the rooms.

What they call the Big Rains have begun and yesterday Kampala was a disaster zone. Muddy floodpools formed at the bottom of Luwum Street where debris came boiling up from clogged drains. A few pedestrians waded through the chaos in galoshes, but most huddled in doorways. The city was a rank, desolate shell. Today the weather is no better, but how different it all appears from up here on Mengo. The balcony looks out on a low, wet mist that has settled over the valley. All that can be seen is foliage drenched and glistening, and the landscape is as unsullied as a Highland glen.

I find Father Grimes is a hard man to forget. By a remarkable coincidence, I met a former Namasagali head boy, Samuel Zinumula, in the *matatu* coming back to Kampala. Immediately, and almost automatically, we started to discuss the priest. Samuel respects him immensely but had obviously found him difficult. 'We had arguments. He pushes and pushes and sometimes you think, when he is demanding 120 per cent, why can't he just be satisfied with 90 per cent? He is never satisfied, and that is a problem in Africa.'

My memory is of two objects which had pride of place in his sitting-room: a portrait of his hero, Thomas More, and a hand-made wooden plaque inscribed by a mother in gratitude to Father Grimes for turning her daughter into 'a promising girl'.

On the morning I left, we were at the office when he noticed a girl standing under the 'arrest' tree and asked what she had done. In a strong South London accent she said she had visited a sick friend in the dormitory without permission. Hearing the accent, I asked her about herself. Her name was Genevieve, and she had spent ten years in Britain from the age of five until quite recently, when her parents decided that Kampala was a better place for children than Brixton, where she was starting to get into deep water. She looked bewildered and defiant.

The plight of an adolescent girl, about the age of my daughter, suffering from a double case of cultural confusion, was infinitely sad. I felt tears coming and I turned away. Father Grimes noticed. 'Don't worry,' he said kindly. 'It was difficult for her at first, but give a child a firm base, be consistent, and they soon adjust. She's going to be fine.'

NEWS FROM THE palace was not good. King Ronnie was still in London and it was not known when he would return. His aide, Mr Kavuma, said: 'We should hear something in the next few days. Keep in touch.'

President Museveni was also inaccessible, according to his press aide, John Nagenda. Museveni was among the most admired of new African leaders. A former Marxist, he had spent student holidays at Dar es Salaam university fighting for Frelimo against the Portuguese in Mozambique, then formed his own rebel army to oppose first Amin and then Obote, before coming to power in 1986. As president he had turned his back on socialism and transformed the economy along capitalist lines, while challenging conventional thinking on Western economic aid, declaring it 'a life-support system for something that is already dead. Aid causes dependency and dependency is slavery.'

Museveni had brought political stability too, while arguing that multi-party democracy was a luxury the country could not afford. Societies were like butterflies, he said, passing through stages from egg to caterpillar, to pupa and finally to butterfly; Western societies had made the complete transition. African ones were still at the caterpillar stage. Colonialism, he argued, had interrupted that development, creating a vast divide between the post-independence elite and the peasantry. Race was all they had in common. Until Africa could create a new middle class, so the argument went, voters would be susceptible to ethnic manipulation.

For an African leader to claim that his people were not ready for multi-party democracy had a disturbingly familiar ring, but Museveni had at least introduced a form of no-party democracy. Voters had recently elected a new assembly consisting of 214 individual members and sixty-two others representing interest groups – thirty-nine women, ten soldiers, five disabled, five between the age of eighteen and thirty, and three trade unionists. Museveni himself had won 74 per cent of the vote in a three-way contest for the presidency. The benefits of ten years of stability were evident. Yet Museveni's middle class was growing restive; with economic growth settled into a comfortable average of 6 per cent for a decade, more and more voices were saying that the country was ready for the next big step, the legalisation of political parties. For a long time beyond criticism, Museveni was starting to come under fire in a flourishing English-language press. I had been looking forward to meeting members of my own trade and set off across town to find them.

Africa never had a free press. In colonial times the papers were dutiful towards authority and their focus on white interests did nothing to illuminate the rise of nationalism. The doyen of journalism in East Africa, Charles Harrison, now living out his days in Nairobi, freely acknowledged that the paper he had edited in colonial Uganda was no more independent than the post-colonial versions that succeeded it. Nor did he have any doubt that any paper which had challenged the Mau Mau emergency regulations in Kenya would have been instantly closed down.

For a journalist, this history made the robustness and diversity of Kampala's publishing industry all the more appealing. Although new titles popped up like rabbits from burrows and almost as quickly vanished, there seemed no limit to the appetite of readers, or the inventiveness of journalists. Laid out in piles on the pavements, newspapers and magazines vied for attention with headlines both lurid and earnest – here an eye-catching contribution in *Chics* to the debate over female circumcision, 'Don't Clip Your Clit!', there the latest official proclamation in the semi-official *New Vision*. And, to top it off, an invigorating circulation battle between two independent newspapers which used the English language with real gusto.

The office of the *Crusader* (motto 'Truth Always') crackled with youthful energy and the joyful air of a shoestring enterprise. The year before George Lugalambi and a few other young journalists had broken away from the highly successful *Monitor* to start their own paper and were now producing a pin-sharp, mature paper that was its genuine rival. Their problems were daunting – contract printers who went broke, power cuts that halted production, scarce advertising revenue. But there was a familiar, heady air in the newsroom as deadline approached. Sub-editors hunched over terminals while a lanky reporter in black jeans and flashy white shoes cradled a phone and murmured reassuringly down the line as he extracted confidences and jotted them down in his notebook.

That day's edition had an especially crusading flavour, with a splash demanding the dismissal of an incompetent regional administrator, a feature headlined 'Bravo Prostitutes, Law Unfair To You', and a thundering editorial about 'mind-boggling corruption in the districts'. George explained the paucity of international sport or news with an apologetic grin. 'We have to crib it off the Internet,' he said.

While the *Crusader* survived on a wing and a prayer, a new building across town had arisen on the profits of a publishing phenomenon. Started from scratch by six journalists who found the semi-official press too ano- dyne, the *Monitor* had turned in a few years from a two-page weekly into Africa's most successful independent daily on a diet of aggressive political reporting and news largely devoted to sex, witchcraft and crime.

David Oma Balikawa, one of the paper's founders, did not look like the sort of news editor to be excited by stories with headlines like 'Brother Attempts Incest', 'Villagers Banish Witch' or 'Python Eating Goats'; nor even by the most compelling story in that day's edition, which was about villagers who caught an armed bandit, shot him with his own gun and then 'built a fire on which they roasted the thug for two days'. David was small and piercingly intense, and prefaced most statements by saying 'I will tell you something very interesting . . .' Instead of scandalous disclosure, however, this introduced a serious discourse on Ugandan politics. For what really excited David and his *Monitor* colleagues was the nature of power. They suffered from the political journalists' disease, a love of intrigue and polemic, as severely as any reporter on the Whitehall or Washington beat.

His case was no less sound for being familiar: Museveni had served his nation admirably, but after a decade in power was starting to believe he was indispensable. It was time to test Uganda's increasing maturity by unbanning political parties. For adopting this editorial line, the *Monitor* had incurred official displeasure, including a withdrawal by the government of all its advertising, a main source of revenue.

'Mild by Ugandan standards,' David agreed, 'but press freedom should not be a negotiating chip in political debate. Our leaders believe if you are not with them, you are against them.'

THE PRESIDENT'S PRESS aide, John Nagenda, was the complete Bagandan gentleman and, having spent twenty years as an exile in Britain, he moved effortlessly between cultural landscapes. Sitting on the verandah of his

bungalow at Mengo, he pointed out the highlights of his garden and welcomed the arrival of the rains. From a compact disc in the living-room
behind us came the sound of Mitsuko Uchida floating a cantabile line over
the bass of a Mozart sonata.

Nagenda had cut a dashing figure in London. He was a big, handsome
man, sporty as well as cultivated, and a regular at the Hurlingham Club.
His passion was cricket. He opened the bowling for East Africa at the
inaugural World Cup and chuckled ruefully at the memory of having Glen
Turner dropped when he had scored just four. Turner, the finest opening
batsman produced by New Zealand, went on to make 170.

Up to his meeting with Museveni, Nagenda had been a Muganda first
and last. 'One simply thought of Bagandans as superior,' he said. Museveni
made him see the bigger picture: the country had been destroyed by ethnicity;
to rebuild, its people *had* to shed tribal politics and work as a unit. Museveni,
he had no doubt, was a great man.

So what, I asked, did he make of the *Monitor*'s criticism of his boss?

His face turned to stone. 'I say bash them, and no apologies,' he said.

Perhaps I looked stunned. 'I don't mind if they are robust,' he went on.
'But those guys just dream up stories to say what a terrible fellow Museveni
is. Recently they wrote that he had chartered a Concorde to fly him to New
York. Utter fabrication. They didn't even try to check it. When I pointed
this out, they put in a small retraction – bottom of page two. By then the
damage was done. People said, "You see? He's the same as the rest."'

How then did he propose to bash the press? 'In the old days, that journalist
would have been picked up on a Friday night and spent an inconvenient
weekend in jail. I must confess there are times when I am tempted by those
techniques again.'

The Mozart came to an end. 'Do you care for the Salomons' version of
the Haydn quartets?' he asked.

8. The Mountains

THERE WAS ONLY ONE good reason for going to the Mountains of the Moon, and that was the sheer romance of the name. I had also heard an intriguing but vague story about a man living there named Keith who was supposedly the last white farmer in Uganda. But to see the mountains would have been enough.

On the road running south-west from Kampala, mist shrouded the hills and settled in valleys covering the *matoke* groves with a glistening sheen. The skies sat low and heavy on this sombre green bed so that even as the bus crossed the Equator north of Masaka I could look out the window and see in my mind Cumbria and the hills over Coniston on an overcast day. The bus ground on through the morning, passing villages which were sinking beneath a tide of mud, until, leaving Mbarara, the road turned north and started to climb. Rising on either side were estates close-carpeted with tea bushes which rolled into the distance like mounds of soft, furry moss. Now the gentle contours started to sharpen and darken. As the road wound upwards, small lakes appeared below against grim faces of shale, the craters of extinct volcanoes. Then, without warning, the land fell away as we came to an escarpment and looked across the great plain stretched out below of the Queen Elizabeth National Park.

The park had recovered to some extent from the pillaging by Amin's army. Kob and bushbuck dotted the plain as the road passed over the channel linking Lake Edward to Lake George then, about ten miles to the north, crossed the Equator again. Since leaving Kampala, the bus had covered 250 miles encompassing a whole world of geographical diversity. Now I peered out of the window again, anxious for a first glimpse of the mountains, but still the cloud hung heavily on the land.

In his timeless saga of exploration, *The White Nile*, Alan Moorehead traced discovery of the Mountains of the Moon to the legendary Greek traveller, Diogenes, who landed on the East African coast in the first century AD and reported that he had 'travelled inland for a twenty-five days' journey and arrived in the vicinity of two great lakes and the snowy range of mountains whence the Nile draws its twin sources'. Ptolemy used Diogenes's report in his *Geography*, showing the Mountains of the Moon watering two lakes. No advance on this study was made for 1,700 years, until the Germans, Johann Rebmann and Johann Krapf, made the sensational discoveries

of the snow-capped peaks, Kilimanjaro and Kenya. Then Burton and
Speke discovered the lakes. The broad sweep of Ptolemy's thesis was thus
verified, if flawed by the fact that Kilimanjaro and Kenya were individual
peaks rather than a snowy range and were too far to the east to water the
lakes.

Then, in 1889, more than thirty years after the start of the Nile quest,
Stanley made the last of his great discoveries. Far to the west of Lake
Victoria, he came to a smaller body of water which he named Lake Edward,
and on a clear day saw a range of lush green and snowy mountains at an
altitude of about 18,000 feet running north from the Equator for eighty
miles to a latitude of about one degree. Local people called the mountains
the Ruwenzoris, meaning 'the place which brings the rain', by which they
are now usually known. But Ptolemy's name, as evocative and lovely as
any in travel, has stuck.

Nine hours from Kampala, the bus heaved into the little town of Fort
Portal. For an extortionate fare, a youth took me on the back of his moped
the two miles out of town along Lugard Road, past the golf course and up
Stanley Drive to the hotel.

Mountains of the Moon Hotel, Fort Portal: Saturday, 5 April

THE ROOM MAY be grubby and, at $25, overpriced, but the setting is incom-
parable. This morning the cloud lifted briefly and, over omelette and coffee
on the verandah, I looked on the snowy blue massif of the Ruwenzoris that
arise behind a neatly trimmed hedge across the garden. This was once one
of the legendary colonial watering holes, famous for week-long parties of
planters down from the estates. Now the linen is tattered and the rusty
corrugated iron roof sags in places, but the garden is still invested with love
and retains an English touch, a few roses and a flagpole amid the canna
lilies and the palm trees lining the drive.

The Zaire border lies less than twenty miles off, across it Conrad's Heart
of Darkness – pygmies and the rank gloom of the Ituri Forest, where Stanley
hacked his way through clinging undergrowth and hostile tribes on his last,
hellish march. A *matatu* goes as far as a pygmy village near the border but
it sounds like a sad and tawdry place; the custom of other picturesque tribals
like the Maasai who demand fees from visitors has touched the pygmies,
and they are being destroyed by alcohol.

Nor will I be going up the mountains. At this time of year, they are
constantly swept by mist and rain, and all climbs have to be accompanied
by guides and porters. I am content with the view. Though it is impossible

to see the twin peaks of Margherita and Albert, the range is a constant presence even when cloud shrouds the higher reaches.

I am on the trail of the white man named Keith, however. When I asked the young girl at reception, she said she had heard of him and directed me to a bar in town where I had to ask for Joy. I found the place and was gratified by Joy's astonishment at my enquiry. 'Keith Anderson? He is my uncle. Do you know him?' Apparently he lives some way out of town and Joy has arranged for a friend to take us there in the morning.

The paradoxes of this wonderful, dazzling country never fail to amaze me. This evening, drinking a Nile Special in a bar fifty miles north of the Equator, I was grateful to be sitting beside a crackling fire.

'WELL, IF YOU want to have a chat you'd better join us for breakfast,' Keith said.

A hearty affair it was too: sausage, tomato, egg, fried potatoes and baby onions. Keith's wife, Tereza, brought it in, still sizzling from the kitchen. 'She won't have much to say,' Keith said. 'She doesn't speak much English.'

The little homestead stood on top of a back-breaking hill. Their land, ninety acres of tea and *matoke*, fell away sharply so that we seemed to be perched on top of the world, looking due west across a great, green void to the snow-flecked mountains on the other side. Keith found the spot when he was still in the colonial service and took the better part of his pension in a lump sum to buy the land on which he built the bungalow himself. It was the most tantalisingly lovely farm I had ever seen.

He was sixty-eight, born in Beaconsfield, a tall, lean man with snow-white hair who continued to run the place despite the effects of a botched hip operation which had left one leg shorter than the other and forced him to use a stick. He went to Uganda in 1951 as a surveyor, a job which entailed long spells on his own in the bush, and had mapped the entire northern sector of the Ruwenzoris. That was how he and Tereza came to be together.

'There were damn few white women up-country. The last time I had a chance with one was in the 1950s. Smart piece she was – got snapped up by a pal of mine. So a few of us started forming local attachments. I had a previous liaison – my daughter's forty-four now, she's a doctor in South Africa – and Tereza had a chap before me. Of course, you didn't go round too openly, but it was generally known which of us had African girlfriends. We were not ostracised but we were looked down on by the clubby types.'

Where had he and Tereza met? 'We met in a bar in 1964,' he said tartly.

Tereza, who had been dealing with her breakfast, grimaced reproachfully at him. That was the only indication she gave of understanding English. They spoke in Rutoro.

Keith had found the sly snobbery easy enough to deal with, but his friend Chris Marshall, the district commissioner, who also had an African woman, did not. One day he went berserk in his own office, setting fire to the files and almost burning the place down. On being sacked, he too bought a small estate about twenty miles from town. Then came independence and the mixed couples felt able to come into the open. 'Quite liberating, really,' Keith said thoughtfully. 'That was when I decided that I would stay.'

A number of other planters stayed on as well but that all changed when Amin came to power and issued an edict that all property had to be handed over to Ugandans. At a stroke, white and Asian landowners were dispossessed. Only Keith and his friend, Chris, retained their land because they had Ugandan wives. The same act that had cut them adrift from their own kind secured their place here, two old *mzungus* who had become true Africans. Chris had died two years earlier, well into his eighties, so Keith was, indeed, Uganda's last white farmer.

'Funny how it worked out because I was quite improvident. Just lived from day to day until I bought this place.' They managed now on the remains of his pension, which helped with the upkeep of a battered Land Rover, and income from *matoke*, which he sold at a local market, and tea. They wore second-hand cast-offs from Britain and America bought at the same market. Once a week they went into town together to see friends and Tereza's relatives, and sometimes Keith went in on his own for a night with the boys in Joy's bar. In the evening he read or pored over his collection of twentieth-century British Empire stamps.

'I like a drink. Can't afford to go out too often, but we get this banana beer' – he gestured to a large plastic barrel – 'which works out at about 30p for five litres. Try some.' I did. We agreed that it was an acquired taste.

There was work to be done and we went down to the groves where he and his one full-time worker had to cut *matoke* for market. Somewhat idly, I asked how serious Aids was locally. 'About a fifth of the people we have known between fifteen and forty have been taken off,' he said briskly. 'Tereza lost her only daughter. There have also been three nieces and any number of more distant relatives. We've reached a stage where some people go to funerals once or twice a week. I suppose we have been to about fifty funerals ourselves in the past two years.'

He started cutting clusters of plantains with a wicked-looking machete, weighing each bunch and stacking it in the back of the Land Rover. 'Now take Peter,' Keith pointed to his sole labourer, a man in his thirties. 'He's a bit of a ladies' man. I showed him a johnny recently and asked if he used them. He didn't know what it was.'

I asked if he saw any similarity in the attitudes to Aids and driving. 'Oh yes,' he said. 'They are a thoroughly irresponsible lot. At least that's the way we see it. To them it's destiny, fatalism or whatever. Aids has become an accepted part of life. They're very stoical about it. They know they are dying, but they carry on living normally up to the end. I mean, you'll see someone who seems to be perfectly all right, then you hear two or three days later that he's dead. Of course there's a lot of malaria as well, and that speeds things along.'

Later, back at the little bungalow, Tereza summoned us to tea with a burst of Rutoro in which I caught the word 'darling'. The sitting-room looked out on the mountains over a sea of soft green tranquillity. It had been from this region that Museveni had launched his guerrilla war; for years a low-level conflict swirled around the hills without touching Keith and Tereza directly. Recently, anti-Museveni forces based across the border in Zaire had been operating in the district but, as had often been the case in remote parts of Africa, being white, far from attracting hostility, was a kind of protective badge.

So had he never had any unpleasant experiences himself? He shrugged deprecatingly. 'There was just one bit of nonsense. Amin in one of his madder phases ordered that miniskirts were not to be worn higher than four inches above the knee. The next thing I know, in town one day, the police stopped me and measured my shorts. Too short, they said. I was in the cells for a few nights before coming up before the magistrate – a Goan, a chap I knew quite well. I pleaded guilty, of course, and he fined me some small amount.'

The interesting thing about this episode, I suggested, was that once he had been arrested, it was unthinkable that he should simply be freed. No matter how absurd the charge, the fact that he had been picked up by the police in the first place meant that he had to be punished for something.

'That's very true,' he said. 'It goes with the culture. Still, we do well to remember that there's a lot to be said in favour of that culture.' He laughed drily. 'Particularly as you get older. If I was in the UK I would be in some dreadful old home. Here, Tereza and I look after each other, and if she dies before me, someone from the family will come in and take over.'

It was late in the afternoon when I said goodbye to them. Tereza smiled gravely and said 'goooobyee'. Keith smiled diffidently. 'Well, I don't suppose it was of much interest, but you're welcome any time,' he said.

In Conrad's novella, *The Heart of Darkness*, Kurtz, the imperialist who has gone native, is left at the end muttering 'The horror! The horror!' Here was a figure no less isolated than Kurtz, living in serenity with his stamp collection and extended family. A man of simple needs, he had become part of Africa just by submitting himself to it. In the end, it was as simple as that.

I had walked about three miles back towards town when a car stopped and a young man offered me a lift the rest of the way. He guessed that I had been to see Keith, and asked why. I said I was visiting old *mzungus* and wanted to tell their stories because people in Britain might be interested. He took the point at once. 'Yes! Because they cannot understand why they are still living in Africa!' he said triumphantly.

HOW DIFFERENT IT might all have been if sexual contact between members of the colonial service and native peoples had not been prohibited in 1909. Up to then, relations between single officials who kept local 'wives', concubinage as it was known, were tolerated by the authorities to the benefit of social contact and general understanding; local mistresses, known as 'sleeping dictionaries', helped many a young official acquire fluency in a dialect. Lord Crewe's threat of 'disgrace and official ruin' for officials with concubines changed the entire character of relations between African and European.

Africa was something of a sexual wonderland to early visitors. Ronald Hyam's study, *Empire and Sexuality*, describes how the colonies liberated young Victorian men. Casual sex was a routine ingredient of life in many postings and, moreover, the status of being white put the single man in a strong position to get his way. In sex, as in so much else, the Empire was a kind of limitless playground for young, adventurous Englishmen. In the 1830s, an Indian Army officer, Captain Edward Sellon, celebrated the 'salacious, succulent houris' of the East after a 'regular course of fucking with native women' who he found expert 'in all the arts and wiles of love'. The memsahibs soon put a stop to that sort of thing in India, but Africa, in which millions of square miles were administered by a handful of white officials, was far less responsive to similar treatment. As the European settlers at the Cape fanned out in the mid-nineteenth century, hunters and traders set up outposts in the Far Interior, as the region to the north was known. Most of them established relationships with local women.

Because of the fundamental inequality between the white male and his black concubine it became fashionable to see these liaisons as simply another symptom of racial oppression. It is true that black women never won the status of wives and many were discarded along with any offspring when the relationship became inconvenient for the man. It is also the case, however, that most girls in East Africa lost their virginity during puberty and enjoyed no rights while they were single. Some at least of the white men who crossed the colour line sexually did so socially as well.

The French saw concubinage as a positive force. Temporary unions 'with well-chosen native women' were officially encouraged, Hyams wrote, 'as being as desirable for the health, discipline and prestige of the French official as it was for his imperial authority and linguistic competence'. (Keith told me that, even in his time, black mistresses were still referred to as 'sleeping dictionaries'.) In the Britain of the 1880s, however, a doctrine of imperial race purity was on the rise, one which had as its goal the restoration of social distance between the ruling elite and the ruled. Administrators arriving around the turn of the century in territories from Rhodesia to Uganda were horrified to find that many, if not most, single officials working in outlying areas had black concubines. Matters were brought to a head in 1908 by a scandal involving a district official in Kenya, Hubert Silberrad, who acquired two mistresses from his predecessor, who had paid forty goats in bridewealth for each. The London press worked itself up into a righteous froth and soon afterwards Lord Crewe issued his edict. Henceforth colonial administration was to be entrusted almost exclusively to men drawn from a social base that was aloof, conformist and, above all, respectable.

A similar metamorphosis took place forty years later when the Afrikaners acquired political power in South Africa. They were the longest established and most deeply assimilated of Africa's white people, as the large Afrikaans-speaking, mixed-race population at the Cape known as Coloureds bore witness. An act outlawing inter-racial marriage, in effect denying three centuries of cohabitation and blending, was one of the first laws of the race purity doctrine that came to be known as apartheid.

MY ATTEMPTS TO meet Ugandan royalty needed fresh impetus. Having established in a call to Kampala that there was still no news of the Kabaka of Buganda, I set out with the help of my helpful hotel receptionist to find the Omukama of Toro.

In truth, I was more interested in meeting the Omukama's aunt, Princess Elizabeth of Toro. Now usually known as Elizabeth Bagaya, she had made

the remarkable transition in 1974 from international model and social orna-
ment to Idi Amin's foreign minister after her predecessor was found floating
in the Nile – only to be sacked when an alleged sexual escapade in an Orly
airport lavatory gave birth to the *Private Eye* phrase 'Ugandan discussions'.
Well-connected in Western capitals and highly capable – she took a law
degree at Cambridge, and won £50,000 in damages from newspapers which
repeated the *Eye* allegations – she was still Fort Portal's most celebrated
citizen. 'You must see her,' the receptionist had said. 'She will tell you
wonderful stories.'

I found the Omukama's compound about ten minutes' walk from the
hotel. A whitewashed bungalow was surrounded by a high wire fence and
had a guard house at the entrance but I walked up the drive without being
challenged. The door was answered by a young man named Moses. He
seemed genuinely sad as he explained that it would not be possible to meet
the Omukama as he was away at kindergarten in London, being, at the age
of four, the world's youngest monarch. Even more distressing was the news
that I had just missed Princess Elizabeth. 'She was here for Easter, but we
think she is in Nairobi or London now,' he said. It was all most dispiriting.
The rains had set in and I had to move on or risk being stranded here by
flooding; time was running short and I had to press on to Kenya.

It was still raining when I got back to the hotel. In the darkened sitting-
room was a dog-eared copy of the local paper some four weeks old, containing a report on the killing of a rainmaker in a nearby village. Evidently the
district had been in the grip of a drought until recently and the rainmaker,
an elderly man known as Rubalema, had offered to work his spells on
payment of a fee by the village of about £800. Far from being pleased, the
villagers were so incensed by this attempt at extortion that they set upon
Rubalema and beat him fiercely. With his dying breath, he uttered a curse
that the district would not receive a drop of rain for another year. It promptly
started to pour and had hardly stopped since.

ON THE MORNING I left Fort Portal, cloud had clustered around the peaks of
the Ruwenzoris but the sun was out, casting a sharp, clear light across
meadows through which a stream burbled. The rucksack felt by now familiar,
even comforting, on my back, and I swung along with a light heart, past
the old colonial headquarters in Lugard Road, taking a short cut across the
golf course. Near the clubhouse of the Toro Club (Members Only) stood a
stone cairn marking the site of the first fort, established by the British in
1893.

In town, a *matatu* was just about to leave for Kampala by a less scenic but more direct route than the way I had come. The ample forms of Mr and Mrs J. M. Kironde were already ensconced at either end of the back seat. 'You can take your place,' Mrs Kironde said, indicating a rather small space between them. He was a Muganda, she an Ankole, and they were on their way back to Kampala from visiting her family.

'*Sprechen sie Deutsch*?' asked Mr Kironde, a small tubby man in a baseball cap. Barely waiting for an answer he went on: 'I speak *Deutsch* because I studied there. Three years. Engineering. Munich.' Had he liked Munich? 'Yes, but the Bavarians, you know, they are very proud.' He puffed out his chest. 'They say, "*Ich bin ein Bavarian*."'

Like the Baganda, perhaps? 'Ha ha, very good,' he chortled. 'But now . . .' his voice dropped and he looked around like a conspirator, 'now we are being suppressed.' He put his finger to his lips. After a while he went on: 'You see, you people, you are very democratical. I wonder at it. But African leaders do not like their people to be democratical. They want to keep their people like a poor man coming to ask for a little bread.' He sighed.

Mrs Kironde was terrifically turned out in a high-shouldered, traditional dress with a grand gold-braided sash and lashings of jewellery. She giggled fetchingly at Mr Kironde across me. Whenever the *matatu* stopped, and the horde of vendors descended with skewered meat, nuts, pineapples and drinks, the Kirondes spent liberally and pressed offerings on me, squashed like a child between them.

Mr Kironde appointed himself our guide and made emphatic pronouncements which were promptly disproved. 'We will be in Mubende in ten minutes,' he said. Half an hour later we had still not reached Mubende. 'Bushenyi is just over that hill,' he insisted. The hill was surmounted to reveal an expanse of verdant but empty bush. 'This is a good driver,' he said happily. Just then the *matatu* swerved sharply to avoid dashing a cyclist to death. I wanted to be left alone with my gritted teeth and my terror, but Mr Kironde, sensing my anxiety, was determined to reassure me. 'Do not worry, my friend,' he said kindly, putting a hand on my knee. 'If our time is up, there is nothing we can do. Believe me, I know all about this.' He tapped his heart. 'I am DMC.'

What, I asked, was DMC.

'Dangerous Mechanical Condition.' And he roared: 'Like the *matatu*.'

We reached Kampala in mid-afternoon, coming in via Mengo Hill where

I got out. As the *matatu* sped off, Mr Kironde waved cheerfully through the rear window.

KING RONNIE WAS still in London. The Baganda who I spoke to were unsurprised. 'He's such a disappointment,' said John Nagenda. 'He's become the sort of fellow who spends all his time overseas and ends up joining a mediocre club like the Travellers' or the RAC.' I was deeply disappointed myself, but another individual who embodied the Anglo-Bagandan past agreed to see me before I left.

It was hard to imagine that Abu Mayanja had ever been an anti-colonial firebrand. He was an owlish man of about seventy with virtually no neck and glasses so thick that his eyes seemed to be looking up from the bottom of a pond. He had been arrested twice by the British, detained for very much longer by Obote, and served virtually every other Ugandan ruler, whether as Amin's education minister or Museveni's deputy prime minister. Somehow, he had survived.

'Well, I was never terribly ambitious, and I was always quite poor,' he said, triggering a burst of the wheezy, convulsive hilarity which his own sallies brought on. That response was typical; asked a serious question, he took the Englishman's refuge in a flippant reply. At one stage, when I pressed a point, he said: 'You musn't take everything I say too literally, it takes the chaff out of it.' Then he dissolved into mirth again.

He was the son of a Mugandan peasant. At primary school, his brightness came to the attention of teachers who secured a place for him at King's College, Buddo. From there he passed to Makerere and another King's College, this time at Cambridge. I had first heard about Abu from one of his former lecturers at Makerere who remembered an angry student leader in the 1950s, parading around campus with a poster that read 'Down with 19th century Tory despotism!' Expelled, he was taken up by Sir Andrew Cohen, Uganda's last governor, who arranged a place for him at Cambridge.

'I didn't feel as grateful as I ought to have. I thought they were trying to keep me out of politics.' He cackled. 'Of course they were. But Cohen was still a great man.'

He was at Cambridge for four years from 1953. There, he said, he discovered the key to liberalism from his history lecturer. 'He put it like this. He said, ''There is the Light Programme and there is the Third Programme. The Third Programme is very good for you, but I would not stop you listening to the Light Programme if that is what you want.'' ' By the time he returned to Uganda, the anger in the agitator's breast had been soothed and the transition to an Anglo-African had begun.

For an hour he talked pungently and wittily about political affairs: Museveni was extremely able, his trouble was that he was so sure of his own position he believed he could argue everyone else out of theirs; it was pleasing that King Ronnie's mind was stimulated by London, but worrying that he needed to spend so much of his time being stimulated.

The banter was set aside briefly just once, when he spoke seriously about the relationship between Buganda and Britain. The eyes rolled behind the glasses like stones in the pond. 'In most places, the missionaries went out and converted the small man. Here they started at the court, and everything else followed. But that would not have been enough on its own. The people who were sent out were of the very highest calibre. Tucker, Cohen, the Cooks . . . these were people who made the greatest impact on the Baganda. I don't want to be coy about it, Cook was a great man – a missionary and a physician, like St Luke.

'And we made an impression on them too, because they paid us the compliment of showing us that we deserved their best.'

BEFORE LEAVING KAMPALA, I walked up the hill one last time, to the cemetery on the hill at Namirembe. My own sense of impending loss at departing from Uganda added to the power and mystery of the place. The spirits of Speke and Mutesa, Mackay and Mwanga, might be moving with the hint of breeze that rustled the palms.

With Abu's words still freshly in mind, I went back to the spot where the Cooks were buried but was drawn to a small grave nearby. The stone was inscribed 'Christopher, darling son of Roy and Dora Billington. Called Sept. 1944 aged 4'. On the grave lay a floral display with a card dated 23 February 1997. It read: 'Dear Christopher. We remember you as we celebrate a hundred years of the hospital in which your Dad and Mum served for many years. Glory be to God. From the Staff at Mengo.'

I had started my journey with anxiety. Uganda and Tanzania had represented a compendium of African woes, and on my previous attempts to visit them I had been arrested and thrown out. I had feared, moreover, that I might find I did not like Africa any more, might feel myself a stranger among aliens. Yet at this moment, I could think of nowhere I had felt so completely at home. For the first time in my experience, being a *mzungu* had not mattered. It felt too good to last.

9. The Valley

MALABA WAS THE NAME of the border post. Fifteen years on, the memory was still sharp, but as we filed off the bus and into the immigration hut, it was hard to associate the place with menace.

The idea had been to pick up a car in Nairobi and drive it to Uganda to follow up reports about atrocities by Obote's army. The problem was that the car, belonging to a BBC colleague whom I will call Walker, was 'hot'. I was unaware of this. The discovery was made by a Ugandan border official who studied the log-book and noticed, as I had not done, that it had been doctored. He was polite but the air was suddenly still. I was taken to an office where a man was being beaten. He cowered on the floor as a soldier lashed him with a weighted length of hosepipe. The man uttered no cry but his feet scrabbled on the boards as he tried to escape and the pipe made a flat, whistling sound in the air. Then the official said something to the soldier in which I caught the word *mzungu*, so he took the man out the back to beat him where a white would not see.

I produced a letter from Walker, authorising me as his friend to drive the car wherever I wished. They were unimpressed; the engine number had undeniably been altered in the log-book. 'Did you murder Mr Walker for his car?' asked my interrogator.

They kept me for a few hours, unsure of what to do, before passing the buck. A call was made to the Kenyan post and a posse of police came roaring across. They were furious at being shown up by Ugandans, but once the car had been impounded they lost interest in me. I was taken before a magistrate and fined for driving an unlicensed vehicle.

When I confronted Walker later, he was unabashed; indeed, he was aggrieved that I had not bribed my way out of the situation. 'I should have known they would have picked on you,' he grumbled. We had been arrested together on an assignment in Zambia once before. 'It's that squint of yours. The blacks think it's the evil eye.'

BACK THEN, UGANDA was the country visitors approached with apprehension. Kenya was an African success story. Westernised, prosperous Kenya, with its modern capital, pearly coastal resorts and safari lodges, was the kind of place where white people felt comfortable. Expatriate businessmen, aid workers and journalists used it as a base for covering the hard parts of the continent. Now the shadow had shifted from Uganda and Kenya's success story had soured. Visitors were routinely mugged in Nairobi, tourists had been robbed and even murdered in game parks.

Kenyans claimed that the view projected of their country in the press was distorted, if not racist. Why, for example, was there so much coverage of one case, the murder of Julie Ward in the Maasai Mara reserve, when at least half a dozen backpackers had been killed in the Australian outback? This was perfectly true, but – as in Uganda in the 1980s – the main victims of a régime as corrupt as it was tyrannical were not whites, but the common folk known officially, with bogus reverence, as the *wananchi*. A state where the murder of the foreign minister could be covered up as a suicide was no respecter of human life.

Despite these drawbacks, I was looking forward to enjoying some of Kenya's creature comforts. I might find a comfortable hotel in Nairobi, have a hot bath for the first time since setting out, and even – sweetest of all – exchange chicken and rice for a steak and chips. These visions tempered my regret at leaving Uganda as we filed back on to the bus. The officials on the Kenyan side were surly but disinterested and my passport was stamped with barely a glance. Beyond the border, the change in landscape was almost immediate. Gone was the deep green lushness of papyrus swamps and *matoke* groves. In its place was a spare, lean savannah – long plains of yellowing grass and acacia trees. The land defined the contrasting character of the two countries and their peoples, fecundity and sparseness, the agricultural Baganda, the pastoralist Maasai and Kikuyu.

For all its associations with Britain, Kenya was never visited by any of the great explorers. Stanley, the 'Smasher of Rocks' himself, thought it far too dangerous. In 1878, he told the Royal Geographical Society: 'I do not know in all my list of travels where you could become martyrs so quickly as in Masai [Land].' It was an unheralded Scot, Joseph Thomson, with his expedition for the Royal Geographical Society five years later, who started demystifying the territory, but to the outside world it remained a nomadic wilderness until the construction of the Uganda Railway from the coast to Lake Victoria. In May 1899, the line reached a swampy plain roughly halfway to the lake. It was a featureless and unhealthy spot, but lay at the foot of the eastern escarpment up which the railway had to climb to the Great Rift Valley and was therefore suited for a supply station. And so Nairobi was born.

Empire was at its zenith. Two years earlier Britain had celebrated Victoria's golden jubilee with the last empty spaces on the globe neatly

demarcated and coloured. In the past decade the energy of the Lugards and
Johnstons in East Africa had been more than matched in the south by Cecil
Rhodes. Using the Cape Colony as his political platform and diamond
earnings as his bankroll, Rhodes had sent mounted cohorts to occupy the
so-called Far Interior, the region stretching north of Kipling's 'great, grey-
green, greasy Limpopo' beyond the Zambezi, and all the way to the shores
of Lake Tanganyika. As Jan Morris has written, it seemed that dominion
had become Britain's destiny.

> The mystique of it all, the legend of blood, crown, sacrifice, formed a sort
> of ju-ju. The red looked ingrained on the map, as though it had been
> stained there in some arcane ritual, and the vast spaces of Greater Britain
> were like a field of perpetual youth, where future generations of Britons
> would for ever be regenerated.

Yet already there was a coarsening of the imperial spirit, especially in
Africa. Livingstone had seen Christianity and civilisation as the means by
which blacks would free themselves from slavery and ignorance. Rhodes
saw only commerce – and British domination. Five months after the Uganda
Railway reached Nairobi, Britain went to war for gold against the Boers,
Africa's original white settlers, who had done everything in their power to
escape the clutches of Empire. In defeat, the Boers were hate-filled, the
British shamed in victory. Theirs was to be a strange and poignant partnership in Kenya.

Appropriately enough, it was sport that made the territory a homeland
for officers, gentlemen and the lotus-eaters of the Happy Valley. The Third
Baron Delamere hunted there long before his colonial evangelism started
the transformation of the White Highlands. Frederick Selous, most renowned
of all African hunters, visited in 1902 and after that could hardly bear to
tear himself away. Quite simply, the plains were alive with game on a scale
and variety unknown anywhere else in the world – elephant, buffalo, lion,
and antelope and gazelle in unimaginable numbers.

Delamere was not Kenya's first settler, but he was the most vigorous
and influential. As a pioneer-cum-politician he went out in 1902 proclaiming:
'We mean to make East Africa a white man's country.' Unlike densely
populated Uganda, large tracts, including those most suited to European-
style agriculture, were uninhabited. Elsewhere, gaunt and bloodthirsty
nomads preyed on numerous but unwarlike folk. At the outset, the Kikuyu
actually saw the whites as a bulwark against the Maasai. At the time it

seemed the only problem was that few whites were willing to throw in their hand with a new, self-supporting colony.

Then, in 1908, the Afrikaners came, riders moving across the plains. Leonine and guttural, with wide-brimmed hats, they lived outdoors as naturally as the wildlife they loved to hunt, and in their wake followed covered wagons with their women and dirty, half-naked children as wild as Africa itself. The wagons, pulled by a span of sixteen oxen, passed through the Great Rift Valley where Delamere had his ranch at Soysambu, and climbed up the Mau escarpment. They trundled on across the Uasin Gishu plateau where their leader, Jansen van Rensberg, called a halt. A solitary hill named Sergoit broke the plain that ran from horizon to horizon and teemed with game. Here the wagons were outspanned and the men rode out to mark off their farms. After a time they called the place Eldoret, as if this were to be their Eldorado, a new promised land for the Boers.

I first heard the story about the Boers of Eldoret from one of their own, a woman named Minnie Bothma, farming with her husband in Zambia in 1976, and was struck by the tragedy and romance of it: the irreconcilables, *bittereinders*, as they were known, who would not submit to Britain after defeat, and trekked away from their homes in the Transvaal just as their forefathers had once trekked from the Cape, and kept going for thousands of miles until they found a new Arcadia in west Kenya, only to fall again under the British yoke. It was a wonderful story, almost biblical in resonance, and for years I believed it was absolutely true.

FROM THE BUS station I hauled my pack up to the Eldoret Wagon Hotel and, after luxuriating in the bath for almost an hour, went to change some money. There was another white man at the bank. Hesitantly I asked if he knew how I could get to Fanie Kruger's farm. He drew a map on the back of an envelope.

The only taxi in town stood at the corner of Kenyatta Street, a London cab painted red with a driver wearing a black suit and tie. The meter had been taken out and I asked the fare to Sergoit. I had to hold my breath, but there was no other way of getting there and I reasoned that it was not every day you got the chance to ride in a London cab to visit the last Afrikaner farmer in Eldoret.

Acacia scrub passed outside the window amid the familiar clatter of the diesel engine. All this had been the Boers' domain. After word went back that the trekkers had found fine wheat-growing country, others followed. By the 1940s, Eldoret could have been a *dorp* on the *platteland*. The Dutch

Reformed Church congregation alone was six hundred strong. The farmers held fêtes, with stalls selling *melktert* and *koeksusters*, and games of *jukskei* and the wheezy accordion dance known as *tikkiedraai*. They had their own schools, churches and clubs, and the Eldoret rugby side was the most feared in the country. Now they were all gone. Abandoned farms had been occupied by squatters, the Van Riebeeck School was Nakuru Secondary, and African gospellers had taken over the Dutch Reformed Church. The Boers' Eldorado had suffered the fate they most feared.

As so often in white Africa, it was the power of the imagination that had been most destructive. Kenya had its Mau Mau troubles in the 1950s, but Eldoret was relatively untouched. Then murder, rape and chaos came to the former Belgian Congo, and in far-off Eldoret the Boers were gripped by fear. As the British negotiated with the Mau Mau leader, Jomo Kenyatta, to lead an independent Kenya, fear turned to dread. From 1961, stories about Kenyan 'trekkers' arriving by road at the South African border started to appear in the local press. The following from the Cape *Argus* of 23 February was typical: 'Piet Olivier, a prosperous farmer from Eldoret, said: "It will be much worse than the Congo when independence comes. The only reason we came now, at the risk of being called cowards, is that we would probably have to leave half our families behind – dead – afterwards."'

'It was sheer, blind panic,' said Fanie Kruger. 'There was no reason for it, but that's the way it can happen. Suddenly, all our people were talking about being murdered in their beds. And once it started, there was no stopping it.'

Among those who joined the exodus was Fanie's father. 'So eventually the old man gets to Middelberg in the eastern Transvaal, which is where our people came from, to have a look around. Now it's July, and you know that is the prettiest time of year here. Down South it's the middle of winter and the land is brown and burned. Next thing, the old man is back in the truck – drives non-stop, three days. He gets back and it's one of our fantastic mornings, quite wet but bright sunshine, and he says "*Nee, ons gaan nie*" (We're not going). But the others just kept leaving. By the late 1960s, there were just a handful left. Now it's just me.'

The last Afrikaner farmer looked typical of the breed, a rugby prop in khaki shorts and ankle socks, with a wry humour that split his face in boyish laughter. The laughter came easily but there was an edge. He had not endured without compromise and his situation was not without risk. The Kruger homestead was a military-style compound with guards and two-way radios. Fanie pulled his weight in the local community – he was a stalwart of Kanu, the ruling party, sat on a number of committees and was a member of the police reserve. He had no time for the languid recipe of the White Highlands for survival – which was to stick with the herd, enjoy life at the club, lie low and steer clear of politics.

'That lot are living in a nice little cocoon. It's okay for them, they've still got numbers. I'm on my own here, and we've had to look after ourselves.' Quickly he went on: 'Look, this government was very good to my dad and me, hey? But at the end of the day, if Kenyans don't own a piece of land, they will feel dissatisfied.'

So what, I asked, if Biwott decided that he wanted the Kruger farm? Nicholas Biwott was the local MP, the most powerful man in Kenya after his mentor, President Daniel arap Moi. He was also the most feared, the thugish minister who acted as Moi's enforcer. Stories of sinister doings circulated constantly around Biwott's name. He had a finger in every pie in a notoriously crooked administration, and an appetite for land. He was also Fanie Kruger's neighbour.

Fanie's eye narrowed, and he spoke a little too fast. 'Biwott could have had me out, no problem, but he's been a very good neighbour and if I can help him I will. I don't judge people.' He went on hastily: 'And it's not just me. I know three or four palefaces who were destitute – I mean *destitute*. Who paid the hospitals, the funeral charges? Biwott. He had no obligation. Don't ask me why he did it, but I respect the guy.'

Conversation veered back to safer ground. The Kruger homestead, set on a little *kopje* sheltered by blossoming trees, and 4,500 acres on which the wheat swayed like a veil of golden silk on the plain, was a place any Boer would be proud to pass on to his son. Fanie's own boy was seven. Hell, he said, things were still good. So much so that now the families who went Down South in the 1960s were coming back to look around. 'They used to call me *kaffirboetie* [kaffir brother] when I went down,' he said with grim satisfaction. 'Now things are starting to get a bit hard there, they want to try here again. I say to them, "Dream on, pal".'

I asked him about Eldoret's *bittereinders*, the heroes of Boer legend who gave up everything, joining Jansen van Rensberg to trek halfway across Africa in ox wagons to escape British rule. 'Hell, man, they weren't trying to get away from the Brits, they were trying to get away from their own people. The Brits *had* to move them – they were outcasts.'

The final phase of the Boer War brought shame on Britain. Unable to bring the mobile *kommandos* to battle, Kitchener set up camps in which Boer civilians were interned and where typhoid rapidly took hold. Up to

20,000, mainly women and children died, and the seeds were planted of a terrible hatred. Their men, the *bittereinders*, dreamed of revenge, not only against the British but those who had collaborated or resisted with less resolve, the *hensoppers*. Eventually, Britain had to provide a bolt-hole for them, far from the hand of vengeance. So Eldoret had been founded as a colony for pariahs. Not for the first time, the Afrikaner love of mythology cloaked a darker secret.

What about the wagons, though; surely that part was true? 'They all came up by ship to Tanga and Mombasa,' said Fanie. 'Then they went by train to the railhead at Londiani. If there was any trekking by wagon, it was no more than forty miles.'

The Afrikaner fondness for a past embroidered with nostalgia and fantasy should not obscure a reality that was often just as compelling as the myth. The story of their diaspora – not the Great Trek of innumerable and interminable South African school history lessons, but the more gradual and individual dispersal of hunters, farmers and downright nomads, beyond the Vaal, and Zambezi and the Kafue, settling in small clan-based colonies far distant from their Cape origins – was the very stuff of frontier saga.

Although most Afrikaners had lost that frontier edge, Fanie retained it. So did another figure a few hundred miles down my road. Her name was Katrina. I had no idea how I was going to find her, but her story was fascinating. Fanie had been jeered at as a *kaffirboetie*, but what Katrina had done was utterly beyond the pale. As a young Afrikaner in the colonial society of Tanganyika, she had eloped with an African servant.

AT THE HOTEL there was a message from the Soysambu estate: I was welcome to visit Lord and Lady Delamere. Details of just how I was to get there were garbled, but I boarded the bus with an assurance that if I alighted at the 133 kilometre peg, just beyond Nakuru, I would be within an hour's walk of the homestead. From Eldoret to Nairobi was about 250 miles, and Soysambu was roughly halfway, in the pastoral country of the Great Rift Valley.

The bus rattled south-east until it reached the edge of the plateau, the Mau Escarpment, which plunged away to the floor of the Rift. There, laid out below, was the land Delamere had seen as a realm for his settlers, a new South Africa or, better still, a new Australia. He visited East Africa for the first time in 1897 on a hunting expedition after a youth in which he had shown every promise of bringing dishonour to the family name. A failure at Eton, he was, in the words of his biographer, Elspeth Huxley,

intemperate, unconventional and rash. Immediately, he fell in love with
the country which Lugard had been the first to extol as suitable for
white settlement. Lugard's idea was that Kenya might develop a fruit-
exporting economy, like California. The ever-contrary Delamere, however,
employed by a colonial administration to promote settlement, took Australia
as his model. Wool and sheep would bring prosperity to white settlers
at the edge of the Rift Valley, on land regarded as useless by the natives.
Like many of his ideas, this turned out to be fundamentally flawed, but
Delamere was never discouraged by practical considerations, and his overall
vision – that European-style agriculture would have a vital role to play in
the future of Africa – was entirely sound. Undaunted by repeated failure,
and mounting debts which eventually ruined the family estate back in
Cheshire, he continued to farm experimentally until finding success with
wheat and varieties of cattle which thrived in areas disdained by the Maasai
pastoralists.

There is a point, coming down off the Mau Escarpment at the edge of
the valley, where the light seems to acquire a new quality. It is perhaps
partly an illusion, brought on by the sudden opening up of a landscape so
fresh that one might have just emerged from a tunnel, but look at it again
and you feel sure it is more than just new shapes and colours: there is a
clarity, a soft sparkle on the blue bank of the eastern ridge fifty miles across
the valley, and on the craters below of extinct volcanoes, etched in pinks
and purples, and on the lakes of Nakuru and Naivasha, shining a tingling
image of the world back at itself, which can only be explained in terms of
the light. In the years when things were not easy for the settlers – and there
were many such times, for most were starting out on their own, and were
at the mercy of an obstructive bureaucracy as well as disease, stock thieves
and the elements – there was always the country to turn to for solace and
renewal. As Mrs Huxley wrote, these highlands had a peculiar capacity for
inspiring love among those who made their home here. Partly it was 'the
space and freedom, the grandeur, and the hospitality of comfortable, irregular
homesteads with bright and carefully tended gardens'. But perhaps even
more significantly it was 'a country that always holds the unexpected in
store, that rouses high hopes and seldom satisfies them, and yet charms the
bitterness out of disappointment'.

The bus dropped me a few hundred yards from the 133 kilometre peg.
A few hundred yards away lay Elmenteita, a soda lake six miles long with
its surface coated white and pink in the late morning by flamingos. Down
here the valley had that same luminous quality, but as the clatter of the bus

trailed into the distance, it also fell silent. I started walking up the road. Then a smart black estate car appeared, throwing up a cloud of dust on a dirt track. Lord Delamere had thoughtfully sent a chauffeur to collect the backpacker.

Soysambu: Monday, 12 April

IT IS LATE afternoon on the verandah outside the guest-room, looking across the floor of the Rift where rain swept up from the south after lunch. The only sound is a light wind rustling in the bougainvillea and occasionally the soft rumble of distant thunder.

The Delameres always had a reputation for eccentricity. The Third Lord, who built Soysambu, so objected to the introduction of street lights in Nairobi that he rode up and down shooting them out; the Fourth vowed never to allow the scandalous Diana Broughton to cross his threshold, then married her and shared her with his friends; the Fifth, my host, is thought of as a recluse who spends most of his time playing with his model railway. In fact, he likes the trains well enough but his real love is the estate. He is a very tall man in his sixties and resembles portraits of his imperious grandfather but is missing two front teeth which can give him a piratical, even predatory, look. 'People can't be trusted,' he grumbles. 'Steal things, that sort of thing.' But pepperiness is a mask for a kindly man. My rucksack and scruffiness were accepted as naturally as if I rightly belonged on Soysambu's grandee guest list, which has ranged from the Westminsters to the Mountbattens. The Baron is funny, mordant and indiscreet. Lady Delamere is as little as he is large. A daughter of the last Governor, Sir Patrick Renison, she resembles a roly-poly version of the Queen. Like her husband, she is unguarded and drops verbal firecrackers and the occasional expletive with her eyes screwed up in wicked delight, like a little girl's.

It is all a long way from the discomforts of the road. Breakfast is served beneath an arbor on a vast, cool patio where birds flutter in search of discarded morsels. Dinner is served at a rosewood table by the light of silver candelabra. A magnificent allegorical Breughel hangs on one wall, various Cholmondeley ancestors on the others. Once there was a set of de Lamerie silver but Diana disposed of quite a few treasures to sustain her extravagances. The meal is served by two chatty and far from overawed maids. The wine, South African plonk, comes round frequently in an exquisite claret jug.

Like all great homes, Soysambu is full of ghosts. The Third Lord came here in 1910 when the valley was an empty wilderness. For the first few years he lived in a mud and grass hut, while he wrestled with his latest crop or livestock venture and found company among the Maasai. Like many settlers, he was drawn to the physical beauty and pride of the Maasai warrior *moran* and marvelled at their courage in the lion hunt. More unusually for a European, he shared their indifference to comfort, learnt their language and adopted certain Maasai customs. 'I loved them and they loved me,' he once said. He became disillusioned when pressure on land increased and they continued to reject European-style pastoralism. 'I would take land from Maasai tomorrow for farms,' he said later. 'I would take it from any nomads. They don't use it.'*

His grandson still regards him as a hero. 'Wonderful ideas, utterly hopeless with cash,' he says. Delamere was a figure on the grand scale, able to intimidate colonial governors as well as inspire 'his' settlers. The aristocratic pedigree must have helped, but there was steel too. As its leading citizen, its uncrowned head, he set what was to be the tone for Kenya colony, a combination of hard work and hard play of the high-jinks public school variety. Along with shooting out the streetlights of Nairobi, in protest against creeping civilisation, he bought the Nakuru hotel where he set about smashing all the windows. Eventually he fell out with the colonial authorities, but continued after his death in 1931 to be revered by the settlers who subscribed to a statue which was set up on Delamere Avenue in Nairobi. After *uhuru* the street was changed to Kenyatta Avenue and the statue was taken down. There was some suggestion that it might be melted down and refashioned in the likeness of Kenyatta. Instead, it was brought here, and stands now beside the homestead – 'looking out at his cows', says his grandson.

Diana is also a presence. She was the queen of Soysambu. Delamere had eventually got round to building a homestead to replace the mud hut, but never had much interest in it. Diana married his son, the Fourth Lord, and spent lavishly, adding guest wings and much else besides. She was his third wife, he her fourth husband, but although she was still a promiscuous as well as lovely woman, the marriage was happy. Her stepson recalls her as a fabulous creature, fragrant, glamorous and bejewelled. 'She was much

---

* A thesis could be written about the worship by upper-caste Englishmen of the Maasai, a people who, as Mrs Huxley has said, were intrinsically both fascist and racist. She herself made friends among the Kikuyu who adapted more readily to European ways, and produced Kenya's first political class; whites have expressed similar ethnic preferences, between 'warrior' and 'philosopher' peoples, in Zimbabwe (Ndebele and Shona) and South Africa (Zulu and Xhosa).

nicer to me than father, who was a horrible man,' he says. 'Her indiscretions were many and varied, and she gave the impression of finding them highly enjoyable. Extravagant woman. She did a lot for the estate but sold off masses of pictures, silver and jewels, particularly after father's death when she was quite gaga but still my guardian and there was nothing I could do to stop her.'

The Kenya in which the Fifth Lord lives is a far tougher, more lawless place than it was in the time of his father and grandfather. He took over the estate in 1979, just after the death of Kenyatta, under whom the country prospered. Since then Moi has plundered it, and there is intense demand for land, for simple survival reasons. Only 17 per cent of Kenya is arable and the population is recording the fastest growth of any country in history – between 3.8 and 4.1 per cent. White farmers are feeling the pinch from rustling and squatting. Although reluctant to get involved politically themselves, they are furious with Richard Leakey who attracts unwelcome attention to *mzungus* by openly opposing Moi, and seem to expect Delamere to act as some larger-than-life figure, like his grandfather, who can somehow fix things with an unsympathetic government. They grumble that Delamere is playing with toy trains while the country goes up in smoke.

The Baron has problems of his own. Thanks to his father's improvidence and Diana's extravagance, the estate has been whittled down from a high point of 200,000 acres to about a quarter of that, and has more serious problems with rustling and theft than most. At present my host is plagued by a neighbour who regularly sets fire to pasture on the western boundary. The intention clearly is to intimidate and force a withdrawal from the land.

'I shan't go,' he says. 'I will send for a Kamba witchdoctor. They are the best. He will find out who this fellow is – they go about secretly and are very good at wheedling information out of people – and that will be that. I will not want to know about it.'

He rails against the improvidence of his neighbours. 'Delamere will pay, that's the motto of Naivasha,' he grouses. The fact is, that as the last of the major ranchers of the valley, he is a baron in every sense, a feudal lord with an estate that supports 5,000 workers and dependants in conditions that are the envy of the district. Staff refer to him respectfully as Lord Delamere but there is no fawning and his manner with them is easy and relaxed. In addition to direct dependants, his boreholes provide water to 50,000 people dwelling in the valley, at the estate's expense. It is fair to say that if the Delameres were ruined, their successors would not be half so paternal. 'I am the tenant of this land,' he says, 'and will be to the end of my days, and I hope to be able to pass it on in a good state of preservation.'

THE LIVESTOCK BARONS – Delamere, Gilbert Colvile and Galbraith Cole, old Etonians all – lived in the valley. The lotus-eaters dwelt across the eastern escarpment in the Aberdares, the White Highlands. The thread that connected them was Diana, one of the great *femmes fatales*.

She was improbably middle class for so grand a courtesan, being born into a solidly prosperous Hove family. But Diana always wanted more – more jewels, more luxury and more men – and working at a cocktail club called the Blue Goose off Berkeley Square was a natural first step. Her weakness was aristocrats and guns, and it was a combination of the two that ignited the great Happy Valley scandal of 1941. The story is too well-known to bear detailed repetition: a few months after arriving in Nairobi with her second husband, the baronet Sir Henry 'Jock' Delves Broughton, Diana became the mistress of the dashing but odious Josslyn Hay, Earl of Erroll and playboy of the Aberdares; Erroll's murder, after dining at the Muthaiga Club with Diana and Broughton, created sensation but no lamenting, a process repeated when Broughton was brought to trial, acquitted and soon afterwards killed himself.

Diana continued to move from bedroom to bedroom. She started an affair with Gilbert Colvile, another well-born if eccentric rancher, who married her in 1943 and then encouraged her to take other lovers, including a game warden and an army colonel, in the hope that she would provide him with an heir. She remained a striking woman in 1955 when, at the age of forty-two, she made her greatest conquest, marrying Colvile's friend, the Fourth Baron Delamere. Still she scandalised colonial society, although her most tempestuous affair, with a white hunter named Peter Leth, was hushed up when she wounded him with a pistol. She died in 1987 and was buried on a plain near Soysambu, between her last two husbands and with two favourite pugs at her feet, beneath the inscription 'Surrounded by all that I love'.

In the meantime, publication of a best-seller about the Erroll case, *White Mischief*, started a small industry. Theories about the identity of Erroll's killer abounded, from scorned lovers to other cuckolded husbands, but Broughton remained the main suspect. Surprisingly few suggested that Diana herself might have had a hand in the murder.

Her stepson, however, who knew her incandescent temper and her readiness to use firearms, believed that it was not Broughton but Diana who murdered her most notorious lover.

FLYING WAS PART and parcel of life in Kenya colony, even its culture. In the 1920s, Denys Finch-Hatton gave Karen Blixen what she called the greatest, the most transporting pleasure of her life in Africa, which was to fly over it. Their friend, the aviatrix Beryl Markham, wrote in words that sang about the exhilaration and uncertainty of first-born adventure at taking off over the Ngong hills. Flying in Kenya was almost a metaphor for freedom, and I jumped at the chance to join Delamere on a hop to another farm.

We had been flying for no more than thirty minutes when the descent started towards the western escarpment of the Rift, where the land rises in tiers over a series of spurs decorated by delicate umbrella acacia trees, all the lovelier when you are descending between them.

'If you don't like small planes you might want to close your eyes for the next bit,' he shouted over the growl of the engine.

I would have, but found myself transfixed. The Cessna banked vertically, bringing my stomach up to my throat as it dived and weaved its way down among the folds of the hills. The next thing I knew, we were wheeling towards two large gum trees. We hurtled between them before I could scream. But now the landing strip raced up, with hills on either side like Sheba's breasts. We hit the ground with a terrific bump, before finally coming to a halt just where the landing strip dissolved into a valley below.

'Beastly place to land,' he said.

After lunch we flew home. At cruising height he turned to me. 'I've got to fill in the log. You take over. Pedals to turn, joystick to climb or dive. But hold her as she is.'

I must have held my breath for ten intoxicating minutes, feeling the controls responding gently to my touch and the buck of the little aircraft buffeted by wind carrying rain up the Rift. Then it was time to come down. Through a film of cloud, we caught glimpses of a million flamingos on Elmenteita.

ON MY LAST night at Soysambu the choice was between playing model railways with Lord Delamere or going on a buffalo hunt with his son, Tom. The estate supported giraffe, buffalo and leopard as well as antelope. Hunting was prohibited by law but a herd of buffalo was causing mayhem on a citrus plantation and permission had been granted to cull a single bull.

We found the herd almost at once near a corner of the lake. In the dark, the animals' eyes glinted as the spotlight picked out their shadowy bulk. The objective being a cull, rather than sport, we were in an open four-wheel drive *bakkie*, with two riflemen, four trackers and myself. The herd, about fifteen animals including young, moved off almost at once and the *bakkie* began a pursuit. Once we got reasonably close and Tom took aim, but the herd thundered off again before he could be sure of a clean shot.

The buffalo soon realised they were being harried and a few big bulls dropped back, like cavalry defending a column of civilians from mounted raiders. Tom was able to take steady aim at one, held in the glare of the spotlight. Even anticipating it, the blast from the .375 Magnum came like a thunderclap. The bull staggered at the impact and fell momentarily to his forelegs, but was instantly up and galloping away.

Again we started in pursuit, the *bakkie* careering across open ground, the spotlight dancing crazily in the sky. In the back we struggled to keep our feet by holding on to a rail. I soon went down and was joined by two or three others, thrown around like logs until we came up again on the bull. He was turned towards us, about twenty yards off, his chest heaving blood, a dying heavyweight. The guns roared and two more bullets slapped into him. Almost imperceptibly at first, he sank to his knees, then his side. But still the great head stayed up, glowering hatred into the glare of the spotlight. Two more shots and at last the horns went down. He lay there for about ten seconds, and then expelled a long, low rumble, the echo of a bellow, as he died.

There was no backslapping. The air was even solemn as the men set to work with their skinning knives, murmuring softly to one another. A cut was made from ribs to testicles to remove the stomach, a large white bag steaming in the cool night air as it flopped to the ground. Tom came across to apologise for the shaking-up. 'You just can't let a buffalo get away with bullets in him. It's like leaving a hand grenade lying around with the pin out.'

It had been savage and exhilarating. Tonight, and for nights afterwards, there would be feasting in the Delamere compounds. I looked at Tom, a bloodstained public schoolboy with a gun in his hands. He had lived in London, seen old school friends climb the golden ladder, might indeed have made a career as a merchant banker himself. But in the end, between the City and the Rift Valley, there could have been only one choice.

UP IN THE Highlands, farming could be precarious – more *Flame Trees of Thika* than *White Mischief*, notwithstanding the rather frayed graciousness of polo and lunch at the club, sundowners under an umbrella tree. The farmers did not fear that Kenya would go the way of Tanzania, where white farms were nationalised, or Zimbabwe, where a similar threat was in the air. Agriculture was big business, the mainstay of Kenya's economy, and – so the story went – the government appreciated the efficiency of the white farming sector. So there were still opportunities for the man able to take care of himself.

In the western highlands, I met a tough former British Army officer who had bought a 600 acre farm mixed equally between coffee and tea, but in a state of gross neglect. Almost £500,000 was needed for refurbishment and new equipment, and he prepared a prospectus which won the approval of the European Investment Bank. Soon afterwards the money was forwarded via the Kenya National Bank, at a 5.5 per cent interest rate. Having acted as a conduit, the Kenyan bank stated that it would charge 11 per cent. The farmer had no option but to accept this, but now, two months later, he had still not received the funds and, being committed to projects for the growing season, had been forced to take a bridging loan elsewhere at 28 per cent. In desperation, he had been back to the local representative of the European bank, who threw up his hands in horror but was no more successful than the farmer in extracting the money from the Kenyan bank.

This farmer employed about 100 full-time workers and another fifty as casual pickers. With dependants, however, the farm provided a livelihood for about 700 people. 'If I go, we all go,' the farmer said.

A nearby farm was one of many enterprises owned by Kenya's richest man, Daniel arap Moi, the president. It was of similar size, and had employed a similar number of people until the previous year. Then the entire workforce was dismissed, losing their homes as well as their jobs. A skeleton staff now ran the farm. Those who had been full-time workers had become squatters. They were hanging on in the hope of casual picking work.

The farmer spoke with icy fury. 'We have state-sanctioned murder, legalised gangsterism and, now that Mobutu is gone, corruption on a scale that puts us top of the league in Africa. You're writing a book? Well, I think someone should do a book on Kenya – as a straightforward study in evil.'

10. The Plains

THERE IS A LONG tradition of extracting money from the traveller in Africa. In the explorers' day the practice was called *hongo*. A chief would pounce on a caravan passing through his country and demand a portion of the travellers' goods as a form of tax for his safe passage. There was nothing vicious or even hostile about the custom, which was rather a form of exploiting opportunity in a cruelly hard world. It had its modern equivalent in dash, the bribe sometimes demanded by customs or immigration officials. Nairobi's variation on *hongo* was mugging.

It is hard to find anyone who ever liked Nairobi, with the possible exception of Karen Blixen, who loved all things Kenyan. The Africanist academic Margery Perham was almost as sanguine, but even she detested Nairobi, describing it in 1929 as 'one of the shabbiest and shoddiest towns I have seen in my travels . . . you either stumble through mud or are blinded by gritty dust'. Almost seven decades on, things had got a lot worse.

Coming into town, the bus window framed snapshots of Nairobi's underclass at the business of survival, a panorama of street children sniffing glue from plastic bags and vagabonds picking through piles of fetid trash. Heedful of the warnings about mugging, I walked purposefully from the bus station as if I knew where I was going and after a few false starts ended up at a cheap, sleazy joint a half hour's walk from the city. It was full of other backpackers and had a cowboy-style bar and restaurant with a menu boasting T-bone steak. It was my birthday, and I set out to celebrate entering my fiftieth year in style.

The place was seething with hookers vying for the attention of a handful of tourists. Only one of the girls accosted me at the bar, but three more waylaid me on the way to a table. T-bone was off, so was sirloin. The last steak in the house came looking like a small piece of grey chapati. I tried to think of the hungry scavengers but it still tasted foul. Amid the thunder of the disco, white men traipsed past with girls into a lavatory. Off to one side, I caught sight of a tired, bewildered looking *mzee*, trying to interest tourists in his carvings.

I felt so depressed I did not even stay for another beer. On my way out, a girl barred the way. 'Don't you say excuse me?' she demanded. I had just got to the door when another girl grabbed my trousers, leering, 'Is this my darling, will I be lucky tonight?'

It soon became clear that I had bigger problems than my seedy surroundings. I had planned to spend a few days in Nairobi, seeing a few people like Richard Leakey, the palaeontologist and dynastic head of a remarkable white Kenyan clan, and then moving to Thika to explore Huxley country. But Leakey was away and the contact in Thika who had offered to put me up was cut off because the phone lines were down. The time factor, too, was preying on my mind: I had barely three months for the entire 8,000 mile journey; more than half my time was up, and I had not yet covered a third of the distance.

Heading into town in a crowded bus, I was mulling over my options when I became aware of a sudden press of bodies. Two men were squeezing up against me, it seemed with the intention of getting to the exit. I leaned back as best I could to let them pass, but the pressure persisted. Thinking no more of it, I extricated myself and eased my way towards the front of the bus. Only when I found the pressure being renewed did the alarm bells start ringing.

He was tall and in his twenties, with a beard. The most remarkable thing was that his eyes were not on me, but were fixed off to one side. I never did get a clear look at the other. Together they formed a kind of phalanx and were now pressing me further towards the front and away from the exit. I became aware of a buzz from the other passengers. Bizarrely, I thought I heard the bearded man mutter, 'Don't worry'. I started to resist and move towards the exit. They pressed in closer, both bodies now hard against me, hands working at my bag. A voice in my head screamed 'Get out' and my body responded with a surge of adrenalin, barging a way between them as the bearded man cried out to the passengers, 'What's the matter with this guy?' Then I was at the exit and out.

What made it unsettling was that I had rehearsed in my mind how I would handle a mugging. The only item of real importance in my bag was the journal I had been keeping since setting out, so when the mugger produced a knife or some other form of threat, I had planned to co-operate, and disarm him by saying something like, 'Help yourself to the camera. Tape recorder? No problem. Just leave me that little black book, if you will.' I felt an utter fool.

The next day I was walking through the back streets, looking for the dive where my wife and I had stayed more than twenty years earlier when we were what used to be called hippie travellers. It had always been a cheap part of town, but now the pavements were broken and piled with rubbish, the buildings were ruins. This time at least the alarm bells started ringing early – as soon as I spotted the gang of hard-faced youths. Clutching the bag hard under my arm, I walked on quickly. About twenty paces on, there was suddenly a sound of running feet behind me and a split second later a hand plunged into the trouser pocket containing my wallet.

He was too eager and he botched it. I was alert and full of anger. I swung round, catching him solidly with my left elbow and slinging the bag on my right arm at him in best Thatcher fashion. He went flying off the pavement, sprawling into the road on his bottom. For a moment he sat there, looking up with a mixture of consternation and pain. He was thin and very young, perhaps sixteen, about the age of my son. My first instinct was to give him a good kick – I think I had the ribs in mind. Instead I shouted: 'Now, just you fuck off!' He did, but not with undue haste, looking back at me as he went. The rest of the gang watched with seeming indifference, like spectators at a rather dull sporting event. An old man sitting on a crate in a doorway smiled and nodded. 'Hauw. Very good,' he said.

That night I was thinking of giving up on Nairobi entirely when I got a message from my contact in Thika. He would meet me at the Muthaiga Country Club the next day.

BY ALL ACCOUNTS, the Muthaiga of the 1940s fast set resembled Paul Scott's memorable caricature of the colonial club, 'so self-conscious about its exclu-siveness and yet so vulgar . . . as though there were inviolable rules for heartless gossip and insufferable behaviour'. Now its character was more that of a reformed rake or alcoholic – diffident and a little dull. Here, it seemed to say, we maintain the standards of a white man's country, but discreetly. The roast of the day circulated through the dining-room on a spectacular carving trolley, a great silver chariot with ball-and-claw legs. Jam roly-poly was served on Thursday and steamed pudding on Saturday. Yesterday's London papers were in a sunny reading-room with Lloyd Loom chairs. Blacks and Jews were no longer barred but the membership remained overwhelmingly white; the notion of paying a membership fee for a place where you still had to buy the drinks struck most Africans as quite mad.

The club was a haven for those whose formula for staying on might have gone something like this: leave us with our privileges and rituals, and we won't get involved in politics; we have to buy our place in the sun, and the price is that we keep our noses clean and stay out of the way; African politics is a dirty game and if a few heads have to get broken, well, we can rub along with that, too; we will also keep silent on all matters of public interest, with the possible exception of wildlife and tourism, in which we have a stake as well.

As a code for survival it was unexceptionable. It was also symptomatic of a failure not only to integrate – insignificant in itself – but to assimilate. White Kenyans belonged nowhere else, but with a few notable exceptions, they seemed not quite to belong here either. Their numbers had held up reasonably well: thirty-four years after independence there were still about 20,000 of them. But conditions were changing quickly. As a result of Kenya's rapid economic slide, the good life was no longer so good and the protective cocoon was at last vulnerable.

I was in the reading room with a copy of *The Field* when the man who I will call Angus came in. He had written to me in England after hearing of my journey, offering to put me up as a paying guest and to arrange meetings with people he said I would find interesting. Angus was about sixty, a former district officer and safari manager with the brisk manner of a man used to giving orders, and the suspicious air of one convinced they are not being properly carried out. He bustled me out to the car and made a peremptory introduction to his wife, Linda. They were retired, living near Thika, about twenty-five miles from Nairobi, on a corporate agricultural estate where they rented a spacious bungalow and took in overseas visitors. They lost no time in briefing newcomers on the country's problems.

'Of course I know these chaps,' Angus said. 'Speak the language. Years in Mau Mau, then a DO in Mweiga. Can't trust a word they say, you've got to do the thinking for them. And standards . . . well, there aren't any. It's just take the money and run. Greedy beggars, hands always in the till. Even my own chaps, good enough in their way, but you've got to watch them all the time.'

Linda chimed in. 'Angus understands the way they think, their psychology. He's very good at sorting things out. He's firmer with them, I'm the soft one.' She finished brightly, 'But together we manage pretty well.'

I confess it came as a surprise. Most racism had acquired a harder or more subtle edge than this sort of parody of a home counties colonel, and I wondered for a moment if I was being teased. So they used a sort of good cop, bad cop approach, I suggested. Linda nodded happily, pleased with the metaphor.

On the way, we stopped at a bus station to ask whether a bus I intended to catch on leaving Thika ran from a particular stand. The counter clerk told me in English that the service had been stopped for lack of demand. As Angus came bustling up, I passed on this information. He ignored me and went to the counter, speaking in execrable, sing-song Swahili. The clerk repeated that the service had been discontinued. Angus was not satisfied and started a cross-examination which went on for some minutes as he exhausted his suspicion that the clerk was misinformed or merely an imbecile. Finally he said in English, 'So there is no service at all?'

'Affirmative,' said the clerk wearily.

Angus stood bolt upright. 'Hrrmph,' he said to me. 'There's no service.'

They lived in the rolling golden savannah north of Nairobi, where the Athi Plains start rising towards the snowcap of Mount Kenya and early settlers built homesteads with blackened, wood-burning ranges and floors of red-polished cement. William Northrup Macmillan, an American magnate whose girth was as vast as his wealth, founded an estate here in 1904 near a hill named Donyo Sabuk, and Elspeth Huxley passed this way in a wagon as a child in 1913. Flame trees were in bloom, and the acacias had lush new leaves after the rains. The bungalow looked over to Donyo Sabuk and the blue ridge of the Ngong hills. Hippo grunted in the dams, and after a while I felt I could just about cope with Angus for two days.

That evening I asked about the people he had said in his letter I would find interesting. The question was left hanging in the air as he began talking about himself, his work on behalf of various colonial societies and his passion, which was golf. He played at Muthaiga but, he explained, preferred a nearby club which had no black members. In an attempt perhaps to ease the constraint that had quickly developed, he leaned over confidentially while Linda was out of the room and said: 'I've got nothing against them really, but we've just got nothing in common. You can't tell them a dirty joke, or talk about sex or anything like that.'

By breakfast I was no longer in any doubt that Angus's interesting people were himself and Linda. We had soon explored all the possibilities of conversation about his career as a district officer, which appeared to have been pretty uneventful, and his subsequent job as office manager for one of Kenya's big safari companies. He did tell me one interesting story, about the time, a few years earlier, when he shot and wounded an intruder and called the police. The senior officer, arriving to find the man bleeding outside, despatched him with a single pistol shot to the head; it had become common, Angus said, to shoot criminals out of hand to spare an overburdened justice system.

What was more intriguing in a way, however, was his almost total detachment from the place in which he had lived his entire life. His grumblings against African incompetence and corruption were in the nature of confidences shared among whites. He would not have thought of openly criticising any member of the government, and loathed Richard Leakey for kicking up a fuss which had attracted unwelcome attention to the white community. Angus and Linda might almost have been contract expatriates whose enjoyment of the country extended to the weather, the servants and the golf club. Although he had an excellent collection of Africana books, including signed first editions by Elspeth Huxley, he seemed ignorant of their contents, and I suspected that he collected rather than read them. The lives of endeavour, joy and disappointment, chonicled with such passion by Huxley and Karen Blixen, appeared to have no echo in his own experience of Kenya.

Under our arrangement, he had agreed to show me around the district and I wanted to see the home at Kitimuru where Elspeth's mother, Nellie Grant, had spent her last days. Shortly before leaving Britain, I had written to Elspeth who responded with an invitation to visit her in Wiltshire. Aged eighty-nine, she had sounded astonishingly sprightly on the phone. 'There's a pub on the corner where we can have lunch,' she said. A few days later she phoned to say she had to go into hospital. Two weeks later, on 10 January 1997, she died.

Nellie's place was a sweet, whitewashed Cape Dutch cottage with twin gables and a green corrugated iron roof, set in an English garden with a lily pond. The occupants were named Harries, a well-known Kenyan clan; Sarah Harries pointed out the flame tree from which blooms were cut and flown by Kenya Airways to Elspeth's memorial service. As we were leaving, we bumped into a small, wizened man driving a *bakkie* who turned out to be Allen Harries, now owner of the Macmillan homestead, Juja House, who invited us to call by. I said that was most hospitable of him. 'Ah, well, let's just hang on,' Angus said, and speaking as if I was not there, he went on: 'This chap's a sort of writer, but we've got a full schedule and now there's hardly any time left.'

When I got him alone I was almost shaking with rage. I reminded him of our agreement and said that as a paying guest, I would decide who and what I wanted to see. At first he was huffy but I suspect that by now both of us recognised we had made a mistake and it was with a sense of mutual relief that we agreed he would take me out to see the Harries, then drop me off for me to get back to Nairobi by *matatu*.

AS WELL AS being immensely wealthy, Macmillan was a flamboyant figure who was knighted by the British for his services to Kenya and had hosted great parties at Juja House. The once-vast sisal estate had long since been broken up, however, and the dirt track to the homestead threaded a way through peasant smallholdings, past shanties and unkempt children. Angus, who had set out in buoyant mood, was appalled, muttering darkly about African waste and ineptitude. At the same time, he seemed uneasy at finding himself off the fairway for once. He remarked how intrepid it was for the Harries to be living out here on their own; and when he was obliged to ask directions, he did so circumspectly.

Allen and Jean Harries were a bony, leathery-faced couple in their seventies who looked like figures from *The Grapes of Wrath* but were members of one of Kenya's most respected families. We sat on a verandah cluttered with chairs and dogs, and mounted heads of buffalo, wildebeest and antelope shot by Macmillan. Juja House was a clapboard bungalow set among a grove of flame trees looking out across the Athi river and, once again, I could feel the magic that had worked so powerfully on the early visitors. Allen was laconic, Jean wry, with a sense of humour as dry as dust. Both puffed constantly on cigarettes while Angus talked about himself. They listened patiently as country people do, until eventually Angus remembered himself and asked about their security problem.

'Security? There is no problem,' Jean said. 'No fence, no *askaris*, no problem,' she laughed wheezily. Armed guards known as *askaris* were employed by virtually every farmer and resident of Nairobi's better suburbs. For two elderly *mzungus*, surrounded by squatters and smallholders, to be living in the bush without protection was almost unthinkable. Angus looked awed.

'We went into town recently and I left the key in the door,' Jean went on. 'A week later I noticed it was still there.' And her laughter trailed off into a rattling cough. Allen grunted. 'Making a fuss about security only attracts attention,' he said.

Angus was now thoroughly respectful. Indicating me, he said: 'I told him you were real Kenyans, the kind of pioneer type who threw in their lot with the country for better or worse.' Allen and Jean looked embarrassed but for the first time I warmed a little to Angus.

Allen's grandfather, a poor Essex farmer, took his wife out to South Africa at the turn of the century and lost his land in the Boer War. He arrived in Nairobi in 1904 to try again and, after covering hundreds of miles on foot, chose a site at Thika. There a piano and other possessions were transported by wagon while the family walked beside the oxen, sleeping in the open beside fires which kept lions and hyenas away. There were to be nine children in all, including Allen's father, and the Harries became a clan as important in their way as the Leakeys, industrious and successful farmers. Most, like Allen, had taken Kenyan citizenship and stayed on, although a Harries family newsletter was a kind of atlas of the post-*uhuru* diaspora, bringing with it news of clan members in Australia, New Zealand, South Africa, Zimbabwe, Canada and, more rarely, Britain.

Allen and Jean had retired from their farm recently and, looking around for a place to see out their days, had found Juja House vacant, dilapidated, the garden overgrown. They showed us around the house, where Teddy Roosevelt stayed during his African safari in 1909 and Frederick Selous was a regular guest. The rooms were small and spartan. The glory was the view from the verandah, looking down over the Athi. There was plenty of game, including the occasional giraffe and hippo in the river, and the birdlife was dazzling.

As we drove off, Angus said he was sure I had found this useful – meeting some interesting people. I thanked him and said I had indeed.

IF FEW WHITE Kenyans acted like citizens with a legitimate right to speak out about what was happening to their country, it was perhaps not all that surprising. All those I met who had, had run into trouble. Richard Leakey had been arrested, severely beaten and, while piloting his own plane, had a suspicious air crash which cost him both his legs.

Leakey was unquestionably the leader of the activists, a magnetic figure with successful careers as palaeontologist and conservationist behind him, who had now dared, as had no other white in post-colonial Africa, to challenge politically an incumbent head of state. There were those who argued that he was the wrong man, that he was too much a maverick, that far from representing independent interests, he was a Trojan horse for the Kikuyu, the majority tribe sidelined from power since Jomo Kenyatta's death. But no one questioned Leakey's ability or commitment. He also had an indefinable star quality, a dazzling talker who could hold his own in any company. At first I thought I had caught him on a bad day. A big stocky man of fifty-three, he stumped across the room with narrowed eyes, a disconcerting combination of wariness and truculence.

Like Allen Harries, Leakey was a third-generation Kenyan, his missionary grandfather, Harry, having arrived in the Kikuyu country in 1902. Harry's son, Louis, grew up speaking Kikuyu as his native tongue and with a command of bushcraft that those who observed him found uncanny. Louis became a palaeontologist but his greatest genius was for showmanship and spotting women of talent. With his second wife, Mary, he excavated Olduvai Gorge in Tanzania, discovering fossil fragments 2 million years old which proved beyond reasonable doubt that *Homo sapiens* evolved from primate stock on the plains of Serengeti. Later Louis encouraged and launched a trio of young women, Jane Goodall, Diane Fossey and Birute Galdikas, on their studies of the great central African apes. As if emulating a primate himself, Louis's son had meanwhile emerged from his father's shadow to tackle the old male on his own territory. Richard's excavations at Koobi Fora, in the sun-blasted wastes east of Lake Turkana in 1972, turned up a skull of *Homo erectus* dating back 2.6 million years, older than any of his parents' finds.

Despite his somewhat fearsome appearance and reputation, he spoke quietly, with great intensity and fluency. We passed quickly over his years at Koobi Fora and work at the Kenya Wildlife Service which did much to save Kenya's elephant from poaching; at that time he had been the darling of the government, a *mzungu* who identified with African aspirations and had helped raise the international profile of the country, a friend to the president himself. Then Leakey broke cover, linking himself with a pro-democracy movement. At the same time, he joined a group of Kikuyu friends, notably a lawyer named Paul Muite, to form a new party, Safina. Moi was enraged. In 1995, Leakey and Muite were set upon at a rally in Nakuru and thrashed with whips. It was a commonplace incident in Kenyan politics, but the fact that a white man, and a well-known one, had been severely beaten, exercised a foreign press fatigued with African affairs. Leakey was embarrassed at being singled out.

'Politics here are very violent,' he said. 'Young thugs are used in order to intimidate and there is no reason – if they are going to use that technique – why it shouldn't be used on me. The bruises are the same, whatever the colour of one's skin.'

Did he sense hostility from other whites? 'Oh yes, a lot,' he said with relish. 'They resent deeply anything which polarises their position. But then I am acting not as a white but as a Kenyan. This is where I belong, this is where my friends are. The fact that I feel sufficiently at home to question and criticise came as a bit of a shock apparently to them and to Mr Moi. Now I think we are seeing a new generation – I see it in my children – which has a far stronger sense that this is where we belong. It's natural. My father was very firm and sincere in his love and commitment to this country, but he also thought of England as a home. I don't at all. I feel a foreigner anywhere else but here.'

Printed in England 0396

N P G
NATIONAL
PORTRAIT
GALLERY

HERD OF BUFFALO OPPOSITE GARDEN ISLAND, VICTORIA FALLS
Thomas Baines, 1859
Oil on canvas, 46 x 65.7 cm
© Royal Geographical Society

Sold to support the National Portrait Gallery, London

I said while he was a white Kenyan, it was also said that he was more a white Kikuyu. Politics in Kenya were notoriously ethnic and other groups, the Maasai and the Kalenjin to which Moi belonged, feared Kikuyu domination. 'My father's close association with the Kikuyu inevitably gave me friendships, and yes, President Moi has accused me of being a Kikuyu. But I can't be a foreigner and a Kikuyu. When it has suited him, I have been both.' Was it not true, however, that his friends were mainly Kikuyu? 'Not entirely. I've got some very good friends from . . .' he hesitated briefly '. . . from the coast, some from western Kenya.'

I braced myself and plunged in at the deep end. I said that perhaps he could explain whether there was a cultural factor behind the corruption and venality that plagued African leadership. Quite simply, why had so many African governments proved themselves incapable of delivering on behalf of their people?

'I think you are right, and yet you are wrong. The implication is that they are a flawed part of the human race.'

'No it is not.'

'Okay, good, because there is nothing flawed about Africans. This continent, this country in particular, had a society before colonial penetration that was organised in a traditional but sophisticated way, with a strong sense of accountability in the leadership. Whether you were a chief, an elder, or the head of a family, you had responsibilities and if you did not meet them, society had a way of dealing with you. It is clear that there was a series of law-abiding mini-states and that all these people – the Kikuyu, the Maasai, the Luo, had their own accountable society. Christianity and colonialism said, "That's all rotten. We'll start afresh with a society based on a fear of our God." The trouble was there was not long for that to take root. It may work for the church, but does it work in terms of those values being passed down through several generations? Remember that, at the same time, different standards of fairness pertained under colonialism and there were a lot of confusing signals.

'We get up to independence and suddenly you have a great number of people who have had very little and now they have high expectations, even though the country remains undeveloped. Lots of people have jobs for which they have not been properly trained, and all the while values are shifting. On top of this you have a tremendous pull between East and West which says, "Values are unimportant, you're our client, we'll back you anyway." Venality and corruption will arise from a situation like that in societies black, white or brown.'

I said that those of us who lived outside Africa but loved it suffered from a continual mood swing. Just when it seemed that the continent was on the brink of collapse, something would happen that made you think it was on the verge of revival.

'We are in the process of an immensely painful transition. It is no longer possible to live off the land. For school, for healthcare, even to get a burial permit, you need money. But there is no money and there are no jobs. The vast majority of people are increasingly unable to cope. Those who do have access to money – the policeman, for example – are almost forced to be corrupt, because they are expected by the extended family to look after them.

'So we have to collapse the old systems. In Zaire, sadly, it was necessary to have a civil war, to chase the bastards out at the point of a bayonet. It had to happen in Uganda as well. Is it necessary in Kenya? I hope not. But ultimately you have to collapse old systems to build new ones, and the capacity of dictatorships to give up their protective infrastucture is not characteristic. Now some of the changes we are seeing – in Uganda, Malawi, South Africa – are part of a new sense that says, "Dammit, you see, we *can* do it."'

What did he make of events in South Africa?

'They have managed to get across some very sticky ground quite success-fully. I think actually they may have a slow-curing gum on their boots and when it does cure they may stick solid. The Mandela magic is working, but if he were a younger man he would have had to bite the bullet and deal with some of the issues which so far have just been set aside. The delay in acting may make the ultimate crisis worse.'

That, I said, could be disastrous, because if South Africa went off the rails the international reaction would be to consign Africa once and for all to the failure basket.

'Ah, but you see . . .' and he leaned forward eagerly, '. . . if by that stage Kenya is working again – like we are now seeing Uganda working again – you will get an international reaction that says, "Ah, you have to go down that road first in order to get on to this one."'

We laughed. 'You may not have to go all the way round,' he went on, 'but I think you *may* have to go all the way round, and my hope is that Kenya has been virtually all the way round. We've got to put the past behind us. We've got to stop getting angry, we've got to stop feeling guilty – we've got to develop the confidence to be citizens of the world. We're like teenagers, terribly prickly. But think of it – the Americans are as well and that is after several hundred years. And Africa is not so young – the real Africa is not young at all.'

So, Africa's time would come? 'Oh, I'm sure it will, I'm quite certain of it. But we're in a very difficult phase at the moment, and with everyone else so concerned with their own preoccupations, we're not getting much help.'

Perhaps that was for the best, I suggested. Western involvement had generally been harmful even when well-intentioned. 'It probably is for the best, but they should stop making it more difficult. If they don't want to help us that's one thing, but they should stop hindering us, and their blind support for dictatorships is no help at all.'

TALKING TO LEAKEY helped bring Kenya back into focus. At first I had been lulled by the country, then confused. There was a constant ambiguity between, on the one hand, the occasional glimpses that reflected Blixen's lyrical *Out of Africa* and on the other the Kenya of state-sanctioned murder and glue-sniffing street children. Young whites tended to respond in one of two ways. A new generation of wastrels who called themselves Kenya Cowboys lived a pallid imitation of the old sybaritism, doing odd jobs, smoking dope, getting drunk. Others were inspired by Leakey, insisting that they had a stake in the country and demanding the rights and responsibilities of citizens.

Robert Shaw lived on what was once part of Karen Blixen's coffee estate in the Ngong hills south-west of Nairobi. A decline in services in the fashionable suburb of Karen had galvanised local residents into that most English form of protest, a ratepayers' rebellion. Shaw, however, had really put his neck out. Soon after joining Leakey in forming Safina as an opposition party, he was hijacked, probably by a security police unit. He was driven around for two hours, blindfold and threatened, until he was certain he was going to be killed, before being stripped of his clothes and abandoned.

Shaw and his wife, Judy, were in their thirties with an acre of land, still largely indigenous forest, and a house they had built themselves. Light danced on the leaves in late afternoon and birds sang in a way that brought to mind Huxley's limpid phrase about 'doves calling with notes like a mellow wine dropping from a bottle'. Shaw, a businessman, spoke coolly about fear and phone-tapping, scams and rottenness. 'It's been a bad ten years. There was a feeling that Kenya was different. This was the jewel that still shone while everything around us had gone to pieces. We've got to get back there – and it can be done. There are a lot of able people in the private sector, a lot of Kenyans who are sick of Moi and his gang.'

Would he stay, come what may? 'A few years ago I would have said, absolutely, there's no way I'm leaving. Now . . .' he looked at his toddler son '. . . it is not so simple. We live with the threats and intimidation, but things like the hijack do work on you. If I'm in Europe, I find I'm looking over my shoulder automatically. Then you realise you don't have to look over your shoulder. If it got to the point that I thought we were in real danger, I guess we'd go.'

Dominic Martin also ran a successful business. As a result of printing opposition publications, his premises and home had been repeatedly raided, and he had been detained and charged with sedition. He was about forty, a big man with a wide smile and a fondness for food, drink and enjoyment. We had a couple of hectic nights out which were as much fun as I had had since Kampala. He was dashing, too, in a public school sort of way, indeed, had been educated in England although there was nothing he missed about it now. 'Full of bovine arseholes who have given up on living,' he said cheerfully.

'The trouble is,' he went on, 'that in guaranteeing your rights and freedoms, the state has become an interfering busybody. Your macro freedoms are assured, you take them for granted. But in the meantime, you've given away your micro freedoms without a struggle and you have to conform in a very tight way. Because one man gets into a car and kills four people, the whole population has to be ringed in. Here we have no macro freedoms at all – we can get shot one night or put away and that's the end of it. But we have micro freedoms.' He exploded: 'Boy, do we have micro freedoms. This is just the most exciting place to be. There's no one to fall back on, no welfare state, no dole. But I have freedom and opportunity. I've bought a bit of land up on the edge of the Rift Valley which looks out on Lake Naivasha and Mount Longonot. There's something special about the valley – a primal calling, a distant memory, call it what you will. And when you look up to a blue sky and open space, you feel better, no matter how oppressive the political environment. If it came to a fight here, I'd be very happy to join in. The bottom line is, we still have a chance to change our system of government, and I don't think you do.'

MY TIME IN Kenya was nearing an end. Meeting Leakey and the others had raised my spirits and made me think again. There was something immensely exciting about a society in which there was everything to play for. We in Europe *had* become smug about our freedoms, and complacent about threats to them. Men like Leakey and Martin were nourished by challenge, while too often now, we tried to avoid it.

I was preparing to head south, back to Tanzania, when there came a message from Kampala. 'The Kabaka is back, and he wants to see you.'

11. The Steppe

'MOST REGRETTABLE, REALLY MOST regrettable,' said Mr E. W. Kugundu, private secretary to the Ssabataka Ronald Muwenda Mutebi II. 'Please accept my apologies. Your letter went to the Katikiro's office. We in the private office know more about His Majesty's movements. If your letter had come to us in the first place, we would have been better able to organise things and spare you all this confusion.'

I waved the apology away. Although I had barely slept on the fourteen-hour bus trip overnight from Nairobi to Kampala, I was rejoicing inwardly. I said it didn't matter, the important thing was that we had got there in the end, or something equally banal.

Mr Kugundu was a tall, graceful figure with long fingers. He was in his sixties, his assistant Peter Mpanga, equally elegant, much younger. They looked at me intently and asked solicitous questions about my journey. I had made a reasonable fist of my appearance with a shower and change of clothes at the Namirembe Guest-house, but was conscious of looking far from courtly for meeting a monarch and it seemed somehow unbecoming to admit that I had made the 410-mile journey by overnight bus. 'Tiring, but not uncomfortable,' I murmured.

We sat in a spacious office in the Lukiko, the old Bagandan parliament on the hill at Mengo. From a window I could see the Lubiri, King Ronnie's palace, on a ridge about half a mile away, and wondered whether the meeting would take place here or there. Mr Kugundu explained that King Ronnie had asked a close friend to brief me beforehand, and said that in the meantime he would show me round while Mr Mpanga settled a few final details.

Our tour took in the chamber, a Westminster model with banks of leather seats on either side, a speaker's chair and a podium on which the sovereign's throne had stood. Wistfully, Mr Kugundu said the last time the chamber had been used was in 1966 when Bagandan MPs voted to demand their autonomy from Obote's federal Uganda. Soon afterwards Obote ordered the attack on Mengo and the Kabaka fled into exile. In the looting that followed, the throne was lost.

Mrs Mpanga, the friend deputed to brief me, was from an old Bagandan clan and had shared the royal family's exile in London. She was jolly and unstuffy, recalling years of penury living in a one-bedroom flat in Belsize Park, long bleak winters, and working as a nanny for a Tory cabinet minister whose wife was flabbergasted when she discovered that Mrs Mpanga had lectured at Makerere in civics. She gave an outline of King Ronnie's role in the new Uganda which sounded much like that of constitutional monarchs elsewhere: 'He wants to be a social influence in helping to bring back the spirit of volunteerism. His big interests are street children and the environment.'

I had begun idly to wonder when the meeting would actually take place when she called across, 'Kugundu, we need some tea.' The old man, who had been busying himself at his desk with calls, brought across his own vacuum flask. I had the only cup, she drank from a glass and he used the plastic cap.

We were sipping the hot, milky liquid when Mr Kugundu leaned across and said gravely: 'Mr Taylor, I regret I have learnt that the Kabaka is indisposed and will not be able to meet you.'

Mrs Mpanga did not miss a beat. 'I remember Museveni once serving tea in a glass, but really Kugundu, you should do better for our guest,' she said.

'Oh, that's quite all right,' I heard myself say.

After a long pause, I wondered aloud whether the Kabaka might be less indisposed by the following day. Peter Mpanga hustled off and was back in a few minutes. His information was that this was unlikely. The Kabaka was unwell. By now Mrs Mpanga had remembered that at his birthday party a few days earlier, King Ronnie had been off colour and said he thought he was coming down with a cold. They agreed, the signs had been there. Peter Mpanga wrung his hands, Mrs Mpanga sailed off majestically and Mr Kugundu, shaking his head sorrowfully, saw me out. At the entrance to the Lukiko we stopped to look across at the palace: there lurked the indisposed monarch, here stood the rejected supplicant with his petition unanswered and a long trail ahead.

'Most regrettable, really most regrettable,' Mr Kugundu said. 'If only your letter had come to our office in the first place all this would have been avoided.'

In the evening I caught the bus back to Nairobi.

TIME HAD BECOME a source of worry. By my rough timetable for the journey, I ought now to have completed the circuit around the lakes, returned to my starting point of Dar es Salaam, and continued on to Malawi. As it was, with only a month left, I was still 4,500 miles from the Cape. Facing hard travelling by bus and train through Tanzania, I chose the fastest and most comfortable option for the first leg, an express minibus from Nairobi to the town of Arusha. From there the road ran south across the Maasai Steppe to Dar, where I intended to take a train on the Chinese-built Tazara line, alighting at Mbeya and crossing by road into Malawi.

The minibus contained an assortment of other white backpackers, a couple from America carrying hundreds of pounds of equipment to climb Kilimanjaro, and a gaggle of middle-aged Italians on their way to the Tanzanian game parks. During neighbourly spats the border between Kenya and Tanzania used to be closed quite regularly, but now travellers were taking advantage of cut-price air fares to Nairobi and catching a bus the 180 miles to Arusha for Serengeti and Ngorongoro. The driver, an animated little wisp of a man, said we should be there in four hours.

In the event, it took twice that. Rains brought by the El Niño phenomenon were continuing unabated, visiting East Africa with the worst floods in memory. The Athi river had burst its banks and spewed through the valley south of Nairobi, cutting the road to the border. We spent hours marooned with other traffic at a submerged bridge. The sensible thing would have been to wait until the water subsided or return to Nairobi, but the driver was labouring under the imperatives of time and delivery. He decided to drive through the flood, even though it was by no means certain that the bridge was intact.

The extent of the risk became clear about halfway across the thick brown water that churned and boiled a few feet below the window. A *matatu*, inexplicably empty apart from the driver, had been swept off the bridge – or it may have come too close to the edge – and was wedged diagonally on its side against a tree. We passed a few feet away. The scared face of the driver was frozen at a window. As we reached the other side, a cheering crowd gave the thumbs up sign, heedless of the unfortunate stranded in mid-river.

TANZANIA GAVE ITS curiously beguiling, crooked-smile welcome. Arusha was a garden-like town at the foot of an extinct volcano, Mount Meru, with a stream through the middle set about with flowering trees; the jacaranda were over but the cassia and spithoedea were bursting with yellow and orange blossoms. All this lay amid the usual *ujamaa* disaster zone of pot-holed roads, collapsed pavements and empty shops. The smart hotels used by safari operators were self-contained enclaves on the outskirts of town. I found a joint called Pallson's off a muddy side street which had the defeated air of a place which had not put up a proper tourist since the 1960s. The restaurant was decorated with empty South African wine bottles and the bar, called the Brasserie, had just three bottles of drink on its shelves – two Cokes and one Safari, all warm. The next discovery I made was that my travellers' cheques were gone.

After dismay came anger. For some time I had been conscious of failing concentration, of carelessness that had led to mistakes and missed opportunities. How the travellers' cheques had been lost or stolen I had no idea, but the incident was symptomatic of a trend that needed to be arrested. I would teach myself a lesson: I still had a reasonable amount of cash – £140 and $100 – concealed in various places. By rigorous budgeting, travelling third class on the trains, staying in the scruffiest places and rationing myself to one beer a day, I could complete the journey on what I had. It would be a challenge as well as a lesson, more like the old days when my wife and I had managed in India on a pound a day between two of us. I began to feel quite pleased with the idea: I could do with a touch of missionary asceticism.

Chicken and rice was exactly as I remembered it. The eating-house was dimly lit but I could just make out the yellowing wing of a scrawny bird and the undernourished little grains swimming in water and fat. I had already drunk my Safari for the day so the repast was unaccompanied. The road back to the hotel passed a bar dispensing lively Zairean music. Resolutely, I walked on. Pallson's was utterly deserted. I went to my room and took up *The Last Chronicle of Barset*, and was shocked and ashamed to find that even the venom of Mrs Proudie and the agony of Josiah Crawley seemed insipid. Asceticism had already lost its appeal.

In the morning I went to the pouch and felt my heart leap at the touch of plastic which I found at the bottom. At one of the smart safari hotels outside town there was a bureau de change where I was allowed to draw £200. It was a sobering moment to discover that credit cards could work magic even in this cash-starved backwater.

Arusha: Friday, 25 April

ALL ALONG I MUST have been at least subconsciously aware that this was to be a search for phantoms. There were intimations in the weeks before I left England, like the death of Elspeth Huxley. Frailty winnowed out others. I had hoped to visit the last old white savage himself, Wilfred Thesiger, living with his extended family of Samburu at Maralal in Kenya, where he had intended to die, then heard that he was back in London. That came as a shock. Surely Thesiger, I had thought, will be there to the end. When I went to see him at the cosy flat off the Embankment which he had inherited from his mother, he seemed slightly defensive, though heaven knows he had no cause to be. 'It was the people I was there for, and once Lawi and Laputa died there was no reason to stay,' he growled.*

The indications of withering have only multiplied on the journey, among the dying – like Daudi in Kunduchi or Gosbert in Bukoba; the frail – Ron in Kampala; or the merely elderly – Father Grimes in Namasagali and Keith Anderson in Fort Portal. And there is so little *regeneration*. Today, more ghosts passed across my trail, like figures in a Shakespearean procession. At least two old-timers living in these parts have died in the past few months, among them Brian Hartley, who spent the last years of his life on the quixotic quest of trying to persuade the Maasai that, if their pastoral traditions were to survive, they had to change livestock; depredation of the steppe by cattle has been so severe that Hartley, who had also lived in Arabia, introduced the Maasai to camels. In his case, at least, his work is being carried on by his son Kim.

So, more ghosts, and one outright phantasm. I have failed to find Katrina.

Katrina was among another colony of Afrikaner exiles, a small group who settled just north of here at a place they called Kampfontein in the western lee of Mount Meru, around the same time as their fellows went to Eldoret. The Boers of Meru lost their land when Nyerere nationalised the commercial farms, but whereas they had returned to South Africa, Katrina stayed, along with her dark secret. For she had violated a shibboleth of her people, stealing away from her family in the night to find love in the arms of a black man. They had two children, and Katrina became an outcast. When the Boers left, she stayed with her lover. I had heard that she was still here, old and wizened, a bit *manyatta*, as those touched by the madness of the wilderness are called, living in a *shamba* with a handful of other peasants.

Asking after her around town proved pretty hopeless, but I finally found a man who might have known where she was. To his old friends in Oxford, Marius Ghikas was a near-mythical figure himself. Marius's ancestors lay in Izmir and Alexandria and he recalled a time when the settlers here were Greeks and Germans rather than British. This was always the best land in Tanganyika, capable of producing two crops of wheat a year and good for cattle and sheep as well as coffee. It is lovely with it, out there on the green slopes of Mount Meru and Kilimanjaro, and the Germans mourned the loss of their colony. Marius recalls as a boy before the war when his school-fellows, with boyish defiance, gave each other the Nazi salute and cried

---

* Lawi and Laputa were Thesiger's foster sons. Both died aged about thirty-five, he believes of Aids.

'Heil Hitler!', and later how they and their families were interned and had their goods seized as enemy property.

The Greeks prospered during the war though, and by the end of it Marius's father was a millionaire, with sisal and coffee estates and the hotel at Moshi. Marius was sent to study law at Oxford, where his contemporaries remembered him as a brilliant student, but he never practised. For him, it was always the land. 'Greek by ethos, British by education, African by inclination,' he declares in accentless English. So it was hard when the government took everything. He survived as his father had done during the Depression, growing vegetables, and by running cattle across the border to Kenya. Even when things were at their worst, he never considered leaving. 'They would have had to kill me,' he says with grim satisfaction. Now in his sixties, his tenacity has at last reaped benefits, with the restoration by the government of some of his property.

I asked if he knew of Katrina. His eyes widened in surprise that I had heard of her. 'I know the stories, but I've never seen her,' he said. 'Maybe she went crazy, maybe she died.' It is almost as if she was a chimera, as remote and exotic as a mermaid.

THERE WAS ONE last ghost to be laid to rest before I left Arusha. I set out in a taxi without directions, knowing only that she lived somewhere west of town on an estate called Mringa. The road passed beside acres of coffee and cereal crops rolling into distant hills. We stopped at the occasional roadside store but my questions about Mringa and an old *bibi mzungu* (white woman) met with blank looks. About ten miles out, the road reached the main highway for the Kenya border where it was clear we had gone too far. Turning back, we left the main road and started venturing up rutted tracks. After an hour of this, I was beginning to have doubts about my original information. But by now the driver had entered the spirit of the quest. I was thinking of giving up when he spotted a group of women sitting under a tree and stopped the car. He returned smiling and gesturing up the track, '*Bibi mzungu.*'

The house had a red corrugated iron roof dappled by sunlight and was shaded by eucalyptus trees. The swing door, covered in mesh to keep out flies, was opened by a maid who showed me into a darkened sitting-room. Daphne Mahon, aged eighty-seven, was dozing in an armchair, her legs up on a footstool. Her eyes flickered open. In a voice that started feebly but grew stronger, she told me the story of Ol Molog, the colony founded by Sir Archibald McIndoe.

McIndoe was a medical man from New Zealand who, at the outbreak of the Second World War, was posted to a cottage hospital at East Grinstead for RAF fliers. His patients were distinguished by the hideousness of their injuries, not to limb or organ, but to skin, mainly facial, melted and destroyed by burns. For McIndoe was a plastic surgeon and, drawing on techniques pioneered by Sir Harold Gillies in the 1914–18 War, he remodelled and rebuilt men's features. In addition, as was testified to by the 600 servicemen for whom he cared at the Queen Victoria Hospital and who were known as the Guinea Pig Club, he helped rebuild their lives, instilling in them a will to conquer disability and face the world. He was a great and much-loved man.

Not all McIndoe's wards could be completely rehabilitated, however, and for those whose physical and mental scars went too deep for resuming normal life, he lobbied tirelessly. One of his campaigns was for disfigured airmen to be made grants of land in the fertile regions of Tanganyika colony. Eventually, the scheme won official approval and a community of about twenty-five farms for former airmen was established north-west of Kilimanjaro at a place called Ol Molog, which was just about the finest wheat-farming area in all Africa.

Daphne Mahon and her husband, Brian, had lived in South Africa and India before coming to Arusha after the war and buying Mringa, an estate producing arabica coffee. In that immediate post-war period, Tanganyika was the place for settler farmers, Kenya having become more attractive for commerce and light industry. Like other Europeans at that time, the Mahons saw no cloud on the horizon. Although a few African nationalists had come back from the war talking about independence, the prevailing wisdom in the Colonial Service was that African self-rule was unlikely before the millennium. Once the Winds of Change started to blow, events moved bewilderingly fast, but even then there seemed no reason why the settlers should not simply continue with their new life in a country to which they had already become extremely attached.

Daphne and Brian had made friends with two of McIndoe's airmen, Peter Head, an Englishman, and Peter Hugo, an Afrikaner originally from the Karoo. Both were decorated war heroes, and Hugo had one of the highest tallies among Battle of Britain fighter pilots. Soon after independence, squatters started to appear on Peter Head's farm and he wrote to the department of agriculture, asking for them to be removed. Both men were at a lunch given by the Mahons when the police arrived. 'It was all very bizarre. They were asking about Peter and said they wanted to see gun licences. It was obvious they meant Peter Head, and that it involved the letter about the squatters, but for some reason they took it into their heads that the man they were after was Peter Hugo. Anyway, he said no problem, he would take them and show them his guns and licences.'

Later that afternoon he was back. The police had told him the licences were not in order and he had twenty-four hours to leave the farm or go to jail. 'Of course, he refused to leave, so they arrested him. We went to see him in jail. I remember he was cold because they had taken away his jersey and shoes. We got him out the next day, but everything had changed. The whole world had been turned upside down.'

Peter Hugo's estate was sequestrated. Guards were put on his farm, but one woman, Joan Fryburg, said two could play at that damned game, took a pick-up round and told them some of the pictures and carpets in the house were hers, so reclaiming at least some of his property. Other neighbours and friends raised enough to send Hugo back to the Cape. 'It was shameful that the British did nothing about it. He was a nice man, and he was a real *man*. All the Africans loved him.' The words came out with surprising force from the frail figure in the armchair. I looked up. She was crying.

After a while I asked what had happened to Peter Head. 'Nothing. He sold his farm soon afterwards, got his money out of the country and went to Australia. That was what made it frightening. It was all so . . . so arbitrary.

'Oh well,' she went on, 'I suppose they saw us as taking advantage of the country, instead of advancing it. Dear Mr Nyerere. Say what you like, he took 120 tribes and made them into a people. "Country before tribe", he used to say. I take my hat off to him. As a statesman, anway.' She emitted a girlish giggle. 'Not as an economist. Goodness me no.'

She did not know what had happened to the rest of McIndoe's airmen, but one by one the farmers left. 'Your friends got fewer and fewer, and so you were drawn closer. When one left, you felt it quite badly, but we stuck it out because we still liked the life.' Then came the final blow, the nationalisation of agriculture. All the remaining white farms around Arusha were taken over. Apart, that is, from the Mahons'.

'I will never know why. We must have been in line for it along with everyone else. Brian had given some land to the local chief for a school, I ran a clinic, but we were not alone in doing that sort of thing. We were a little out of the way here, and I think they must have forgotten about us. We just slipped through the net. So here I am. Still here.'

*   *   *

TO START WITH the bus was blissfully empty. I had bought a ticket the previous evening and my heart leapt as I boarded to find space all around my seat. No more than a dozen other passengers were seated, some cracking peanut shells or tearing at sugar-cane sticks, tossing husks and stringy fibre on the floor. The engine was already running. I spread myself on the seat and took out Trollope and warmed immediately to the prospect of a brief escape from Africa to the English countryside. After the wasted overnight journeys, a comfortable run in the company of the characters and among the spires of Barsetshire would be a pleasure.

Departure time came and went, the driver revved the engine, more people boarded. Outside the touts were shouting the fare and destination, inside it was starting to fill up. Half an hour late, the bus started to move. It got 10 yards and stopped. In the next half hour more passengers piled aboard. Two others joined me on a seat for two. It was now standing room only. I asked my neighbour how much she had paid. 'Six thousand bob,' she said. Why, I wondered, had I paid nine thousand. 'You booked early,' she said.

It came welling up from a long way down. All the bottled-up fury over my treatment by King Ronnie, the by now familiar contempt shown by service operators for consumers, and the submissive complicity of us all in this ill-usage, boiled over. I stopped a passing conductor and demanded to know when we were leaving.

'Just wait,' he said dismissively.

'I am waiting,' I shouted. 'That's all I am doing, waiting. This is supposed to be an express bus leaving an hour ago. And I paid more than these people. You keep us waiting and waiting so you can fill up the bus.' He was turning away. 'You are not an express bus, you are . . . you are a *matatu.*'

Everyone laughed and I felt better. As the bus eventually pulled away, I put Trollope back in my bag. The big disappointment was that the clouds had closed in around Moshi, blocking out the snows of Kilimanjaro. But about two hours from Arusha the road turned south, and all through the afternoon, for 200 miles, the bus hugged the Usambara mountains, a chain high and green with granite cliff faces like the bergs and winelands of the Cape, only here empty and sublime, while away to the west the Maasai Steppe fell in rolling folds into a golden void hundreds of thousands of square miles deep.

I had encountered enough ghosts. They betokened a kind of failure, testimony that once whites had been a part of Africa, but no longer; only the lost and the hardiest endured and they had all but died out. The words of the historian John Iliffe came back to me: Africans deserved admiration for colonising an especially hostile region of the world on behalf of the entire human race; the unspoken implication was that the rest of the species, and our kind in particular, were not of the same mettle. Perhaps this was true, but after all our roots in East Africa had been shallow, a trail mapped by explorers and adventurers leading to colonisation and then withdrawal, all in the space of seventy years, so that those who remained were but an appendix of Empire. Southern Africa, the place of my childhood and to which I had returned with a young family, was different. There, generation after generation had given bones to the earth. There, if anywhere, we belonged.

PART TWO

COMING
BACK

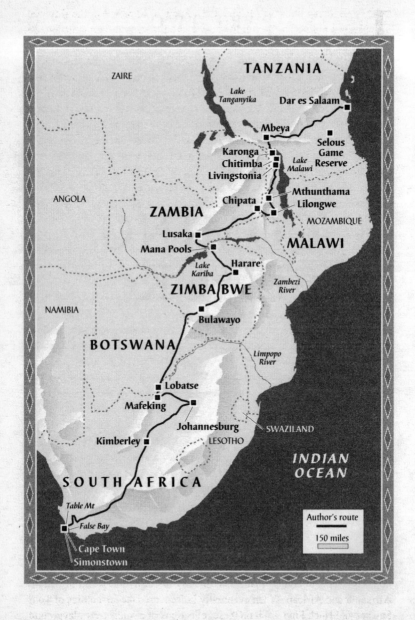

I HAD NEVER BEEN TO Malawi, but I knew it. I knew it in the way one knows a place most vividly – as a child, and in the imagination. In those days it was Nyasaland and then its appeal was strongest. There was something about the sibilance of the name, the sinuousness of the sound, which set it apart from the other countries to our north. My consciousness of Africa stemmed mainly from my father's travels. He would take off by train for the Rhodesias or, on longer trips, to the Belgian Congo and Angola, which years later were invested with dark, mysterious events. Perhaps because he never went to Nyasaland it always seemed to me more exotic. From my British Empire stamp collection, I knew it as a place of elongated stamps with the Queen's head above the image of a leopard astride a rock. But most of all I knew Nyasaland because of Sinclair.

The *dorp* in which we then lived was only twenty miles north of the Reef of the White Waters, the Witwatersrand, but trips to Johannesburg were like ventures to another country. And when I started school in the suburbs, a twice-daily bus trundled me back in the afternoon to the rolling veld, a dusty main street with a post office and a general store, a dingy chamber with a heavy, musty smell of hessian sacks, sweet tobacco and Lifebuoy soap. In the early 1950s, nothing distinguished Rivonia from dozens of other Transvaal *dorps*.

Our home was a tin-roofed bungalow looking out over a line of willow trees which marked the course of the river, and miles of open savannah. With my friends, Mike and Malcolm, I used to wander the veld in search of wild creatures, like the snakes which we took to school to awe our urban fellows. Usually, though, we lingered by the river, a sluggish, muddy *spruit* said to be infested with bilharzia, a disease spread by a flesh-boring snail. We kept rudimentary canoes, made from a sheet of corrugated iron flattened out, nailed at either end to wooden stanchions and sealed with pitch. These wobbly craft often tipped us out into the river and eventually we ignored entirely parental admonitions about bilharzia and swam freely in the brackish waters, basking afterwards on the rocks in mud-smeared contentment.

Most of our neighbours were Afrikaners, and they were different. My parents did not pay homage to our anglophone heritage – never was England spoken of as 'home' – but I imbibed an association with things English from reading. Alongside my life in the veld, I had a voracious appetite for popular fiction. There was no South African culture that reflected our lives, no books, films or comics that spoke directly to our hybrid world of Briton, Afrikaner and African. When eventually I discovered the adventures of Tom Sawyer and Huck Finn, I fell on these reflections of a sunlit river playground touched by darkness. As a boy, however, my social reference points were English novels and comics, the comradeship of Holmes and Watson, the grittiness of Biggles, the savoir-faire of Simon Templar. These influences knitted an internal landscape of cosy rooms in Baker Street and foggy London streets which was every bit as real in my mind as the sunburnt veld outside my window.

Fantasy and reality came closer in tales of school and sport. From a grandmother in Cape Town, I received each fortnight a tightly-bound roll of English comics – *Tiger*, *Lion* and *Comet* – which I collected from Miss van Harmelin at the post office before racing home across the veld to immerse myself in the further adventures of Roy of the Rovers and other heroes. Roy even made a football fan of me for a while, but it did not last and I returned to my passion, which was cricket. My most treasured possession, after my stamp collection, was a 1930s annual of the boys' magazine *Chums*, hundreds of yellowing pages of Hentyesque fables about British pluck on the North-west Frontier, in the Great War and in Darkest Africa. Above all, though, what I loved were the tales set in the English public school with their feats of sporting prowess, especially at cricket.

When I was nine, Peter May brought to South Africa an MCC side that included Compton, Cowdrey, Tyson and Laker, and on a honeyed evening at the Wanderers ground I sat beside my father, spellbound by the climax of a Test match. Needing 231 to win, England were bowled out in a marathon spell of off-spin by Hugh Tayfield who took nine for 113 for South Africa to win a famous game by seventeen runs. The scenes that followed – a milling, cheering crowd, Tayfield being chaired off the field – were more than merely joyous to a cricket-mad boy. They were a reassurance that in the strangely un-English world which we occupied, the stories in *Chums* could come true.

It was at around this time that Sinclair became our houseboy. He came to the back door with a letter saying he could cook and read and was hired because our last boy, Chesa, had gone back to Nyasaland. Sinclair was from Nyasaland, too, which was a recommendation because we had loved Chesa and because, like most Nyasas, he was mission-educated. Local natives, on the other hand (we called blacks natives to distinguish ourselves from those who called them kaffirs) had been left without schooling and were widely held to be good for nothing beyond brute labouring.

Chesa's decision to return to his family had mortified me and I was suspicious of the newcomer. He was slight, yet had a full jet-black beard and a natural baritone voice, which gave him what seemed to a child of

David Livingstone before
his final return to Africa
in 1865.

Richard Burton in his tent.

The Nile expedition of Speke and Grant, as reported by *The Illustrated London News*.

Speke and Grant at Mutesa's court in what is now Kampala, Uganda.

Henry Stanley, 'the Smasher of Rocks'.

Daudi Ricardo.

The Anglican Cathedral in
Zanzibar, built on the site
of the old slave market.

David Bartlett, the vicar of
Zanzibar, on his rounds at Mbweni.

Ruins of the missionary school at Mbweni.

Dhow in the harbour at Zanzibar.

Bagamoyo, Tanzania.

Beach at Bagamoyo, where slaves began their journey into bondage.

Police parade, Dar es Salaam, Tanzania.

Ujiji on Lake Tanganyika, near the spot where Stanley met Livingstone.

Bismarck Rocks at Mwanza on the southern shore of Lake Victoria, Tanzania.

Central *matatu* station, Kampala.

The tomb of the Kabakas, Kampala.

Cemetery on Mengo hill, Kampala, with the graves of the Cooks in the foreground.

The Nile at Namasagali, just north of the source, Uganda.

Father Damian Grimes outside one of the college houses, Namasagali.

Namasagali boys boating on the Nile – Bob, Monavi and Adam.

Keith Anderson weighing his matoke crop before heading to market, Fort Portal, Uganda.

Road outside Fort Portal.

London cab and driver, en route to the Kruger farm, Eldoret, Kenya.

Lord Delamere at Soysambu, Kenya.

Reception committee for Delamere's plane in the Kenya highlands.

Elspeth Huxley's mother's
cottage, Kitumuru, Kenya.

Charles Ngwira at
Lake Malawi.

Musa Zulu.

Judith Todd and
Malcolm King, Bulawayo,
Zimbabwe.

The author with elders of the Khumalo clan at Lobengula's indaba tree, Old Bulawayo.

End of the line – the railway to Simonstown, South Africa.

nine a patriarchal air, even though he must still have been in his thirties. Chesa had smiled with the world, even when stupid kids said things like 'Hello Chesa, can you sell me some cheese?' and ran away shrieking with laughter. I used to visit him in his room, a dimly-lit windowless place smelling of wood smoke and sweat. Mocking Sinclair was inconceivable and the first time I wandered into the room he gave me a stony, wordless look, and I backed out.

It was his teacakes and my comics that broke the ice. I got home from school one day to be offered a batch of cupcakes with raisins; they were probably quite ordinary but I had never come across such things before and thought them delicious. After that, Sinclair produced them on request. In return, I showed him my comics, which he read avidly. He became especially keen on Roy of the Rovers, although we agreed that as an overall paper, *Comet* was better than *Tiger*. From there it was a short step to games. Sinclair was familiar with football, but I insisted on cricket and he indulged me. Our matches were played out on a dirt pitch next to the big syringa tree. It took him a while to got the hang of bowling over-arm, but when he got through my guard and rattled the orange-box wicket, the big black beard would part in a shout of glee.

I write this conscious of the nostalgic tendency in the white South African memory to recall a childhood arcadia involving black or coloured playmates. A good deal of mawkish and self-serving guff has been written about multi-racial rites of passage in a racist state. Yet it seems to me that there was often deep attachment and a humanity in these relationships which largely transcended social inequality. Partly this was inevitable: it was difficult to live in close proximity to another human being without being touched by their lives, learning about one another's families and hopes. Many white children had a degree of intimacy with Africans that no legislation could prohibit – or can now coerce – and which was itself subversive of attempts to separate the races in adulthood. For it was among those whose experience with blacks were closest, rural Afrikaners, that the principle of racial purity as enshrined in the Immorality Act outlawing sex across the colour line, was most frequently compromised. By the time I entered into adolescence, I was more able to confide in Sinclair about the stirrings in me of sexuality than I could in my parents. And I dare to say that he saw something of a son in me. When his wife in Nyasaland gave birth, the boy was given an African name and a European name, as was the custom. His European name was Stephen.

I think what made Sinclair so memorable had something to do with the duality of his nature. It was like having not one additional member of the family, but two. There was the gentle figure, almost feminine despite that luxuriant beard, who took pride in the kitchen, in his baking and in a repertoire that rapidly expanded under my mother's teaching. He turned into a truly excellent cook whose talents excited compliments from guests. Among them he became a celebrity and we took pride in his renown, in the grave reserve of his manner and excellent English, and we used to boast about his other accomplishments, his neat handwriting and fondness for reading.

Yet he had his demons too. Mostly he kept them at bay with *dagga*, marijuana which was the common man's intoxicant and which he grew at the bottom of our land. But every now and again he would be moved by a wild spirit and would concoct in his room a vicious home brew called *skokiaan*, which would consume him and render him at first fierce and then insensible. Once, when my mother had an important dinner party for overseas visitors from my father's firm, she went to the kitchen and found Sinclair hopelessly drunk. Furious, she ordered him to go to his room. He rose up and turned on her with flashing eyes, and for a moment she thought he would strike her. Then he stumbled out and stayed away for three days.

It was drink rather than any political activity that brought him to the attention of the police, but the effect was the same. Most whites detested mission-educated blacks as troublemakers with ideas above their station and, although Sinclair was no political activist, he had a dignity outrageous and provocative to the police in a Transvaal *dorp*. An informer told 'Blackie' Swart that Sinclair was brewing *skokiaan*. After his first arrest there was no chance that he would be forgotten.

Sergeant Swart, head of Rivonia police, was a boulder of a man with black eyes and the moustachios of a South American revolutionary. He seemed to exist in a permanent state of quiet ferocity. 'Hey, that Blackie,' one might hear someone say with a shake of the head and a wry, half-admiring smile. 'Man, he sure knows how to keep the kaffirs in line.'

Once, crossing the veld on my way home, I met a group of blacks going in the opposite direction. Among them was a short, smiling man named Clever whom I knew. As they passed, a blue police van rattled down the dirt road to intercept them and crunched to a halt on the stony surface. From it leapt a bristling young *konstabel*, followed at a leisurely pace by Blackie Swart. The *konstabel* squared up to Clever. *'Kaffir, waar's jou pass,'* he shouted. From a trouser pocket Clever produced a worn piece of paper. The *konstabel* handed it to Blackie who examined it briefly. Then, without a word, his arm shot out, hitting the side of Clever's head with a crack like a whip. Clever went down in a heap. Blackie moved on to the others, now cowering apart, but he was not really interested in their passes. The ritual of power was over. The police clambered back into the van and accelerated away in a cloud of dust.

I never saw Blackie beat Sinclair but I know he did. Once he became aware of Sinclair, the little room at the back of our house was often visited by the police and, because of Sinclair's habits and bearing, they rarely went away empty-handed. Then my father would go up to the police station and, after he had paid an admission-of-guilt fine, Sinclair would be brought in from the cells. For a few days we would mentally tiptoe around the house in guilt and shame about the welts and swellings on Sinclair's face. But to my knowledge, nobody ever challenged Blackie. We used to joke about how stupid they were, but the truth is there was nothing funny about it; the South African police were always above the law.

WITH MY FRIEND Mike I sometimes walked past Liliesleaf Farm, a typical Rivonia smallholding of a few acres near the aptly named Sleepy Hollow Hotel, on our way to a spot further down the river where there was a dam set about with willow trees that trailed fronds on the surface like plaits of a girl's hair. Once Mike and I spent a weekend in my little bell tent beside the river, at the bottom of Liliesleaf. I remember that it rained a lot and we could not start a proper fire and ended up eating half-raw *boerewors*.

It may even have been then that I saw Nelson Mandela for the first time. I realise that this is fanciful, but I like to imagine that, as we swam in the river, I might have looked up and seen him there, wearing his simple blue overalls. He was a terrorist then, of course, a tall, slim man with almond eyes, a small beard and a rather severe expression. On the run after being acquitted in the 1961 Treason Trial, he wore the overalls in his disguise as the houseboy of the tenant, an artist named Arthur Goldreich. In fact, Liliesleaf had been bought by Umkhonto we Sizwe, the military wing of the ANC, as a hideaway, a small farm in a rural backwater where the coming and going of black labourers would attract little attention. In his autobiography, Nelson recalled his time in Rivonia as an idyllic bubble where he could be visited by his young wife, Winnie, and their two children.

Even in retrospect I cannot be sure whether they arrested Mandela before Sinclair or after him. Mandela's name at the time had resonance in a fairly small circle and the news that he had been picked up while driving from Natal to Johannesburg in August 1962 would have caused no great stir in our world. But a few months later, on my way to school, the newspaper banners were full of a real sensation: a swoop on Rivonia had netted the high command of a Moscow-backed revolutionary conspiracy. All along, Liliesleaf had been the headquarters of Operation Mayibuye, a plan for guerrilla warfare in South Africa. As well as Mandela, the commander-in-chief, the farm had been a base for all the Umkhonto leaders, Joe Slovo, Walter Sisulu, Govan Mbeki and Joe Modise. Rivonia was agog. Overnight, the *dorp* had gone from obscurity to infamy.

In the midst of all this Sinclair was arrested again. At first there seemed nothing to worry about, something to do with his pass, the police said. My father went up to pay the usual fine and came back looking serious. There was some crackdown, a new mood in the air. Blackie Swart was moving on and some young man with glasses had taken over. He was not interested in giving Sinclair a hiding and letting him go. An important principle was involved: an alien black's pass had lapsed and the only thing for it was that he should be sent back to Nyasaland.

My parents cajoled and pleaded. Might there not be a way round the problem? Eventually, my father was given the name of an official in a government department and set off for Johannesburg with a small wad of banknotes and a sense of apprehension. In the event, the official took the bribe happily enough but it did no good. A few weeks later we saw Sinclair off at the station, and for the first time in my life I felt a sense of loss.

That was not the worst thing. A few months later we had a letter from one of the Witwatersrand mine managers saying that Sinclair had applied for a job as a cook, and that they would be able to arrange a permit for him to return to South Africa to work at the mine if my mother could verify his credentials. Of course she wrote a glowing reference and some time afterwards we had a letter in Sinclair's neat handwriting, thanking her and saying that he had got the job. The worst thing was that we never wrote back.

I am still not sure why. Partly it was South Africa itself. It produced in us, black and white, Afrikaner and Briton, a paradoxical blend of emotion and inertia, and a certain fatalism. We were not unique in that; everywhere people form relationships and allow them to drift and die. It was also in the nature of things that relations between employer and servant, however close, would stop short of full friendship. Except for a child. So although I know Africa works its most powerful spells in the memory, the lament was real.

*   *   *

GUILT – AND REBELLIOUSNESS – only came later. Sinclair apart, my attitude towards Africans was, for one so young, remarkably condescending. I say this in no spirit of bleeding heart remorse, but to identify a phenomenon. For I had the same attitude towards our white neighours, the Afrikaners. And I believe it stemmed from the fact that I recognised even then that they and the Africans were both of this land in a way that we, the English, were not.

The Rivonia area had been settled during the Great Trek. Each Boer family was allocated a farm based on the distance covered by a rider in a given period, and in this way a trekker named Badenhorst staked out a property on a ridge between two gurgling streams which he called Rietfontein (reed fountain). After the discovery of gold on the Reef, the demand for produce to feed the mines increased and Badenhorst subdivided his farm and sold to Afrikaner small-holders. New migrants, English and East European Jews of various nationalities, brought a property boom, and Rivonia acquired its status as a township between the old Boer capital of Pretoria and the booming new metropolis of Johannesburg.

The biggest Afrikaner clan was the Van Harmelins, among whom Wim, a boy sightly older than me, lived nearby. He was an unnervingly elemental creature. Almost totally incoherent, he had sharp, darting features and resembled a meerkat, a small predator and one of the menagerie of animals, including birds of prey and reptiles, which he harvested from the bushveld. While my friends and I were interested in amphibians and non-poisonous snakes, like the pretty red-lipped herald, Wim was fascinated by the killers of the animal world. In winter, he used to plunder hibernating spitting cobras, or rinkhals, from anthills and sell them to the snake park for serum.

We used to come across him in the veld with a black boy named Sampson. At the time you would not have spoken of black and white teenage boys being friends in the Transvaal, but Wim was never seen with anyone besides Sampson. Once, after Mike was given an airgun, we were walking to the river in search of butcher birds, or shrikes, to kill. We justified this to ourselves as they were vicious little killers which impaled baby sparrows known as mossies on thorns. At the river we found Wim and Sampson. On one hand Wim had a black-shouldered kite, a sleek, small bird of prey, which he was stroking and feeding scraps of frog.

Proudly we showed off the airgun. Wim's eyes narrowed in contempt. 'Gedda reeel gun thut kulls,' he grated. 'Thut kunt kull a mossie.' And he looked back at his kite with wolfish love.

I have mentioned guilt and condescension, but there was another emotion which I was barely aware of then, and only admitted to myself much later, and that was fear. Superficially, this was absurd. Our social superiority to Afrikaners was unquestioned by us: our fathers had office jobs in town, theirs worked for the railways or the post office. Africans were even less of a threat. Yes, by now we knew the horror stories from the Congo, had overheard adults discussing with dreadful zest the rape of nuns by drunken demons, and we knew too that in our own country whites were outnumbered five to one by blacks. But it was inconceivable that such outrages could be repeated here.

No, my fear of Africans and Afrikaners went deeper, and I think was founded in an unconscious understanding even as a child that they were partners in seeing the nature of true power in this cruel, beautiful place. They shared a destiny in it. We were equivocal. The Afrikaners had a term for us – '*soutpiel*', or 'salty prick' which referred to our way of straddling two worlds with one foot in Africa and one in England while our cocks dangled in the sea.

12. The Lake

Tazara Line, Southern Tanzania: Monday, 28 April

H OW APT THAT CECIL Rhodes's dream was pursued by Chairman Mao – the Great Buddha following in the tracks of the Grand Panjandrum. A Cape-to-Cairo railway will never be completed now, but for a while the great Uhuru line brought it closer. And a grand project it was: to build a railway 1,162 miles through virgin bush, across rivers and mountains, and do it in five years. It was Mao's most ambitious foreign adventure, simultaneously to free Tanzania and Zambia from dependence on the transport infrastructure of the white régimes in southern Africa, and open up the African interior to Chinese enterprise. It proved disastrous, and such were the scars it left that Mao never embarked on any imperial venture half so bold again. Twenty-two years on, the 'freedom line' is a rackety white elephant, passing through dozens of ghostly stations marooned in the bush. Yet it remains a magnificent feat, even in the extent of its flaws.

After two pleasant days back in the hospitable confusion of Dar, I went out to the station this morning to find out about Tazara services to find that there was a train leaving in an hour. The genial booking clerk agreed to hold a ticket for me while I raced back to settle my hotel bill, change some money for the fare, and dashed back. This afternoon, while the train click-clacked south, I dozed and my companions argued about democracy. The advocate was the plump fellow in newly creamed white shoes who looked like a fat cat and argued how democracy had brought growth and progress to Malawi and Zambia. Then the bearded man in a blue safari suit snapped that all he could see was that democracy cost a lot of money, and meant that he had to pay for his children to go to school or to the hospital.

They have gone off in search of food and I am left alone to savour one of the greatest treats for the traveller in Africa, to sit at the window of a slow moving train passing through a game reserve. We entered the Selous Park two hours ago, coming upon elephant and giraffe, and herds of zebra and wildebeest. Now a family of warthogs, sublime in their hideousness, glower up at the train. The Selous is Africa's largest reserve, twice the size of Denmark. Just south of here, at Behobeho, lies my old hero, F. C. Selous, killed in 1917 by a German sniper while scouting for the Royal Fusiliers at the age of sixty-four.

What did the Chinese make of all this? The story of how 25,000 of them worked for five years, isolated in the endless African bush, among an utterly alien people, is one of the great untold sagas. It was conducted in almost total secrecy. Not even the casualties were known, although the number who died in accidents, from disease and man-eating lions is believed to be spectacularly high. The workers were kept in a quarantine so successful it became a Chinese boast that not one baby was born as a result of their presence. I suppose there's something laudable about that, but it almost suggests that they feared cultural contamination. From what I have seen, the tendency of Chinese is to regard all other races as inferior, in much the same way that the British once did. So there was something touching about the sight today of a lone Chinese worker at a siding being pestered by a naked toddler for attention: the child persisted until, still engaged in conversation, he picked it up in a distracted way and dandled it on his knee.

The Kipengere mountains, green and heavy, and the wild flowers of purple and gold, make the scene redolent of the Cape. There are still 3,700 miles to go but I am now southward bound. In the morning I alight at Mbeya and take a bus to Sinclair's country.

Chitimba, Lake Malawi: Thursday, 30 April

I HAVE FOUND SOMEWHERE to retire to. By rationing myself to two beers, I can live here on £1.50 a day – 70p for a bed in a shared room at the resthouse, 8p for fruit (pawpaw and bananas), 30p for fish stew with cassava and 40p for beer. The fish is a rather glutinous barbel from the lake but the local Carlsberg is excellent.

If anything, the lake is even more lovely than Lake Tanganyika which it closely matches, both being long, deep rents in the Earth's crust running north to south. At a length of 350 miles and 45 miles at its widest point, Lake Malawi is slightly the shorter and narrower, but it is also the trunk of the Great Rift Valley. Lake steamers used to be the main means of travel in the region and I read in my 1920 travel guide that the African Lakes Corporation at that time charged £22 10s for each passenger to be carried in a hammock the 220 miles from Karonga, the northern port of this lake, to Abercorn, the southern port on Lake Tanganyika. (Baggage, 8s 6d per 60 lb load; about 15 days good going.)

From my room, I can walk down to a broad expanse of soft, fine sand where perhaps a dozen dugout canoes, bleached a pale grey and streaked with black knots and whorls, lie like beached porpoises, and a slumbering sapphire sea falls away on either side. For its entire length, thatch villages rise at the water's edge; here is a pre-colonial world, of solemn-eyed, naked children, and women breaking the ground with simple metal tools, and maize stalks fluttering like leaves among the palm trees, and Africa itself seems blessed.

There is almost nothing in Chitimba, including electricity, so it would be a quiet retirement. The beer comes from the only store, which has a room around the back lit by a paraffin lamp where drinkers come in the evening. I had a beer last night with a man named Delicious. The subject of Banda came up. 'No question, he was an absolute dictator,' said Delicious. 'He fed people to the crocodiles.' Shaking his head admiringly, he went on: 'He was tough. He was a bastard. He was so clever that one . . . hayi, he was a wizard.'

What about his successor, Muluzi, I asked. 'These new ones do not care about the poor people. They look after the rich. Banda was not for the rich. So now we are missing him.'

The proprietor, a man named O. B., joined us. Both of them had heard about tomorrow's election in Britain. Delicious wanted to know if it was for a president. I said we had a queen instead of a president so the vote was for a prime minister. Was the queen like Banda, he asked. Not quite, I said, there was no election for the queen.

O. B. broke in. 'She is like the chiefs,' he said impatiently. 'It is with the blood.'

Delicious was baffled. A woman as chief? 'Yes, of course there are some women chiefs,' O. B. said. I pointed out, however, that in Britain it only happened when the chief had no sons. Delicious looked relieved.

BEFORE SETTING OUT, I had the idea of tracking Sinclair down. Perhaps somewhere, I thought, an old South African police record book might show where he came from and where he was sent back to. It would have meant a lot to me to see him again, to say how much we had missed him, to tell an old man how I had thought about him, and learnt to admire; that, and to find out what happened to Stephen. It proved a hopeless quest, as it was probably always bound to be. Life expectancy in Malawi was forty-six; Sinclair would have been in his seventies. But if we had met, I would have asked him about the changes he had seen in his country.

When he left it was Nyasaland, an impoverished protectorate in which the key influence was the Scottish missionaries who had provided his education. When he went home it was to Malawi, a state under the spell of a figure no less austere, a diminutive man in a grey Homburg who wielded an ivory-handled fly whisk as if it were a wand. Two figures dominated the country's past: the first David Livingstone, the second the former President for Life, Hastings Kamuzu Banda.

Livingstone came upon the lake in 1859, the only triumph on the catastrophic Zambezi expedition. The beauty of Nyasa, meaning 'broad waters', was overshadowed by the slave raiding going on along its shores. Livingstone saw 'a land of darkness and of the shadow of death', but it inspired the vision by which he would be remembered, as the prophet of African colonisation. He anticipated a time when the trade had been eradicated and enthused over the prospect of a partnership between the honest poor of Britain and Africa. 'The soil is so rich it could support millions of people,' he wrote.

Banda was the kind of tyrant whom liberal whites felt secure in denouncing. He looked the part. A malevolently gnomish figure wearing a bleak countenance and dark glasses the size of plates, he might have been taken for a cousin of Haiti's 'Papa Doc' Duvalier. Then there was his ghoulish boast, about feeding his enemies to the crocodiles. Worst of all, however, in the eyes of the comfortably righteous, was that he was prepared to do business with apartheid, that he maintained diplomatic ties with Pretoria in exchange for economic aid.

I would not care to speculate what Sinclair thought about all this. What was clear, as I made my way down the lake, was that Delicious was not alone in mourning the erstwhile President for Life, who was no longer president but was still alive, aged ninety-nine, having lived under house arrest since his election defeat in 1994. In the town of Karonga one night, I met a doctor who had once been at University College Hospital and wanted to hear news about London. He introduced himself half apologetically. 'I used to take the Tube from Finsbury Park, and I would say to myself, "Who will I recognise today?" After two years I had recognised three people, and I said, "no, this place is too big for me". So I came back.'

He was in his thirties, a plump, pleasant-faced man, familiar with the whimsical nature of authoritarianism. 'I was never arrested myself, but I had a friend who went to Essex University. He came home for a break, then was going back to England when he was arrested at the airport. They had nothing on him, but the connection with England made them suspicious. He was inside for two years. Even a passport could be an incriminating document in those days. I suppose I was lucky.'

As the doctor talked, we were joined by a couple of his colleagues from their clinic. The old chestnut about Banda feeding his enemies to the crocodiles came out again, and they laughed, and slowly the conversation took on a tone of wry nostalgia.

'There was no corruption before – I mean political corruption, sure, but not financial. People were too afraid of trying that. Now they all want to get their hands in your pocket. And this new man, this Muluzi, he doesn't know what is going on.'

'He flops whichever way is necessary.'

'That's democracy, baby,' said the doctor.

A male orderly complained about the roads. 'You will see. We used to have good roads – now it takes you three hours to travel a hundred miles.'

Another chipped in: 'If that happened under Kamuzu, he would have said, "Who is the minister of roads?"'

'Then he would have sacked him.'

'Then he would have arrested him.' They roared with laughter.

As we said goodbye, one leaned over and said: 'We liked Banda because he was the chief. That is the way Africans want it. It is our tradition.'

The roads were as bad as they had said, the poverty more dire than anything I had seen in Tanzania. Gangs of ragged villagers with spades filled in potholes with soil and stones in the hope of a tip from drivers.

Livingstone and Banda ... taking a *matatu* south on the crumbling macadam known, with a certain pathos, as the M1, I was bound for the two places where the dreams of each man had been given a form – the colony of Livingstonia; and the 'Eton of the bush'.

13. The Mission

I CLIMBED UP TO Livingstonia on top of a maize sack in the back of an open four-wheel drive *bakkie*. No other vehicle had come by all day so there were dozens of us crammed together on the sacks as it wound up the switchback trail under the stars. At first it was a delight, the night encrusted with sparkle, the cosiness of bodies scented by wood smoke pressed together. But as the *bakkie* ground along in first gear for hours, I grew uncomfortable then irritated. What on earth had possessed Robert Laws to build his mission in such a spot?

The idea of a living memorial to Livingstone was raised within days of his burial at Westminster Abbey in April 1874. For the last eight years of his life he had roamed the wilderness with his handful of African companions like some possessed pilgrim. While not exactly disgraced, he had left England for the last time in 1865 under a cloud, his reputation tarnished by the failure of his endeavours and the cantankerousness of his nature. Quite what it was that Livingstone was engaged upon was none too clear: he was crusading against the slave trade; he was preaching and converting the heathen; he was on his own Nile quest. Then he simply disappeared, for years, the wandering mystic, until there followed in rapid succession discovery by Stanley, renewed fame, martyrdom, and the ultimate redemptive act of love by his bearers, Susi and Chuma. So there had to be a memorial, and the obvious site was the lake which he claimed as his one discovery of significance. The following year, Robert Laws, like Livingstone a Scot and a physician, went out to Lake Nyasa. From a bay on the southern shore he wrote, 'Livingstonia is begun'.

Livingstone is an unfashionable figure now, often spoken of as a failure. The argument goes something like this: as a missionary, he made just one prominent convert, the chief Sechele, who later lapsed. As an explorer, he was inexpert: he was wrong in every respect about the source of the Nile, and quite deliberately concealed the fact that he got directions to Lake Nyasa from a Portuguese named Candido de Costa Cardoso, who was its real discoverer. As a leader of expeditions, he was quite hopeless, consistently failing to take account of, or recognise, practical difficulties, and then blaming everyone else when things went wrong. Perhaps his greatest failure of all was as a family man: he imposed a life so hellish on his pathetic wife, Mary, that she became an alcoholic and lost her own faith before dying on the Zambezi expedition. Their son, Robert, a troubled youth, fled his overbearing father and, while still a teenager, joined the Northern forces in the American Civil War; in December 1864 he was wounded in a skirmish in Virginia and died a prisoner, a few days short of his nineteenth birthday.

Greatness is harder to define than failure and especially hard when it is a greatness of the spirit. Livingstone laid out the chart, so to speak, for African exploration; years before Burton and Speke started for the Nile, he recognised that waterways were the key to unlocking the continent. He was, however, atypical of the exploring breed. Altogether more wild, more dangerous, than the saint of Victorian myth, he nevertheless lacked the sheer ruthlessness, the indifference to suffering, that enabled Stanley to impose his will on the continent, and made him in the end the most redoubtable of its explorers, its Amundsen.

The parallel with the Antarctic travellers is worth pursuing for the light it casts on Livingstone. Polar exploration seemed to draw nobility from those who endured its terrible hardships. Marooned in an uninhabited, icy vastness, men like Shackleton, Mawson, Scott and Amundsen became for all the world knights errant, united by a chivalric code that appeared to embody self-sacrifice and transcend anything base or mean. They might be rivals but still they honoured one another; and even when, like Scott, they were flawed, they were never less than heroic.

In Africa, by contrast, the pursuit of glory was usually selfish and invariably tainted. Burton and Speke ended up hating not only one another but Africa itself. Speke rewarded Grant's loyalty by denying him the reward of a share in their achievement. Stanley's ferocity destroyed the only friends he ever had, and many others besides. Baker's methods were downright brutal. It was as if certain qualities were borne on the air of each world – a purifying iciness at the Poles, a corrupting miasma in Africa. The difference is, of course, that at the Poles men had to co-operate with one another just to survive in a pitiless wilderness, while in Africa it was not only the elements that were hostile, but other humans who were engaged in an equally desperate struggle for survival.

Laurens van der Post once made the point that, while a great deal was written about the devastating effect that the European has had on the native of Africa, no one stopped to inquire into the effect of the native on the European. Frequently those who explored Africa diminished their own humanity by their dealings with its inhabitants, but in this test Livingstone's greatness shone through. It was not just that he liked Africans and befriended them, that he loathed what slavery had done to their society and became by his example its most formidable antagonist. In the end, he *was* an African, a leader among them, but one who shared their world as no other white man of his time did, and who treated them as equals, with respect and understanding.

Even if he was the least of its explorers, Livingstone was far and away the greatest of Africa's travellers, and to describe his final journey as an extended form of suicide, as has been done, merely illustrates how the values of our time have changed since his. Quite simply, he loved to test his physical powers against an unforgiving landscape. Even in extremis he could describe with exhilaration, 'the very great . . . animal pleasure of travelling in a wild unexplored country'. In those last years of his life, he engaged with the continent a bit like a wild animal himself, as one of its own, yet he never lost either his idealism or his faith in its future. Finally, he found in it serenity.

His influence was greater posthumously than in his lifetime. A month after his death, the slave market at Zanzibar was closed. He would have been gratified to know that his example inspired a generation to believe that Britain had a mission in Africa, but saddened that the upshot was to be the 'Scramble'. For Livingstone had no thought that chunks of Africa might be acquired as possessions for exploitation by European powers. His hope was for a partnership between humble white settlers and black peasants. His belief was that, once this was achieved, commerce would drive out the slave trade while, under Christianity, Africa would develop autonomously. 'As the African need not be torn from his country and enslaved, no more need the English poor be crowded together in unwholesome dens, and debarred from breathing the pure air of Heaven,' he wrote.

The Livingstonia Mission, sent to Nyasa in 1875 under Laws, was to be the first step towards this vision.

Livingstonia: Friday, 2 May

HAVING CLAMBERED THANKFULLY down from the *bakkie* after midnight, I was too exhausted to take much note of my surroundings and awoke this morning in a narrow missionary bed with a sense of disorientation. Outside, daylight illuminated a strange landscape. On a plateau looking across green, misty hills, clouds swirled through forests of pine carrying a thin film of rain across a scene from the Scottish Highlands. That there was a tropical lake lying below these chilly vapours seemed inconceivable.

Laws's house, a sturdy Victorian residence of hewn stone blocks with bay and casement windows, is as severe as an Edinburgh nonconformist.

The beds have wooden slatted headboards, the fireplaces are cold and empty, walls and floors are unadorned and, appropriately for a place which takes paying guests, it has all the jauntiness of a post-war boarding-house. At the sight of a flaming red poinsettia flaunting itself against a side wall, my heart leapt.

Laws, a wearyingly pious man, was a member of the Church of Scotland, but in fairness it was not merely a longing for his native landscape that brought him to this rainswept and impractical site. The first Livingstonia was built on the southern shore at Cape Maclear, which was lovely but deadly, being infested with malaria. After the death of five of his brethren, Laws removed the mission halfway up the lake to Bandawe where, in the belief that the fever stemmed from vapours coming off the lake, he ordered that homes should be built with doors facing inland. Bandawe was, if anything, even less healthy than Cape Maclear and the growing number of mounds in the little missionary graveyard attested to the fallacy of Laws's theory. Finally, almost twenty years after arriving at the lake, he gave in to the more conventional wisdom that linked the risk of fever to altitude. He then proceeded to act with true Livingstonian indifference to practical considerations. The site he settled on was the highest point on the escarpment. His road, rising 2,300 feet over eleven miles and hacked out of the mountainside with rudimentary tools, was a feat of astonishing energy and tenacity, but his idea that a settlement could flourish here was as flawed as Livingstone's blithe plan to plant a mission halfway up the Zambezi. Suffering from the obsessive single-mindedness that afflicted many Europeans left to their own devices in the wilderness. Laws went on to build a church, a school, a hospital, a theological college and a teachers' college on the plateau.

These ingredients – Calvinism, medicine, learning and discipline – were to be laced through the career of the mission's most famous old boy. He arrived in 1915, a teenager named Banda, to train as a teacher. His African name was Kamuzu, but he also took the name of one of the Livingstonia missionaries, Hastings.

THE PASTOR OF Livingstonia, the Reverend Anthony Luhunga, was coming out of the vestry. 'I have a wedding to perform,' he said. 'Why don't you attend and we can speak afterwards.' My doubts about gate-crashing were waved away. 'If you have not been to one of our weddings, you must come,' he said.

The church reflected the paradoxes of African Calvinism. A bare, austere shell enlivened by the rhythm from a ghetto blaster and a procession led by a young woman who danced ahead in a dress of electric blue, scattering pink and white hibiscus petals. I soon saw why the pastor had dismissed my reservations about intruding. Anyone could drop in and did, including a lunatic wearing motorcycle goggles and two lads who continued their football game in a side aisle.

Afterwards, the pastor showed me around the little settlement. Here the puny teenage boy, who had been named Kamuzu, meaning 'little root', because a root potion was believed to have cured his mother's barrenness, studied to be a teacher. The event that changed his life, and the country's history, occurred when he sat his final exam. Being so slight, he was unable to see the blackboard and stood up to look over the shoulder of the student in front. An invigilator thought he was cheating and he was expelled.

In his shame was born a fierce, bitter drive. He made his way to Southern Rhodesia, where he worked as a medical orderly, then South Africa. Studying at night school while working in the mine compounds as an interpreter, he came to the attention of American Methodists and in 1924 was sent on a scholarship to Ohio. There he imbibed the doctrine of self-help preached by the black American leader, Booker T. Washington, and began to accumulate medical degrees – first from Nashville, then Edinburgh and Liverpool. By 1945 he had a practice in Harlesden, North London, with 4,000 patients, most of whom were white. In his undertaker-like suits, and with his courtesy and simplicity, he was almost a figure from the Victorian era. The Church of Scotland, proud of the success of a Livingstonia old boy, made him an elder. Only once did his utter probity slip, when his married English secretary gave birth to his child and Banda was cited in her divorce.

With a growing reputation in his native land, he was invited in 1958 by Nyasaland nationalists to return and lead the independence movement. So long had he been away – forty years – that he could no longer speak the local dialect and knew no one. At this point, with the leadership of an emerging state in the offing, the English doctor with the old-world manners slipped effortlessly into the role of an African chief.

At his London home, he had entertained radicals like the Ghanaian Kwame Nkrumah and Kenya's Jomo Kenyatta, while distancing himself from their views. However, the federation of Nyasaland with the Rhodesias, a threat to his own fiefdom, brought out the militant in him. The stethoscope was replaced by a fly whisk, and he started to bare his teeth. Rivals were sidelined and Banda confronted the colonial authorities, earning the aspirant leader's obligatory short spell in prison, followed by reconciliation and tea with the governor. A tape from the BBC archives of an interview in London not long before he became Malawi's leader gives a blackly comedic glimpse of his new style.

Interviewer: Dr Banda, have you come to ask for a firm date for Nyasaland's independence?

Banda [deadpan]: I won't tell you that.

Interviewer: When do you hope to get independence?

Banda [emphatically]: I won't tell you *that.*

Interviewer: Dr Banda, when you get independence, are you going to break away from the Central African Federation?

Banda [irritably]: Need you ask me that question at this stage?

Interviewer [also nettled]: Well, this stage is as good as any other stage. Why do you ask me why I shouldn't ask you that question at this stage?

Banda [voice rising]: Haven't I said that enough for everybody to be convinced that I mean just that?

Interviewer [calm again]: Dr Banda, if you break with the Central African Federation, how will you make out economically?

Banda: Don't ask me that. Leave that to me.

Interviewer [running out of questions]: So which way is your mind working?

Banda [suspiciously]: Which way? I won't tell you that.

Interviewer: Are you going to tell me anything?

Banda: Nothing!

Interviewer: Are you going to tell me why you've been to Portugal?

Banda: That's my business.

Interviewer: In fact, you're going to tell me nothing at all.

Banda [triumphantly]: Nothing at all!

Pastor Luhunga showed me the teacher training college attended by Banda. A shell of a building, it had long since closed. The theological college and an institute for artisans and craftsmen, another idea close to Livingstone's heart, had also been shut. Only the school survived; that, and Laws's old stone house, built by the first generation of stonemasons trained at Livingstonia, which still attracted the odd curious visitor and would stand until doomsday.

The Church of Scotland had kept the mission going for its symbolic significance but the basic obstacle to a viable settlement was insurmountable, and had been from the moment that Laws planted his settlement on the plateau. Perhaps the fall of Banda, the Church's last significant link with the country, had sealed its fate. Financial support had dried up and the mission was dying, strangled by the cost of carrying everything up the switchback trail by four-wheel drive. 'We have many problems, but it is mainly transport,' Pastor Luhunga said sadly. 'That is what is killing us.'

I started walking back down the mountain road. It wound through the kind of thick woodland which in most inhabited parts of Malawi had been stripped for fuel – the rare, mysterious and lovely genus of *brachystegia* – mountain acacia, mufuti and, sweetest of all, msasa – which is found only in central Africa and which wins the heart by its pure perversity, producing in the brilliant flush of spring the glowing pinks, reds and crimsons of autumn. Hoopoes and bulbuls whooped and wittered in the leaves. The only other sound was the crunch of my shoes on the track. After half an hour, the cloud that had lain upon the plateau all the previous day lifted and, as I rounded yet another hairpin bend, the lake suddenly opened up about 1,500 feet below. The afternoon was clear and luminous, the lake immense. For another hour or so, I was alone with both. Each time the water disappeared behind the trees it would reappear at the next bend with added brilliance.

A short way off the track lay a glorious surprise. Across a gorge, the Manchewe Falls plunged in a thin stream for about 600 feet over a cliff of red rock, enclosed on either side by trees clinging like lichen to the face. Under a shelter of banana leaves, an old man was brewing a pot of tea for a young couple from Kent whom I had met a few days earlier at Karonga. They were an intrepid pair, having set out on their bicycles from Dover eight months earlier, and it was a pleasure to see them again over tea in this dazzling spot. Livingstonia, with all its misty Calvinistic sadness, was behind, and I felt back in Africa.

ON THE BUS going south, I sat next to a woman in a granny-print dress with glasses and coffee-coloured skin as smooth as cream. She had the disappointed air of an exile who remembered better times. Prices, law and order, roads – everything had deteriorated. The country was ruled by rascals. As it turned out, she was no admirer of Banda either. She was a monarchist and what she pined for were military parades, governors-general, plumed hats and royal visits.

'The Queen Mother – '62, I think it was. Then we had the Queen herself. It was so lovely. I was in all the parades because I was a Girl Guide. We used to go on camps. Oh, we had such a good time. Then, when Kamuzu came in, they disbanded the Guides and the Scouts.' She wrinkled her nose in disdain. 'They said we all had to join the Young Pioneers' [Banda's praetorian guard]. 'Well, I put them right about that. I said "Certainly not".'

Her speech was accentless and, for all the brevity of our acquaintanceship, I had the feeling of travelling with a spinster aunt. The bus stopped and a very tall man climbed on. 'He's an Ngoni,' she whispered. 'They're terribly conscious of their culture.' The Ngoni were a Zulu clan who made an epic migration in the 1820s to escape Shaka.

I was desperately keen to know more about my companion. That her father was English I had no doubt. Was her mother Ngoni? How had she acquired the manner of a matron from Tunbridge Wells? And how could I find out without being crass?

My thoughts were halted abruptly as the bus came to a stop in Mzimba. 'Can you help me with my case?' she asked. 'I am getting off here.' There was no time for more.

'Give the Queen Mother a wave from me,' she said.

I WAS SURPRISED by how few people of mixed race I saw. In South Africa, the Coloureds, as they were known, had always been a distinct population group. While researching the life of Frederick Selous, a beau idéal of the Victorian era, I discovered that, during his years as a wandering hunter/naturalist in Zambesia, he had formed a liaison with a Mangwato woman and fathered at least two children by her before leading Rhodes's pioneers to Salisbury and returning home to marry a clergyman's daughter. His African family was abandoned.

Of Selous's two English sons, the first joined the Royal Flying Corps, dying when he was shot down in 1918. The second boy, Harold, followed his father to Africa, joining the Colonial Service and serving in Nyasaland until his death in 1954. Although he never married it was rumoured that he too had established a long-term liaison with an African woman. This was confirmed by his will, in which he bequeathed family possessions along with £5,000 invested in securities to a Yao woman named Rose Mary Abba of Mponde at the southernmost point of the lake. The outcome had a sort of satisfying symmetry – the son had made at least symbolic reparation for the father's neglect.

The epilogue to this story becomes a little complicated. In Fiji, reporting on a military coup, I met a British judge who had been briefly detained by the new régime. He had once sat on the bench in Malawi, and somehow the subject of Selous came up. The judge then related how he had been invited to dine by an Asian lawyer in Blantyre. The meal was served off silver salvers, on one of which the judge could make out a copper-plate inscription with the name F. C. Selous. He asked where it had come from and the lawyer told him: 'Years ago I was out walking by the lake when I came to a village. There was a woman there alone, and she was feeding some pigs. The plates they were eating off were unusual and I looked closer. Then I saw the inscriptions and realised they must all be silver. The woman was quite happy to sell them. I asked her if she had anything else, and she came out with this.' And the lawyer produced a cane carved from a single rhinoceros horn with a heavy silver embossed handle. It was inscribed to F. C. Selous from Cecil Rhodes.

A SIGN ERECTED by the Department of Antiquities pointed the way to the Kachere Tree. In a clearing nearby stood a single large *brachystegia* surrounded by white-painted stones. It was an unlikely looking shrine, but just as Bodh Gaya grew up around the tree at which the Buddha attained enlightenment, this quasi-mystical site was founded to celebrate the spot at which His Excellency the Life President, Ngwazi Dr H. Kamuzu Banda, sat as a child at the feet of a missionary named Dr Prentice and drank from the fountain of knowledge.

There were few pilgrims to Mthunthama these days. The *matatu* left the M1 at Kasungu and plunged off into the bush, through elephant grass swaying high beside the road, until it reached a village – just another village with a few wooden stalls and ragged figures. Then one saw a bank, a supermarket – and the sign.

Banda revealed the plan for his memorial soon after proclaiming himself Life President in 1971. Speaking to an education conference, he fulminated against 'progressive' teaching methods. Malawi's need, he said, was for education based on the fundamentals practised by missionaries like Dr Prentice. He had decided to found the Kamuzu Academy, described, in a model of understatement, as 'a first-class co-educational boarding school designed to prepare its students for entry into any of the world's top universities'. It would be run on British public school lines, with an emphasis on conservative and traditional methods. This would be his 'gift to the country's most brilliant boys and girls'.

Over the next ten years the outlines of the Kamuzu Academy took shape. Buildings were designed in accordance with the Life President's insistence on 'timelessness and dignity'. On what had been almost 200 acres of primal bush near his village, the Great Hall and Clock Tower arose in a high-arched arcade beside an artificial lake. The library plan was based on the US Library of Congress. A chapel, art studio, music room, laboratories and resource centre were built beside classrooms. A golf course was hacked out of the bush, along with badminton courts, gymnasium, sports grounds (the football pitch was the best in the country and was used by the national side) and separate Olympic swimming pools for staff and pupils. And because all those associated with the academy would have to live there, a rural suburb of staff houses took shape a short walk from school.

Much attention was paid to the question of uniform and design, a responsibility entrusted by Banda to Mama Cecilia Kadzamira, the 'Official Hostess', as she was known, and his long-term companion. Uniform was a straw boater and green blazer, with gold blouse and pleated green skirt for girls. The school badge was the kachere tree. At a meeting of the uniform and design committee in November 1978, it was minuted that the motto 'Honor Deo et Patriae' was accepted, and copies of the proposed school song, *I Vow to Thee, My Country* (words by Spring-Rice, music by Holst), were studied and approved. It was reported that the police band had been asked to make a tape recording of the song, 'to be heard by His Excellency, the Life President, for his approval or otherwise'.

At the outset, Banda pronounced that, as learning was based on the classics, Latin and Greek would be compulsory. 'One cannot understand European civilisation without knowing the history and language of the Greeks and Romans,' he declared. His insistence 'that all teachers should have had at least some Latin in their academic background' determined that the staff would be British. In private, he spelled it out even more clearly. 'I will not have Malawian teachers at my school,' he said. To emphasise the continuity with British tradition, gowns and mortarboards were worn on formal occasions.

The cost was dizzying. Precise figures have always been guarded but, by the time building was completed, it is certain that at least £12 million had been spent, three times the initial estimate, in a country with an annual revenue of £140 million. After that the academy consumed about 40 per cent of the total budget for secondary education.

But if it was élitist on the grand scale, the academy was no bastion of privilege. Students came from every part of the country, each district presenting its top boy and girl pupils after public exams. The humblest peasant's child could win entry. In offering the finest education without regard to status or gender, the Kamuzu Academy was unique in Africa. And the objective, to create a new intelligentsia on a basis of merit, was brave and noble. Although called the 'Eton of the bush', it was egalitarian – and, therefore, nothing of the sort.

Kamuzu Academy opened its doors for the new school year in 1981. Among those smiling proudly at the opening ceremony were the chairman of the board of governors, Aaron Gadama, and the deputy chairman, Dick Matenje, both ministers and protégés of the Life President. Two years later, as the academy celebrated an excellent first crop of A-level results from the Cambridge Board, the board had two vacancies. Both Gadama and Matenje were dead. It was said that their car, also carrying two other politicians, had plunged over a cliff. All had died of severe head injuries. After a spell of uncertainty at school over the proper response to this tragedy, orders came from Banda's office that mourning was prohibited.

FIFTY YARDS FROM the entrance gate, the dirt roadside verge was brought to an abrupt end by a neat concrete pavement fringed by grass and a painted white line suddenly appeared in the middle of the tarmac road leading to twin gatehouses. This side was Africa. Beyond lay an imperial fantasy in warm, red brick, yellow-blossoming cassia trees and rolling lawns.

The headboy of Kamuzu Academy, Lloyd Mtalimanja, expressed it well. 'You have heard about it, so you have some idea what to expect. But nothing prepares you for that moment when you see this place for the first time.'

The gatehouse guard looked dubiously at me – a dusty figure with a rucksack asking to see the headmaster – but a messenger was assigned as an escort. We walked up the drive, past the chapel and bell tower, towards the ornamental lake fringed with canna lillies standing at the edge of the vaulting arches and clock tower of the administration block. I was ushered into a wood-panelled and carpeted room. On one wall was a photograph showing an inscrutable Banda sitting on a chair flanked by Mama Kadza-mira, while the headmaster and teachers knelt before him like peasants before a feudal lord.

For all the appearance of timeless solidness, Kamuzu Academy was in crisis. It had always suffered from the stress inherent in isolated and inward-looking social cocoons: the teachers feuded like the clergy of an English cathedral, despite living in what still resembled a pastoral corner of the Empire, in bungalows with verandahs, shrub gardens and the services of a cook/gardener. Most got by comfortably on a third of their salaries and remitted about £900 a month to Britain. A staff club, with a pool, golf course and video library, sold cheap drinks. In the old days the biggest discomfort was the occasional bout of malaria and the only panic anyone could remember was the time a suspected rabid dog penetrated the security fence.

Banda's fall brought down the ivory tower. For more than a decade the school had been insulated against Africa. Whatever was necessary, 'H.E.' (His Excellency) or 'the Founder' provided, but one of the first actions of the new government was to freeze the assets of the corporation controlling his financial empire which funded the academy. Now when equipment broke – the photocopier, the dry-cleaner – there was no ready remedy. The grand Library of Congress building could afford neither journals nor books. Those by the pupils' favourite authors – Robert Ludlum (boys), Isaac Asimov (girls) – had been so frequently read that they were falling to pieces. The works of Wilbur Smith, whose staple subject matter of steely white men lording it over savage Africa made him an odd preference, were in scarcely better shape.

Banda's block on black teachers had been abandoned, and there were now eight Malawians and twenty-two Britons. Those who had been at the school longest had found it most difficult to adjust. They recalled the academy's heyday, of 'H.E.' at his peak, and reminisced fondly about the old monster on Founder's Day, when, attired in Homburg and three-piece suit, he lectured an assembly for hours on end in blazing heat on transitive and intransitive verbs, and proceeded through a discourse in fluent Latin on the glories of the ancient world.

Some had been unable to take the strain. They included the previous head, who eloped with a Kenyan woman. Stephen Drew, the deputy head, took over and guided the school over the worst, but he had also had enough and was shortly returning to Britain. The intrigue and plotting over who was likely to succeed him had deepened factions among the staff and others were following him, including Jonathan, the head of English, and the chief party-giver, Ursula, who as Dame was head of housekeeping.

On one thing they were all agreed – the students were a pleasure to teach. 'Mainly it is their spontaneity and enthusiasm,' said Stephen Drew. 'They are keen to achieve and willing to respect achievement by others. It transforms our work. In Britain it has become very uncool to show enthusiasm, to actually be seen working.' Another said: 'There is an innocence here. I have never experienced any insolence in my class. This has gladdened my heart, and so I have never lost my love of teaching.'

Pass rates were uniformly high – 93 per cent A–C grades at GCSE, 98 per cent at A level. But it was in language that the results were most impressive, and where Stephen Drew believed students' greatest aptitude lay. 'English is their second language, sometimes their third. We take their fluency for granted, but it is a most uncommon ability. And just look at our Greek and Latin.' Banda's quirky vision had yielded a record crop of Malawian classics scholars the previous year. In Latin, still compulsory to GCSE, the bottom of the year obtained a B, all the rest got As. In Greek, which was optional, sixteen candidates were entered for GCSE, of whom fourteen obtained A*s. Two laggards got As.

The key question now was whether these results could be maintained. For the biggest upheaval of all had been among the pupils. Cut off from Banda's funds, the school authorities had been left with no alternative but to accept fee-paying students. There was no longer any doubt that the academy would survive, but the egalitarian cornerstone had been lost. New admissions were coming from wealthy families in Kenya, Zambia and Uganda, as well as Malawi, and the transformation to just another African public school was almost complete. At the time, only fifty of the 300 pupils were still there purely on merit, and there would be no more like Nina Kapezi.

Nina was born of humble parents in Lilongwe, her father a clerk for a bus company. Home was a tiny bungalow in which she shared a room with three siblings and the main meal was maize with a vegetable relish. Since winning a scholarship to the academy, she had become used to eating meat daily in the great dining-hall where pupils queued with trays for beef stew with boiled potatoes, and apple pie and custard. She shared her bright, neat room with bunks, desks and reading lights, with just one other girl, walking to class along a path lined with canna lilies.

Nina was shortly to leave, to continue her studies on a law scholarship. What she expected to miss most when she returned to her other life were not the comforts but the school light operatic society, and in particular Gilbert and Sullivan. She had been in *The Pirates of Penzance*, and *The Mikado*, and the experience had opened up a new world. She even thought she might start a light operatic society at university. 'Those of us lucky enough to be here have been exposed to things we would never have known about otherwise,' she said. 'Discovering G&S might be a small thing – but small things can give you some of the biggest pleasures in life.'

BANDA HAD ERECTED a fitting monument to himself, ambitious, perverse, even cruel – for there was a sense in which, for the pupils, life would never be the same, or quite as blessed, again – but above all enigmatic. It seemed absurdly pointless that children in a third world country should be made to learn Greek and Latin. Yet it evidently gave them a grasp of parts of speech that made them able to learn other languages quickly, as well as a capacity for disciplined study beyond price. The students were models of scholarly rectitude, smart, polite and keen. I had sat in on a sixth-form economics class, which went right over my head. If one was to find fault, one might say it all seemed a little bland, a little too perfect, although there was nothing bland about youngsters like Nina.

But was it African? Students learnt no Chichewa, Malawi's main language, nor Swahili, the *lingua franca* of East Africa. More importantly, they studied no African history. They could hold forth on the House of Caesar or Bismarck and the Unification of Germany, but knew nothing of the House of Zulu or Bismarck and the Scramble for Africa. Almost every aspect of life at Kamuzu smacked of what Australians used to term the 'cultural cringe', the conviction that indigenous culture is worthless and only 'the other' valuable.

And would this new intelligentsia, in which so much had been invested, stay in Africa? The indications were not encouraging. Almost a third of A-level students had obtained scholarships to study at universities abroad and experience showed that, given the chance, the best and brightest stayed overseas. In African's case, the loss of skills to the developed world had been less a brain drain than a brain haemorrhage.

The ultimate irony of the Kamuzu Academy was that Banda's hope – that a new generation of technocrats would provide the country's future leadership – had so signally failed to bear fruit. In fifteen years, the school had produced plenty of economists and lawyers, and quite a few doctors. The careers officer proudly cited a former girl pupil who had just been appointed Air Malawi's first woman pilot. But the fate of the school's first two governors, Gadama and Matenje, had provided an object lesson to its students. Not one had followed the Founder into politics.

A year after international pressure brought about the election that was his downfall, and twelve years after the deaths of Gadama and Matenje, Banda was charged with their murders. Exactly what had happened will probably never be known, but it seems they had opposed his choice of John Tembo – a nephew of Mama Kadzamira – as his heir apparent. Orders were then given to the Chief of Police that they were to be eliminated. Along with two other mild dissidents, Twaibu Sangala and David Chiwanga, they had their heads beaten in with rocks to simulate the head injuries of a crash.

Then their car was pushed over a cliff. Banda and Tembo were brought to trial in 1995. Obviously frail and barely lucid, Banda claimed he could not remember events so far back. Both were acquitted.

He died soon after I left Malawi, living in comfort at state expense, taking to the grave a great many secrets, including his own age, which could only be estimated at ninety-nine. That he was a tyrant and a monster was beyond doubt. Even if his personal guilt in the Matenje case remained unproven, his treatment of another former protégé with whom he fell out, Orton Chirwa, who was lured out of hiding and then imprisoned until his death, was not much better. But these were his worst crimes and, despite all that talk about crocodiles, his hands were not steeped in blood, as were those of leaders still venerated, like Kenyatta or Mugabe. And whereas dictators usually raised follies to themselves – Houphouet-Boigny's colossal basilica at his birthplace of Yamoussoukro in Ivory Coast, or Mobutu's marble palace at Gbadolite in Zaire – Banda's grand folly, his quest for immortality, was raised as a service to his people.

I left Malawi with a sense of frustration. The legacies of both Livingstone and Banda had proved elusive. Both were fading, although it was not yet clear that this strange and affecting country had found anything to put in their place. I knew, too, that I would never find out what happened to Sinclair, nor to my namesake, Stephen. One contact, however, had about it an echo of the innocence and hopefulness of childhood.

On a bus, a young man sat down and said: 'I saw you and was stimulated to communicate with you.' What brought this on, I don't know. It was not for help or money because he never asked for anything. His manner was as earnest as his speech. He had a mission background, and being inclined to fancifulness I noted that, at nineteen, he was the right age for a grandson of Sinclair's. He was in Form 3 at secondary school. His interests were reading, chess and church. His desire for self-improvement was almost painful. His name was James Mkandawire. We talked for the rest of the journey and when he said he wanted a pen friend to improve his English, I said I would write to him. Months later, I received a reply.

'Am I dreaming? Are my eyes deceiving me?' These were amongst the questions I was asking myself in silence upon receiving your letter which was much effective and advisable which I did not expect. For that I am very thankful and I hope you will be doing so without drawbacks. Your writing me depicted that I have really found an exact person whom I had been longing for.

I was very much pleased that you have reached your home the way you left. For that I thank God. When one of the family leaves to undergo a long enduring journey, though you give him good wishes, it still more creates suspicions and depressions upon his leaving and after sometime when he comes back it bring a great and immeasurable happiness. I even imagine how your family was enveloped with a terible happiness upon your arrival.

Lastly pass my warm and tender greeting to each and every member of your family. Also our family is greeting you too. I won't forget you.

James

14. The Escarpment

T HE BUS TO LUSAKA was on a sugar run. Like most of life's little pleasures, sugar was in short supply in Zambia, and a consortium of women street traders had made the journey to Lilongwe for supplies. About two tonnes of sugar in five kilogram bags was stacked the length of the bus, under seats and occupying passengers' leg space. The driver started the engine, then turned it off. 'No fuel,' he explained breezily. A length of hosepipe was found and siphoning from a drum began.

I found myself sitting beside an elderly, anxious-looking woman. 'It is the Zambian bus,' she said gloomily. 'We are going to have trouble.' It turned out that she was Zambian herself, but no nationalist. 'It would have been better to wait for the Malawian bus tomorrow.'

We left Lilongwe by 9 a.m. The distance to Lusaka was 460 miles, estimated travelling time twenty-one hours. The seats consisted of bare metal frames with the meanest of padding, and the additional weight of the sugar gave the clapped out shock absorbers all the cushioning qualities of pig iron. Every time I tried to move my legs, they encountered the resistance of sugar bags. It did not help that the traders were a boisterous sisterhood who behaved like football hooligans on a train, being led by a vast, overbearing woman named Maggie, dripping with fake gold jewellery and shrieking like a hyena. Having completely lost my temper before over the contemptuous treatment of the passenger class, on the bus from Arusha, I thought I would leave it to someone else to object to the tyranny of our cargo. No one did. But when we covered the sixty miles to the border in less than two hours, I started to think the ride might not be too bad.

We sailed through immigration in thirty minutes and all got back on the bus. Then Maggie and two others were hauled off by a Zambian customs official in a tattered uniform. The gloomy woman turned smug. 'Now they must pay,' she smirked. For well over an hour they haggled with the official, Maggie making frequent trips back to the bus for another whip-round among the traders. At last he was propitiated.

We set off again, and ran straight into an army roadblock. The CO emerged slowly from beneath a tarpaulin at the roadside, stretching and blinking in the light, but he woke up smartly enough when he spotted the sugar. Once again Maggie, her fake jewellery now stowed, her bluster spent, disappeared for extended negotiations under the tarpaulin.

By the time the bus reached the first Zambian town, Chipata, we had been travelling for six hours and the journey had barely started. The town itself, an unutterably miserable place, was once called Fort Jameson, a backhanded tribute to Rhodes's crony, the disastrous Leander Starr Jameson. In 1919, when 'Fort Jimmy' was the capital of North-East Rhodesia, the guidebook for prospective settlers described it as 'a neat little township with a generally tidy appearance, small white pop., Anglican church, extensive cattle ranches'. Allowing for poetic licence, it had gone a long way downhill since then, and stood now, a lonely outpost, as a sort of pathetic sentinel of Zambian failure.

Between sugar and passengers, the bus had been full before. Over the next two hours, the last nooks and crannies were filled up. Zambians were rightly fearful that any luggage left on the roof rack would be plundered, and consequently took all their possessions into the bus with them. By the time it clanked out of Chipata, every passenger was pressed into place like a butterfly under glass, and the aisle was piled high with baggage. As we were now unable to shift position, the seat felt even more like a slab of concrete, and it soon became evident that the Zambian roads were far worse than Malawi's. We still had fourteen hours to go, travelling through the night. About this time, I started getting stomach cramps and soon afterwards the unmistakable and agonising leaky-bottom symptom of diarrhoea.

Of all the African traveller's dreads, the greatest was of illness. Far more had sucumbed to bacteria and viruses than any other combination of factors, and the continent's capacity for spawning deadly new microbes was terrifying. Maladies as yet undiagnosed but given working names like Rift Valley Fever were even then spreading through the region while the old enemy, malaria, was mutating all the time and killing more people than ever. When I told my doctor where I was going, he winced and arranged a series of vaccinations against conditions which I did not know even existed.

As great as the fear of falling ill was that of having to undergo treatment. I was carrying a medical kit with enough syringes to keep a small regional hospital going for weeks. Despite these misgivings, I had enjoyed rude health for almost three months. Once in Tanzania I had a scare when my temperature soared and for a day I thought I had picked up some ghastly new strain of malaria. Often I had suffered stomach upsets. This latest episode was different.

To start with, I tried to focus on true agony transcended by beauty, listening on headphones to Allegri's *Miserere* sung by King's College choir. The piercing shaft of Roy Goodman's treble only made the banality of my own suffering worse. Surrounded by bodies uncomplaining in discomfort, inured to the worst their world could throw at them, I felt shame, then anger, and finally hate. I loathed Africa and everything about it – the stoicism, the fatalism, but above all the fact that nobody ever complained, and so nothing ever got any better. Authority grew corrupt because it was unchallenged by a cowed citizenry. The transport which moved ever-more mobile populations around the continent could serve as a metaphor for Africa's malaise. The only systems that worked in any ordinarily acceptable sense were the railways, and those were built by outsiders. Road travel was dangerous when not merely uncomfortable, not because it had to be, but because of the 'Chief' syndrome. The Chief was ubiquitous. He might be a president, a soldier, a customs official, or – in this case – a driver or *matatu* operator. What mattered was that he was male and in charge. He could lord it over those beneath him, and they would accept it without resistance. Indeed, they expected it, and in most cases would behave in the same way themselves if given the opportunity.

The sweat-breaking effort of controlling my sphincter was exhausting. Rage and discomfort together rendered time immobile. I took it in fifteen-minute chunks, looking at my watch and wondering how much longer I could hold on before I exploded where I sat. In a state of utter fatigue, the blissful thought occurred that my last act of revenge would be to spatter all those sleeping peacefully around me in shit. Instead, as the cramps came on again, I somehow fought my way over my neighbours and across the mountains of baggage in the aisle, motioned the driver to stop and staggered off to spurt my guts out on the veld. Such was the relief this provided that I found the conditions on regaining my seat almost congenial for an hour or so until my bottom began once again to fibrillate. The final evacuation occurred at a roadblock around 4 a.m. a few miles from Lusaka as soldiers of the Zambian army looked on in awe.

It was still dark when the bus ground to a halt amid a vast pile of rags spread out in the middle of the capital. The pavement came alive as the rags sprang up, clustering around the bus – porters, drivers, touts.

'Taxi, mister, taxi,' said a young man.

The doom-laden lady who I had not seen for hours reappeared at my arm. 'It is not safe,' she said worriedly. 'They will kill you.'

She had been right about everything so far and Lusaka had a reputation for violent crime, but I was past caring. 'Kabulonga,' I said, naming the suburb where my hosts lived.

The young man showed me to a car more dilapidated than anything I had ever seen, parked in the shadows with another youngster at the wheel. It had to be push-started, and the young tout jumped in the back – 'to help'. We set out with one headlight into the night, a cyclops from the breakers' yard.

The engine stalled often and the tout, leaping out to push, was as vital a component of the vehicle as a carburettor. They seemed hopelessly ignorant about where we were going. The tout tried to make small talk while the driver blundered up a succession of darkened streets and, if I had not been so drained, I might have been more concerned that they really might murder me. But finally, after one last push-start, we blundered into the right neighbourhood and I got out. They were good lads, really. I would have been easy meat.

My hosts' house stood behind a high metal security gate and I settled down to wait until dawn. A dog inside set up a howl and a few minutes later an elderly man in a dressing-gown came to the door and called out: 'Is there anyone there?'

'Mr Ellison, it's Stephen Taylor,' I croaked.

'Good God,' he said.

FOR THE FIRST day back in Lusaka I did little but savour hot water and sleeping in sheets. My hosts were a retired couple, Tony and Gabriel Ellison. Tony had gone out to set up the mounted branch of the Northern Rhodesian police. Gabriel was Zambian-born, an artist who had worked for the government and taught Kenneth Kaunda to paint. My debt to them was immense. On the strength of a brief correspondence, they had offered to put me up and their hospitality was all a tired traveller could have wished for.

I had first visited Zambia in 1975. With the clouds of totalitarianism gathering, my wife and I had said farewell to parents and friends, left South Africa and its beauty and cruelty once and for all, and were travelling up through 'Black Africa' to make our lives in Britain. We got stuck in Zambia for a couple of weeks after being thrown out of Tanzania and were taken in by a white farmer couple who saved us by their kindness, even though we were from different worlds. They were shocked when we ranted about South Africa being a police state and the inevitability of revolution. We were stunned when a neighbouring farmer called to ask if he might buy some maize meal for his workers, and Graham refused because it was needed to feed the dogs.

Once they asked if we could help them get some money out to a bank account in South Africa. At the time it was hard to know what they were concerned about. Zambia had been independent for ten years and, luxuriating in the red gold of the Copperbelt, enjoying annual economic growth averaging 13 per cent. Lusaka was among the smallest, and dullest, capitals in the world, what in South Africa we would have regarded as barely more than a *dorp*, with a single main street called Cairo Road running north to south. Above all, there was the reassuring figure of Kenneth Kaunda. With his humility, charm, and a political creed he called humanism, K.K. had a rare capacity to allay white anxieties about African rulers. No uniforms or dark glasses, batons or fly whisks, for him. K.K. lived simply and his trademark was a white handkerchief. He laughed, sang – in a pleasing light tenor – and cried in public with equal ease. He was a genuinely decent man. Even our farmer friends were sure of that.

I was back in 1981, this time as a newspaper correspondent. Six years had wrought a catastrophic transformation. Lusaka was a shambles. Shantytowns burgeoned on the outskirts and unemployed youths scratched and hustled on an unkempt Cairo Road. Much worse was to come. Per capita income fell 30 per cent over the next decade. Rural people abandoned the land for the city, and a country capable of producing enough to feed the entire continent became a food importer. Zambia was turned into the most urbanised country in Africa.

Some of this was unavoidable. A collapse in the copper price and economic sabotage by the hostile white régimes in Rhodesia and South Africa had played their part. But just as much of the problem was dear, benign K.K. himself. Asked in interviews about how he proposed to deal with Zambia's economic woes, he would produce his stock analysis of the problem – 'We were born with a copper spoon in our mouth' – then move on seamlessly to putting the rest of the world to rights. He was especially sound on apartheid, and his other oft-repeated phrase for interviewers was 'When the explosion comes, South Africa will make the French Revolution look like a Sunday school picnic.' Forced into an economic corner, he flinched from the medicine prescribed by the IMF, and so had to borrow at usurious rates. While he waffled on about humanism, unrest brewed on the Copperbelt where the unions had emerged as the only pole of resistance to one-party rule.

Eventually things became so bad that even K.K. got rattled. Frederick Chiluba, the union leader, was one of a number of dissident figures to be detained as meltdown accelerated during the 1980s. Soon after his release, I drove to the Copperbelt with a colleague to meet the challenger. He was a slight, handsome man with delicate hands, and he spoke with quiet determination of the need for economic reform and democracy. Both of us were moderately impressed. Later that night, we were roused from our hotel beds by armed police and taken to headquarters for interrogation. It was routine harassment, done politely enough with just a touch of menace.

All this time, I kept in touch with our farmer benefactors. While the economy disintegrated, their business went from strength to strength. Although they were capable and industrious, all they were doing was working the land efficiently. 'Produce food, and people will buy it,' Graham said. 'Anyone else could do it.' In the end they got enough money out of the country to educate their children in South Africa. When last I heard, they had just been on a trip around the world.

RHODESIAN WHITES USED to be renowned for boneheaded racism. This was mainly encountered in the country clubs of the south, where the settler ethos was most robust, but it was common enough in the miners' bars of the Copperbelt as well. After Zambia's independence, a Freedom Statue was commissioned for the centre of Lusaka from James Butler, R.A., showing an African worker in shorts holding aloft his broken shackles. On the eve of the unveiling it was found that someone had got to it with a pot of white paint and daubed the slogan 'Kaffirs can break anything!' on the base. The ceremony was postponed while frantic efforts were made to clean it off.

Generally though, Northern Rhodesia's white population, never much more than 70,000, was more easygoing and integrated than Southern Rhodesia's, which reached a peak of about 280,000. The two groups never seem to have liked each other much until Zambian independence and Ian Smith's rebellion against the Crown a year later. In the next five years about 40 per cent of Zambia's whites decamped across the Zambezi. For those who stayed, things got tougher as the economy declined. Meanwhile rebel Rhodesia boomed. The watershed, however, came when Kaunda allowed Joshua Nkomo to base his guerrillas in Zambia and Rhodesian forces launched cross-border forays. With fear and hostility riding high, a number of white Zambians were set upon in Lusaka and beaten up. Some with beards, a characteristic of the Rhodesian forces, had them forcibly shaved off.

Paranoia spread. A white cabinet minister thought to have curried favour by denouncing 'spies' was ostracised by the shrinking white community. At the last, even those who had given themselves most wholeheartedly to Zambia's independence decided that they would always be judged by the colour of their skin. More opted to join their own kind to the South. Those who remained were a doughty few.

My hosts, the Ellisons, were among the longest established. Gabriel introduced me to her oldest friend, Fenella Pestel, with whom she had shared childhood on the land, about seventeen miles east of the city. It was a gloriously carefree time; the biggest disturbance they could remember was the restriction during the war of the wife of a nearby farmer named Cholmondeley – an ardent Nazi.

Fenella, a spindly widow of seventy-three with a chin like a shovel and the heart of a lion, was still on her father's farm despite the armed robberies that had started after the economic collapse and increased after the death of her husband. She had been overpowered, tied up and beaten, and shot at three times. Most recently a gang with an AK47 tried to break into the homestead, and blazed away through a window when they could not get in. Rustlers were still a problem and she had decided to sell her last 100 beef cattle. But friends had given up urging her to move to town. 'I am certainly not going to leave the place where I have been all my life when it is nearly over anyway,' she said with asperity. Her spare frame was lost in a rumpled jumper and she looked as though a good breeze would carry her off, but the spade-like chin jutted out a shade further.

I asked if she had a gun.

'I have a pistol.' She said wistfully, 'An AK would be splendid.'

STORIES ABOUNDED ABOUT life in the old days. The Pope family story was a microcosm of southern Africa. Rosemary Pope's father, a Londoner, was posted to Northern Rhodesia in 1922 as a native commissioner. Arriving in Cape Town on the Union Castle mail ship, he travelled almost 2,000 miles by train to Livingstone before discovering that his destination, Fort Jameson, still 1,000 miles away, had been cut off by floods. The only way to reach it was to entrain for Durban, take another ship up the east coast to the mouth of the Zambezi, board a steamer going up the Shire, then slog the last 300 miles by Model-T Ford. Rosemary was born at 'Fort Jimmy' while her father was off on his rounds in the Luangwa valley with porters and tents.

Her husband, John, was born in South Africa but schooled in Devon. When he returned to Africa after the war, to work on the goldmines of the Witwatersrand, the aggressive new mood of Afrikaner nationalism came as a shock. 'The brutality in the mines was sickening, and not just to the blacks. If you were English and you were down in the cage, you got roughed up.' He and Rosemary had been married in South Africa. Neither liked the idea of bringing up their children under apartheid. Rosemary still had fond memories of Northern Rhodesia, so in 1952 they moved to Kitwe on the Copperbelt, and later to Lusaka.

When independence came, they recalled, 'there was never a "stay" or "go" decision. This was our home. There were no hangups about class or race. New embassies were opening up and Lusaka was full of pleasant, interesting people.' When things began to deteriorate, 'we were isolated, so we gradually got used to it. We didn't realise how far down things were slipping.'

It was the war in Rhodesia that brought home to them that paradise was lost. They would head off into the bush for a week, into the wonderful game country of the Luangwa valley, and rediscover the balm for the soul that anyone who has loved the African wilderness knows. Then, returning to Lusaka, they would run into the army roadblocks manned by suspicious, hostile soldiers. 'It was horrible,' said Rosemary. 'Always there was that accusatory tone, as if we were on different sides.'

They never suffered physically but after Rhodesians landed in helicopters on Lusaka golf course, a number of their friends were assaulted in town. In April 1979, the Rhodesian SAS launched a raid on Nkomo's house, itself near Kaunda's official residence, and destroyed the place with rocket fire. 'We had a good laugh because Nkomo was not even there,' John said. But after that, Lusaka was placed under curfew, which curbed socialising until someone had the idea of sleeping-bag parties.

Their son, Robin, was even closer to the ambiguities of their situation. At school in Rhodesia, he felt it most strongly as the sixth form broke up, and the war gathered momentum. 'All the other boys were Rhodies and they were going off to join the army,' he recalled. 'I was going home, back across the border, to rejoin the enemy camp. It was a very odd feeling.'

Robin became a protégé of Norman Carr, who had done more than anyone to preserve Zambia's wildlife, having lobbied successfully for the Luangwa valley to be turned into a reserve. As elsewhere in Africa, game conservation and tourism were the two areas in which whites had remained a dominant force and, after a few years as a game ranger, Robin had started his own camp for visitors to Luangwa. Even there, though, the picture was touched with melancholy. With Carr, he had been involved in a trust to save Luangwa's rhino population, which in 1973 numbered about 5,000, from poachers. By the time of Carr's death a few months earlier, there was not a single rhino left.

'We failed the rhino,' Robin acknowledged. 'About all you can say is that we gained a breathing space for the elephant.'

LUSAKA HAD BECOME a cesspit. Quite literally. The city's waste disposal system could barely cope even with those areas which had drains and water treatment chemicals often ran out. The shantytowns, however, had no drainage of any sort. The water table was contaminated by ubiquitous pit latrines and the water from most wells was poisonous. Diarrhoeal epidemics were routine, outbreaks of cholera and dysentery occurred every rainy season. An aid agency conference had just concluded that the city itself was a seething health hazard.

At the prison, food was irregular because the government had failed to pay the contractor for months. Inmates had taken to eating whatever creatures they could catch, including – according to a *Times of Zambia* report – lizards, owls and cats. However, warders drew the line when they found prisoners roasting two large snakes and confiscated the reptiles before they could be eaten. This squeamishness had nothing to do with concern for the prisoners' diet, rather the belief that snakes were inhabited by ancestral spirits.

Then there was the zoo. Around 1993, the government simply gave up feeding or tending the animals. The task was taken in hand by a group of women volunteers who bullied funds from animal lovers and local firms and then visited the zoo to flout the 'Do Not Feed The Animals' signs still rusting on some cages. The animals were now in a more desperate state than ever – two bears in a pit where they had spent sixteen years, and a pair of tigers in a small concrete cage. The end of their sufferings was in sight, however. Lillian Payne, who had devoted almost four years to the feeding programme, had just decided that the only humane thing to do was to allow the animals to starve to death. 'All I have done is prolong their miserable lives,' she said.

Under the union leader with the delicate hands, Zambia had plumbed new depths of misery. It was fourteen years since my meeting with Chiluba on the Copperbelt, and five since he toppled Kaunda in an election hailed as free, fair, and an all-round triumph for democracy – a harbinger for the new mood sweeping Africa. Kaunda conceded defeat graciously, and Zambians celebrated the benefits which they had been promised market reform would bring. Chiluba, indeed, had so turned his back on his trade union past in the embrace of fiscal rectitude that Zambia was regarded as a model client by the World Bank and IMF. However, economic reform had not been accompanied by political liberalisation and the same ruler who had once spoken up so earnestly for democracy, and had only come to power through Kaunda's (admittedly reluctant) embrace of the ballot box, now declined to extend the same opportunity to his old foe. Constitutional changes were rushed through barring Kaunda from standing again, on the grounds, that his parents were not born in Zambia.*

It was as if the country itself had been born under a dark star. Zambians had just one thing to cheer about – their national football team. They had the best side in the region, serious contenders for the Africa Cup with the near-certainty that they would qualify for the World Cup. When 'the boys' played, the nation stopped to watch. Then, in April 1993, the eighteen-strong squad, flying to Senegal, crashed in an ageing military aircraft in Gabon. Not one player survived, and Zambia lost its only dream.

FOR WHITES, THERE had been a turn for the better. The scrapping of exchange controls meant that foreign travel was again possible, while the shops in the pleasant suburbs of Westlands and Kabulonga were well-stocked with foreign produce. These were also the expatriates' haunts and white Zambians mingled inconspicuously on the diplomatic and aid circuits. This little community had its own handbook, *Lusaka Lowdown*, a monthly digest of news and information which many saw as a survival kit. Here were reviews of the latest video releases and a Music Club announcement that Lorna Kelly, a soprano from Harare, would give a recital of opera arias in the ballroom of the Pamodzi hotel. Although the tone was chatty and light-hearted, the content mirrored a high-risk environment: malaria advice was to be found next to a piece on air ambulances to South Africa, and warnings about a bogus policeman who was holding up motorists beside information on how to make a citizen's arrest.

At any festive occasion, like the Queen's Birthday, they would all turn out. My hosts took me along to a European Union celebration in the gardens of the Pamodzi hotel where ministers and officials vied with the whites and expats to imbibe Brussels's hospitality from circulating trays of sausage rolls and South African chardonnay. Old friendships and old enmities were renewed. An elderly farmer who had been beaten up on the streets in 1979

---

* A few months after my visit, Lusaka awoke one morning to hear a drunk soldier who identified himself as Captain Solo announce that he had taken over the country. This risible 'coup', which involved three junior army officers, was blamed on Kaunda, who was out of the country at the time but was detained anyway and charged.

gestured darkly towards the white former cabinet minister who he claimed
had denounced him as a spy. 'That man is an evil bastard,' he pronounced
loudly.

The quaffing was briefly interrupted for speeches and anthems. As the
strains of the Beethoven/Schiller *Ode to Joy* died away, the woman beside
me sniffed: 'Well,' she said, 'You would think the Europeans could have
come up with something better than *that*.'

IT WAS NOT only elderly farmers like Fenella Pestel who were vulnerable.
Zambia's most prominent white family was the Gore Browns. A grandson
of Sir Stewart Gore Brown still farmed Shiwa Ngandu, the fairy-tale palace
built 450 miles north-east of Lusaka in the 1930s. Shiwa was an epic fantasy
of colonial architecture, like the abandoned Bavarian turrets of Luderitz on
the Namibia coast. The ramparts of a baronial castle emerging from the
bush made Shiwa ideal material for television and, on one of his BBC
journeys, Michael Palin stayed with Gore Brown's daughter Lorna and her
husband, John Harvey. By the time the series was broadcast, they were
dead, murdered by intruders.

And yet among a small, intrepid group of new pioneers, Zambia had a
special allure. This was one of the few places where someone of modest
means could turn the dream of possessing a corner of pure African magic
into reality. Land there was in abundance, rich, dark soil which would
produce not only traditional crops like maize and tobacco, but coffee and
the horticultural vegetables and flowers being grown in Kenya and Zimbabwe for the European market. Quite a few Boers from South Africa had
heard stories about virgin land being distributed free to experienced growers
and come up to explore. About two dozen Afrikaner families had established
themselves on farms along the Tazara corridor, the vast and under-utilised
north-eastern region opened up by the railway to Tanzania.

John and Jane Jellis were Londoners who had made a go of it on a
smaller scale. They came to Zambia for the first time in 1966, he to work
as a surgeon in Chipata, and found when they returned to Britain that they
missed it. They sold their house in High Barnet for £10,000, and went back.
About twenty miles from Lusaka, they found a small farm with a ramshackle
hunter's cottage for £15,000.

John was now a flying surgeon, with a light aircraft that enabled him to
operate in the remotest parts of the bush. Their cottage nestled amid a
thicket of trees, simple and homely with cool stone floors and thatched roof.
They were largely self-sufficient, living off their own produce with power

from solar panels and borehole water. Here it seemed was a perfect existence, a family living on their own terms in Africa, yet giving rather than taking from it. We walked through the *brachystegia* forest which they had set aside as a reserve, and wandered down to the dam where Egyptian geese nestled among the reeds and black-shouldered kites wheeled high overhead.

We, too, had once had a farm in Africa, with a homestead on the hill above the Enterprise valley, where we brought our newborn daughter back from the hospital and once thought we might live for ever. Now, looking out on a pearly autumn afternoon in May, with just a hint of chill coming off the distant blue ridge of the Zambezi escarpment, I felt a tingling, the stirring of an old love.

15. The Plateau

T HE PANGS STARTED AS the bus wound down off the escarpment. I used to travel it regularly, driving between Lusaka and Harare, but the valley had never lost its power or freshness and after thirteen years I found myself eagerly anticipating the next image well before it came into sight. There was the river – mighty and blue, slipping almost imperceptibly by. It had taken its rise in eastern Angola, then turned south through Zambia before plunging over the awesome cataracts of the Mosi o Tunya – which Livingstone came upon in 1855 and renamed the Victoria Falls – then snaked eastwards. Passing here in all its majesty, the Zambezi had come more than 1,000 miles and had another 600 to run before it spent into the Indian Ocean. Across the valley floor, rising in a hazy grey eddy, there was the southern escarpment crested by Makuti. And there beside the road was the giant baobab, with its flailing arms and smooth, waxy skin, marking the turn-off to the place we had once thought of as ours.

Foolish to call it our place, really. It had long since ceased to be a secret and visitors came from around the world now. But looking from the bus, down the dusty trail that disappeared off into the bush, I saw it just as it was when we came here for the first time, soon after the end of the Rhodesian war and Zimbabwe's independence made the Zambezi valley and Mana Pools safe for travel again. We were in an old Mini, bought in Cape Town and driven up to Salisbury. In the back was our son, aged nine months, and a heavy old canvas tent. We reached Mana Pools towards evening and just had time to put up the tent and start a fire before the sun went down in a blaze over the Zambezi. The camp, a long, fenceless clearing on the river bank under marula trees heavy with fruity pods, was deserted. We had eaten meat from the fire, the child was sleeping in the tent and the two of us were sitting, savouring stillness and the snap of the embers, when a massive shape emerged ponderously from the inky blackness. With utter indifference to our presence, the bull elephant started to snaffle pods from a tree less than twenty feet away. Apart from its sheer immensity, seen from down there on the ground, what struck me as wonderful was that a creature of such bulk could move so silently, seeming to just brush the ground as it walked, and eat with the delicacy of a dowager.

An animal fantastic and outrageous, *Loxodonta africana* was the king of the valley, whether as a lone old bull, or a herd wading out into the river at sunset, submerging so just the tips of their trunks topped the surface like periscopes. Then there were the fish eagles, with their long plaintive cry, as if of loss, and the chorus of hippopotamuses guffawing at night, like old buffers at the club with a decanter of port. At the end of the dry season, when the valley shrivelled and crisped under the sun, the place became Eden as game was drawn to the pools – nestling among marula, mopane and umbrella thorns – that gave Mana its name. At a single pool one might find buffalo, kudu, impala, zebra and rhino all coming down to drink. The river had a splendour that not even the Nile or Ganges matched. I could sit beside it for hours, watching the phases of dawn and evening, constantly changing and yet timeless.

But of all the privileges of Mana Pools, the greatest was being left to oneself in the wilderness. There were no fences, so animals wandered into the camp at night; hyenas, elephants and lions could be a hazard. There were no shops, no services of any sort, and at that time few visitors. If you chose to set out into the bush on foot, no one would interfere. You were there, alone, with raw nature itself. That was your privilege. If you ran into trouble, that was your lookout.

On my last visit, I was out walking when I saw a bateleur eagle on top of a distant tree and set out to get closer. I should have sensed danger when a black-backed jackal, a carrion eater, bolted from cover. Suddenly, from the right, there came a heavy rustle and a growl and a lioness charged out of the bush, then halted ten yards away, leering. My heart wanted to stop, my feet tried to flee. Then my mind recalled the cardinal law of the bush, Don't Run. With every nerve end screaming, I kept my eyes on her while circling away. She returned the gaze with an interest that diminished as I receded. When I regained the road, my legs almost folded. Coming back from the other side in my car, I found she was part of a whole pride on a buffalo kill beneath a tree. She had merely been issuing a warning. The males had not bothered to bestir themselves.

There are some places to which we should never return. As the bus reached the other side of the valley and started the ascent of the escarpment, I looked back. I could still feel the pangs for a lost life.

IF A LITTLE on the quiet side, Harare had always been one of Africa's pleasantest capitals. When it was still Salisbury and the world's press descended to chronicle the death throes of white Rhodesia, one American correspondent looked round and said, 'Well, it's okay I guess, but a long way from town.' Right through the war it remained orderly, with well-run services and tranquil garden suburbs. After independence, most of the international agencies, correspondents and other expatriate staff working in what was then called Black Africa, who had fulminated against white rule, gave inward thanks for Rhodesian efficiency and moved their headquarters from Nairobi or Dar es Salaam to Harare.

It was a pleasant place still. The bus from Lusaka dropped me back at our home of four years among tidy streets and people who somehow always managed to look neatly turned out, even when they were hard up. Cecil Square, where the pioneers ran up the flag of the British South Africa Company, was now African Unity Square, but otherwise unchanged, a leafy glade where workers lounged on the grass during the lunch hour. The first Rixi taxi driver I met was a jaunty fellow who eyed my pack and asked where I had been. 'Zambia . . . Tanzania . . .' I replied.

On the way out to the avenues, he asked: 'So how is Zambia, my friend?'

'Zambia is a mess,' I said.

He grinned. 'Here also,' he said. 'It was better under Ian Smith.'

I took it with a pinch of salt. We passed along an avenue of jacaranda trees near our first house in Milton Park. There was the same sense of slowness in a sunny place: a uniformed maid in a starched white cap ambling hand-in-hand with a white toddler, the rows of houses with red-tile roofs and swimming pools that glittered turquoise behind black, wrought-iron fences. Our old home in Lawson Avenue looked just as it did when Ian Smith, erstwhile war hero and prime minister of Southern Rhodesia, declared his rebellion against the Crown in 1965 by a Unilateral Declaration of Independence.

But it was not until the next morning, when I turned on the radio, that I really felt I was back in that bizarre little world of post-Smithy Marxism. The announcer spoke with the flat vowels and pinched consonants of the white southern Africa dialect, once raised in diatribe against 'kaffirs' and 'munts'. The news was about a Hero's Acre burial. 'The President, Comrade Robert Mugabe, paid tribute to veterans of the liberation struggle . . .'

WE WENT TO live in Zimbabwe because of Robert Mugabe. I first saw him at the Lancaster House conference, which he came to with a reputation as a ruthless Marxist guerrilla leader. In the gripping rituals that accompanied the death of white Rhodesia, he was the outstanding figure beside the grimly mulish Smith, the small, frightened Muzorewa, the burly, blustering Nkomo. Without claiming any great wisdom, it seemed obvious to me then that the

British hope of a coalition of these three to keep Mugabe from power was doomed.

White Rhodesians, who saw him as an out-and-out killer, were even more sanguine than the British. Despite the clear evidence of their defeat in the guerrilla war, they continued to insist that their black compatriots, or 'our Afs', were loyal; they would never throw their hand in with the terrorists. When, on 4 March 1980, the country awoke to the news that Mugabe had won an election landslide, whites were stunned. Some started packing immediately. That night he went on television and in a remarkable speech pledged himself to racial reconciliation and respect for the rule of law. 'Let us forgive and forget,' he said. 'Let us join hands in a new amity.' Overnight, the mood of panic lifted.

There was a strong historical precedent for this episode. In 1963, another ex-terrorist was coming to power in Africa and turned around a meeting of hostile white farmers with a message that went in part:

> Many of you, I think, are just as good Kenyans as myself. We must learn to forgive one another. There is no perfect society anywhere. Whether we are white, brown or black, we are not angels. We are human beings and as such we are bound to make mistakes. But there is a great gift which we can exercise, that is to forgive one another.

Kenyatta, then Mugabe . . . They were harbingers for a yet more famous act of reconciliation by Nelson Mandela. The power of forgiveness carries real resonance in the African soul, and it is significant that in each of the three states to have been rent by racial conflict, Kenya, Rhodesia and South Africa, it was a victorious black leader who came forward afterwards, extending the hand of friendship to his former foes. In London in 1980, still with unreconciled longings for my former homeland, it was impossible not to be moved by Mugabe's generosity of spirit. At the same time, my wife and I began to wonder if Zimbabwe might prove the home that South Africa could not be. My employers at *The Times* agreed that I should go out as a stringer with an open-ended arrangement to provide coverage of Zimbabwe and the so-called frontline states.

We arrived determined to prove ourselves on the side of the angels. After finding a pleasant house, we made it known that as enlightened whites we would not be employing a servant, it being demeaning to both parties to have another human being carry out our menial tasks. A succession of women called at our door asking for work, and were no doubt somewhat baffled to be sent on their way with our assurance that this would not be in their interests. It took an old Rhodesian to point out tartly that we were depriving someone not only of wages which we could well afford to pay, but of the even more precious live-in quarters at the back of our house.

It was a time of bewildering change, excitement and tension. Although the war was over and the threat of a coup by Rhodesian military diehards had passed, the wounds remained fresh. Salisbury was full of guns and short fuses. Young whites, former troopies still stunned and hollow after their defeat by the 'terrs', hung around hotels like the Terreskane, drinking too much and getting into fights. A few mad dogs put bombs into radios and left them on pavements in town where they exploded when picked up. It was not just disgruntled whites who were dangerous. In Bulawayo, former guerrillas twice went on the rampage before being subdued by an army still largely consisting of ex-Rhodesian forces.

Culturally the country was going through turmoil as well. So long isolated, it was suddenly the darling of the humanitarian international. Young Scandinavians came to dig wells and third world groupies of all kinds came to dig the thrill of it all. Bulgarians peddled defective goods and Libyans peddled bogus ideology. Rugby was still played but, instead of Transvaal or Natal, the opposition now came from Romania or Russia.

For a white population which had been dependent on South Africa for outside contacts, it was confusing. For that small but distinct group of us who came to Zimbabwe feeling ourselves exiles from South Africa, it was heaven. It was like waking up to find that the pariah state in which we had lived had become beloved by the world. At the end of a week, we could drive out of Salisbury to the lake at Macilwaine, the *kopjies* at Domboshawa, or the park at Mazoe, and we could savour all the atavistic sensations of being back in our old lives, in that lovely landscape – with the light of the evening, the aroma of *boerewors* cooking on an open fire, a *kaffirboom* blossoming red and brilliant on the veld, a lilac-breasted roller on the telephone wires – only now we were without guilt.

We could be better than guiltless, we could be righteous. We could make black friends and have them to parties and bask in the knowledge that we had been right all along, that a multiracial society was only a matter of trying. You learnt quickly to sum up a gathering by its racial composition: all-white usually meant a gathering of unreconstructed 'Rhodies'; those of us who wanted to demonstrate a commitment to Zimbabwe made sure they had black guests. We counted among our friends the handsome government official with the English wife, the genial, chubby journalist married to a former South African, and the promising poet, his French wife and their two children.

Meanwhile we looked across the Limpopo to South Africa with loathing. The apartheid state, at its triumphalist apotheosis, seemed more powerful and brutal than ever. Repression did not stop at its borders. The assassination of Joel Gqabi, the ANC's representative shot outside his home in Salisbury, sent a stark message to exiled activists. Zimbabwe was a prime target for the vengeful campaign of sabotage and economic destabilisation waged by South Africa against its black-ruled neighbours.

Fortunately, there was always Mugabe. Cool and a bit aloof, he was nevertheless the master of every situation. Articulate, clear-thinking and just occasionally drily humorous, he showed up all the mendacious hatefulness of the Neanderthals in Pretoria. Even some whites said they did not know how they could have been so wrong about him. I went down to a small town named Que Que to interview a group who had joined the local branch of the Zanu (PF) party. One of them was Brian Blundell, who had emigrated thirty years earlier from Chelmsford. 'It's high time that whites stopped sitting on the fence and put their weight behind Bob,' he said. 'He's a sensible chap and he's brought us peace.'

WHEN CECIL RHODES conceived of a British settler state north of the Limpopo, he had in mind a new gold reef. Rhodes had built his empire on minerals and was convinced that another fortune lay in the Far Interior. Records of the Portuguese, who had been active on the coast to the east since the sixteenth century, indicated that Mashonaland was the biblical land of Ophir, home of the Queen of Sheba. Here, Rhodes assured his pioneers and share-holders, were riches beyond those even of the Transvaal. The truth was otherwise. The first phase of Rhodesia's settlement was a series of booms, based on falsified prospecting reports, followed by busts.

The ethos that emerged was a hybrid of the East African settler culture and the rough avarice of the Rand goldfields. An early arrival complained, 'Everyone here is either slave to Mammon or to Bacchus.' No less conspicu-ous than the tradition of heavy drinking was that of racism. In 1896, a rebellion by the indigenous Shona people was put down with all the piti-lessness of the Indian Mutiny. An overweening, contemptuous attitude towards 'munts' developed among whites. After 1945, the white population rapidly tripled and, as so often, it was the new migrants who were most inclined to lord it over Africans, most vociferous in claiming to preserve the values of a lost Britain. A Rhodesian, Frank Clements, wrote of the post-war influx:

> They were the misfits of British society; that is, of course, not the same
> thing as the failures and the rejects, though indeed they had decided
> themselves that they were not equipped to succeed at home. In no field of
> activity, from accountancy to welding, from journalism to selling, did
> Rhodesia offer inducements to the successful or the conspicuously
> talented.

Few outsiders found theirs an attractive society. (No egalitarian himself, Evelyn Waugh recoiled in 1960 at the 'abominable rudeness' of white shop-girls to black porters.) But it was easy to underestimate it, too. Smith's declaration of UDI drew from this tightly knit and isolated community of artisans and farmers a resolute capacity to innovate and defy the world and its sanctions. Even seven years of guerrilla warfare, in which the official death toll was 15,705, failed to dent their morale significantly. Although 410 white civilians died (there were 6,091 black civilian dead) and by the end many had taken 'the chicken run' to South Africa, their numbers held up remarkably. From an all-time peak of around 280,000, there were still 240,000 when Lord Soames handed over power to Robert Mugabe, and rebel Rhodesia became the last of Britain's colonies in Africa to achieve independence.

It was then that the real exodus began. Partly because they had believed Smith's propaganda that the war was winnable, and thus never recognised that it had been lost, and partly because a ready and apparently unassailable final white *laager* lay just across the Limpopo, a steady flow of cars and heavily laden pickups and *bakkies* began to wend their way to the Beit Bridge border post. By now they were going at a rate of about 1,500 a month. Like other foreign correspondents, I used to monitor the government statistics, and the shrinking white population. Down to 170,000 by the middle of 1982, it was to fall below the 100,000 mark before the end of the decade.

Initially, they went because the very idea of living under a black government was repugnant. Integration of schools and medical facilities, the removal of statues of Cecil Rhodes, and the renaming of streets after so-called terrorists, like Samora Machel and Julius Nyerere, left them shocked. Restrictions on what property and money migrants could take with them triggered a new wave of departures. Embittered and empty-handed, they went mouthing slogans like 'We made Rhodesia great. They made Zimbabwe ruins.'

There was no lamenting the exodus of racists. Even those who left simply because they saw which way the wind was blowing, and that a black government was bound to make a priority of meeting black needs, were not greatly mourned, although their skills were a real loss to the country. Among the righteous and newly arrived expatriate community, there was a certain *schadenfreude* at the spectacle of 'Rhodies' getting their comeuppance. The prevailing wisdom was that, having prospered off the sweat of black labour and done so little to integrate, whites were long overdue a bit of suffering. Much the same was to be said later amid change in South Africa.

Somewhere along the line, however, a new realism took hold. The whites who stayed, adjusted. Within a couple of years, even the grumblers had learnt to watch their words. Most remarkably, a few of those who had gone Down South and been dismayed by what they found, actually packed up and came back. A farmer named Porky Christie-Smith, who had lost an arm in the war, remained in South Africa only months before returning, certain that for all the white *laager*'s apparent impregnability it was repeating Rhodesia's mistake. 'They're doing exactly what we did with Smith,' he said. 'We were blinded into thinking it had to be that way, when actually we could have talked. You have to negotiate before there is nothing left to negotiate. If we had, there would have been a lot fewer people killed, a lot less mourning.'

I WALKED INTO town past old landmarks . . . the Bronte hotel, where we first stayed, and the Quill Club, court of John Edlin, the only foreign correspondent I ever knew to be fully accepted by black Zimbabweans – *Chibhoyi* they used to call him, 'one of the boys' – recently dead of a stroke on a nightclub dancefloor in Senegal. I went down Second Street to find my old office, but it had been knocked down.

Looking up old friends and acquaintances proved even more dispiriting than Nairobi had been. Among the blacks, Aids had taken off at least four. Well over 10 per cent of the population was HIV positive. But the country's fundamental sickness went deeper still. From being a model medium-sized economy, with a small but inventive industrial sector underpinned by minerals and robust agriculture, Zimbabwe was racing towards economic ruin. Corruption and cronyism had plumbed depths greater than Kenya's. Party and government officials known with conscious irony as 'the *chefs*' grew ever richer by plundering the public purse, while the common people, or *povo*, found themselves further and further adrift from jobs and basic services, such as clean water, education and medical care. From having one of the highest per capita incomes on the continent, Zimbabwe had become another African basket case. About 60 per cent of the population lived below the poverty datum line and the value of the Zimbabwean dollar had declined from two to the pound in our time to eighteen to the pound (in the coming months it was to disintegrate entirely and at the time of writing had reached about sixty to the pound). Our former maid, who had been jobless for months, said, 'Oh, Mr Taylor, what has happened to our Zimbabwe? Now we are crying.'

On closer inspection, the city, which had first seemed as neat and tidy as ever, was frayed at the edges. Grass verges were uncut, litter had been left to pile up in a way that would once have been unthinkable. Harare was still a long way from the decay of Nairobi, Dar or Lusaka, but the decline was unmistakable. It also had an air of emptiness. The wife of the handsome government official had tired of his infidelities and gone back to England. The Frenchwoman had also gone home, having been pushed around once too often by her husband, the poet, who was no longer promising. The third world groupies had found new causes and the foreign correspondents new stories. More damaging was the loss of skills, for example of the paediatrician who treated our son when he was critically ill with pneumonia. By the best estimates, the white population was now down to 70,000.

'No-hopers,' said one old friend cheerfully over a bottle of the uniquely foul cabernet produced by the vines of Zimbabwe. 'The only whites left are the farmers and us no-hopers, and we're only here because no one else will have us. Blacks saying it was better under good ol' Smithy. Ha, good ol' Smithy . . . who would have thought it?'

BILL RHODES (NO RELATION) and his wife, Olive, ran what she called the Old Curiosity Shop, an office on the third floor of a block given over to small African enterprises. It was on the rundown southern side, beyond what used to be Pioneer Street. Nearby, the former Jewish Guildhall, with a Star of David and the year 1920 embossed on a gable, had been turned into Solo's Nightclub. Inside, a passage led to offices in which dozens of women were bent over sewing machines. At the end lay the Rhodeses' curiosity shop.

The metaphor was apt. There was something Dickensian about the two bent, elderly Londoners, the rows of dusty wooden display cabinets and their gleaming, beautifully crafted contents from another age – theodolites, microscopes and compasses. Mr Rhodes ran his business, repairing optical instruments, surrounded by his museum. He removed a theodolite lovingly from a cabinet, wiping a speck of dust from a brass barrel. 'That's a beauty,' he said. 'It was used to survey the Uganda Railway.'

They came out from Ealing in 1956. 'We considered Canada and Australia as well,' she said, 'but I'd married a Rhodes, so I said "let's try Rhodesia".' By the time UDI was declared, he was doing well. Then came sanctions, and things really took off. 'It was the making of our business,' he said.

He had devised a series of instruments, ranging from simple fingerprint optics for the police to a sophisticated aerial survey device used by the air force, which replaced costly or unobtainable imports. This kind of sanction-busting ingenuity, drawing on the craft and improvisational skills of British artisan tradition, became the material and spiritual fuel of UDI. Rhodesia boomed, even as Britain's economic decline gathered pace, and the post-war migrants gave thanks for their foresight in leaving the clapped-out old country.

So did he have any regrets about helping Smith stay in power? He shrugged disinterestedly and turned back to the cabinets. 'Now take a look at this,' he said, removing a miniature sundial of exquisite delicacy. 'Made in Augsberg, that was, around 1680. Early portable timepiece. Bought it from a lady who left in the war.'

They had few savings; these objects were their pension fund. What about robbers, I asked. He laughed drily. 'They've not much regard for craftsmanship here. I suppose you might get enough to buy a second-hand Mercedes, but it's easier to steal the Mercedes.'

He had been back to Britain once and came back saying never again. 'Well, they do say you can't go home again,' Olive chimed in. 'You see, I've never been back, so I still think of it as home. Don't suppose I'll ever go back now. Don't suppose I'd recognise it.'

THE LANES, FATHER and son, had also seen prosperity come and go. I borrowed a car and drove a few miles out to Elizabeth Windsor Drive – despite the name, it had never been a fashionable address – where they lived in an avocado-coloured house poking above a straggly lawn. Eric was seventy-seven, a burly widower who reclined in a leather armchair surrounded by examples of his trade, clocks and engraved tankards set upon white lace doilies. Sitting opposite, his son David, twenty years his junior and a bachelor, had aged prematurely to the point that they might have been brothers. A trio of plaster ducks climbed a wall.

Eric Lane grew up in Kentish Town, left school at fourteen – 'Me old man din't believe in school,' he explained – and joined the RAF. By his own account, he had been a bit of a tough. 'In Cairo once, there was a Gippo 'oo tried to play rough with me. Sorted 'im out with a knife,' he said with relish. After the war he became a watchmaker and emigrated to Rhodesia in 1952 but had retained his Cockney edge.

Lane & Son's best customers had been the Rhodesian military and the government. Among other things, they used to engrave the cigarette cases presented to visitors by President Clifford Dupont, a slick former London solicitor with a chip on his shoulder about Britain. Nowadays there was not much call for their skills and a few years earlier they had been back to the East End to see if they could pick up old strings. They found the folk unwelcoming and work unobtainable. 'It's all machines, see,' Eric lamented. 'No call for hand engravin'.' The only things they enjoyed were the whelks and jellied eels, and they soon came back to the green house in Elizabeth Windsor Drive.

Amid the human debris of white Rhodesia, however, there was a remarkable lack of recrimination. Economic prisoners of another failed African economy, they were grimly stoical about their fate.

'I suppose you *could* say we're stayin' on,' Eric Lane said doubtfully in answer to my question. 'But we're stayin' on 'cos we're bleedin' stuck 'ere.'

16. The Ridge

I N THE BORROWED CAR, I took the Enterprise Road out of town, passing through the leafy northern suburbs, Highlands and Chisipite, to where the houses petered out and the bush fanned back from the road. The road crested a hill among bluegum trees then ran down to Umwinsidale, past the service station where children came down from the local mission to buy bread, milk and soft drinks, then out to where the trees parted and the grass grew high and waving, and past the turn-off to Shamva. Another mile or so along the Mtoko road, a track led off to the right. Up on the ridge I could just make out among the trees, the whitewashed outline of the homestead.

We had been in Harare for almost two years when we moved to the farm, twelve miles from town in the rich agricultural district of Enterprise. To tell the truth, it was more a smallholding than a farm – only 50 acres, of which less than a quarter was arable. The rest consisted of a rocky ridge on which the homestead stood, looking across the Enterprise valley. We were asked to look after it by the owner, a colleague who bought it as a hobby and was then assigned to the Middle East. In the event it ran itself, our two labourers, Frankson and Jonah, drawing wages and using the arable land for their own purposes, which included supporting large extended families, about forty people in all. Our reward was to live in the homestead on the ridge, a curiously misshapen place with a long verandah where we ate breakfast on luminous mornings and had our evening drinks for all but about eight weeks of the year, when the air was too crisp. Even then, a fire was for cosiness rather than real warmth. Every day for two years we looked out on the valley of green scrub, red soil and shimmering dams, and on most of them we gave thanks for our fortune.

Often in the evenings, we climbed the ridge at the back of the homestead where the smell of wood smoke and the sounds of communal living wafted up from the compound. Besides the labourers and their families, we employed a maid, a fine and beautiful young woman named Susan. Some-times we recalled how we had once turned away women asking for work. Now the very idea that we had no responsibility for this little community was unthinkable. They were our people.

There were other places, other landscapes. Our son fell dreadfully ill;

after he recovered, we turned our back on everything, packed him in the Mini and set off around the country, to the Chimanimani mountains and the Matopos hills, with our hearts singing. Soon afterwards my wife fell pregnant again, and we felt our lives complete. With friends, we went to the Eastern Highlands around Chipinga and Inyanga, and stayed in the cottages at Udu dam, fishing for trout below a hillside of umbrella acacias. In years of trying I caught not a single fish, but never found anywhere else half so lovely to cast a line. Always at the end of the dry season, we would go back to Mana Pools and the Zambezi valley.

In the first harvest season, Frankson came in and said he was ready to start sales. He was young and confident and, by the standards of rural Mashonaland, refreshingly bolshy. Workers on the local farms looked to him as something of a leader, and at weekends he cut a distinctive figure out walking in his white shoes, or as striker at football matches played on the hard, red ground at the Pig Research Board.

Soon after we moved to the farm, he and Jonah came to see us. While Jonah hovered uneasily beside him, Frankson said they wanted new overalls, boots and a watch each. Green as we were, we said they must be crazy if they thought we would buy them watches. We would pay for overalls and boots, along with their wages and seeds for whatever they wanted to grow. They would provide produce for the household and could do with the rest as they wished. The proceeds of any sales would be theirs, to buy watches or anything else. Frankson looked pleased with this, Jonah just relieved. During the spring they had cultivated an acre of vegetables without undue exertion. Now tomatoes and eggplants were ready. It was agreed that the best place for a sales pitch was the township of Mbare. We set off with the Mini bulging and the roofrack piled high. I dropped them at the market.

That evening when I got home Frankson looked uncharacteristically subdued. With an aggrieved air, he related how they had been driven away by other traders wherever they tried to set up a stall. Finally they had been approached by a man who said they could trade if they paid him 'security money'. But they had only enough to come home by bus, bearing boxes of unsold tomatoes. Would we advance him the security money?

The next day we went back to Mbare. That night they came home looking again like country boys fleeced by city slickers, having sold enough tomatoes to cover the security money. Frankson's cockiness had evaporated, along with whatever dreams he had of wealth. We suggested that they try a roadside stall. A few boxes were set up beside the road for a day or two with no more success. At that stage Frankson and Jonah abandoned commercial growing altogether. The land reverted to subsistence use, producing enough for the house and compound, with a small surplus that went to Umwinsidale mission.

By then we had almost been seduced – by the beauty of our land and the sense, perhaps illusory, that we were somehow needed. There were times when I thought we might turn our backs on the other life, give up journalism and the cosy bolt-hole of our home in England, and gamble on a farm in Africa. It was perhaps always a dilettante idea, the indulgence of those who could afford to dream. But it did not seem unfeasible. I had seen enough of farming to believe that it rewarded hard work rather than brilliance, and reflect that many who set up in Kenya and Tanganyika after the war had even less experience than us.

Our neighbours would have been convulsed if they had heard this idea. As it was, our set-up was a joke. They were commercial growers with their lives invested in the soil and farms running to many thousands of acres of tobacco and maize. They had, moreover, stuck it out in what had been a hot area during the war and had little time for either foreign journalists or crazy bastards who allowed their workers to run the show. We sometimes came across one another at the Enterprise Country Club, where big-boned, bronzed men in shorts stood up at the bar, drinking cold lager from the bottle. Out on the lawn, under a jacaranda tree, the women sipped tea brought by waiters in white uniforms. Many might have been thought of as racists, but they were pragmatists too, so they observed government directives about workers' wages and conditions; it had become unusual to hear the racially hostile terms 'munts' or 'houts'.

Some farmers were genuinely doing their best for their people, and among this group we made one acquaintance who became a friend.

WHEN I MET Alan he was lecturing in hydrology at the university and using his knowledge of irrigation to grow tomatoes on a rented farm. After a few years, he was able to put down a deposit on a small place of his own. Later he wrote to say that he had done well enough to give up lecturing and had bought a large farm about ten miles past our old place.

I found him again now, a huge man with a disconcertingly ferocious squint who shambled out to greet me in a stained hat, khaki shorts and a wide grin. The open hand could have enfolded a fully-grown chicken. His farm, once given over to maize, was being steadily cleared for horticulture. Other local farmers had gone in for high-earning export crops for the European market – sugar snap peas, beans – but he had stuck to what he knew best, growing tomatoes for local consumption. He was the biggest producer in the district.

Alan's workers had prospered, too. The most junior received well above the minimum wage, while a four-tier pay structure with job titles offered incentive for the enterprising. We drove around the farm and he showed me the compounds where new quarters were being built. He was proud of them, and rightly so. Neat little thatch cottages with large windows, verandahs and electricity, these were far and away the best workers' houses I had seen in Africa.

That evening over drinks, I told him about my idea. I said I knew it must sound crazy, but as a result of my journey I had given some thought to giving it another try, to buying some land – in Uganda if possible, but otherwise Zambia. I had made inquiries and a viable farm could be picked up in Zambia for surprisingly little.

First he looked astonished. 'When you left here you said you'd had Africa,' he said. 'You never wanted to come back.' He paused when I said nothing. Then he scoffed. 'Anyway, you'll never make a farmer. You've got to work in this game, buddy. Up there . . .' he gestured up the valley, '. . . you were like a bunch of hippies. You can't run a farm like that.

'Look,' he went on, 'a white man owning land in Africa is always going to stick out. We produce the only wealth this country has got left but Mugabe goes round calling us "settlers" and "bloodsuckers". Now they're after us, they want the land. He says they can take it without compensating us. I've got neighbours shitting themselves because they just pay the minimum wage, and they reckon they'll be the first to go. I look after my blokes – I treat them well, not just because they are worth it, but because I have to watch my back. I stay in with the local party people, I give to the local schools, it's all very cosy. "Hello, Mr This, Hello, Mr That". But they could still carve me up, chuck us out, and then what have we got to show for four generations in Africa?' He shook his head. 'No, my friend. Stay where you are.'

Later, heading back into town, I looked up at the ridge for a last glimpse of the misshapen homestead. I had an urge to take the turn-off and drive up there, to question the new owners, to ask if I could look around, find out what had happened to them all. The last we heard, Jonah was still there, Frankson was working at the Pig Board, Susan had married George and moved with him to another farm. Suddenly it seemed just too easy to go back, too self-indulgent to reappear briefly to shake hands, embrace, ask about the children, chat about what we had all been doing with our lives, guiltily hand out a few dollars and then disappear again, just another white phantom.

As I drove on, it struck me that the idea – a bit of land, coming back to Africa – *was* absurd, just another hopeless dream of finding home. My journey had reminded me of what I loved; the landscape, the quality of light on an open space; and the people, warm and vital, good humoured and indomitable. These would always be missing from our lives in Britain.

But could we deal with the hardships and the cruelty as well? This was not a place where you dabbled in dreams. You fought tooth and nail for what you had. If there was one characteristic that defined Africa, it was the capacity of its people to endure, and when it came down to it our own sticking qualities had not been impressive. I had come to feel a certain contempt for the mongers of righteousness who had chronicled the death of white Rhodesia with such relish, then raced off in search of new moral mazes – but never returned to re-examine their judgements. But were we any better?

Say what you might about Ian Smith, retired on his farm at Sherugwi, he had demonstrated a certain dour integrity, even if the title of his newly published memoirs, *The Great Betrayal*, indicated that he had not learnt much by the experience. Although Mugabe used to proclaim his own mag-nanimity in allowing Smith to live in peace, I suspected that in fact he had a sneaking regard for another man who had held so grimly to power and who, when he lost it, would not flee to gentler pastures. Ian Smith, let it be said, was an African.

I HAD NO DESIRE, however, to hear Smithy sound off yet again. So I set off to find a friend. I say we were friends although Josiah had worked for me, as an office manager. At first he called me Mr Taylor, then, as we became more familiar, Steve, but when he disliked a story I had written, which he thought was unfriendly to Zimbabwe, he would go back to calling me Mr Taylor. By the time I left, he had had enough of foreign journalists and retired soon afterwards to his land with a second-hand tractor to grow maize.

He was still on his farm in what had been designated Tribal Trust Lands, a phoney term used by the Rhodesian authorities to indicate that these were the inviolable traditional domains of the indigenous people. In reality, they were the poorest soils, the skeleton of a carcass picked clean by the settlers. Josiah was eking out a bare living on a threadbare plot south of Mount Darwin. His dreams of becoming a large-scale maize grower had vanished, his Polish tractor was reduced to a rusting hulk by the unavailability of spares. He and his wife just managed to keep the place going, with good health and the help of their children.

On a wooden stool outside his mud-brick and thatch home, he rolled a smoke from brown paper and rough tobacco. 'What has happened in our Zimbabwe . . .' he shook his head. 'Hai, Mr Taylor, I cannot understand it. Everything is for the *chefs*. The *chefs* have the cars, the *chefs* have the farms. These people are thieves.'

Josiah was a Karanga, the largest clan of the Shona-speaking people. The Shona had produced two successful Iron Age states, the kingdom of Mwene Mutapa, and the Rozwi federation. The Mutapas traded gold with the Portuguese, the Rozwi paramountcy founded Great Zimbabwe and other stone towns. A series of invasions ended the Shona idyll. First came the Ngoni who razed the stone settlements – the zimbabwes – on their bloody passage from Zululand to the shores of Lake Nyasa. Then came the Ndebele, another clan fleeing Shaka, who established a raiding kingdom in the west. Worse followed. When Rhodes's pioneers arrived they were first seen by the Shona as protectors against the Ndebele but they quickly marked out vast estates on the best parts of Mashonaland. In no other part of British Africa was land alienated from its original inhabitants with such casual rapacity as it was in Rhodesia.

Mugabe's victory was a victory for the Shona majority, and his people naturally expected to reap the spoils. No more would the whites or the Ndebele lord it over them. As Josiah once told me, the Ndebele would have to start showing respect for the Shona; as for the whites, they were needed to help run the economy, but the government must buy their farms and give the land back to the Shona. He had a point. The 4,500 white farmers owned more than 60 per cent of the prime arable land.

When Mugabe launched a land reform programme soon after independence, and Britain provided aid to buy white-owned farms, Josiah had hopes that he might get his hands on some of that good land, the dark soil which produced the best crops. In the event, the government had acquired plenty of land with limited potential which it handed over to peasant growers. The good farms, however, the green pastures and golden valleys, had invariably gone to cronies in the party, the '*chefs*'.

I asked Josiah what he made of Mugabe's latest promise, to seize white land without compensation. He thought for a moment. 'It would be good,' he said. 'These whites have too much land. They can give some to me.'

Then he shook his head. 'But the *chefs* will take all of it,' he said.

*   *   *

THE TURNING POINT for us came in January 1983. For some time, even as our love affair with the land was deepening, the natural tension between the authorities and the foreign press had been developing into hostility. As new ministers got into their stride, the mood of government became first over-confident, then overweening. Cupidity gave way to corruption. Comrade ministers trailed around in black limousines, acquiring farms and luxurious homes, while peasants and former combatants were publicly patronised and privately ignored. My own relations were especially bad with the head of the information department, a former BBC correspondent named Justin Nyoka, who made regular if empty threats to have me expelled for 'unfriendly stories'. It was not until 1982, however, that things started to go seriously wrong. Then Mugabe engineered a confrontation with Nkomo, his nominal coalition partner, and former guerrillas from Nkomo's powerbase, the Ndebele minority, started to desert from the army with their guns and head off into the bush. Matabeleland, in the south-west of the country, went back to being a low-level war zone.

The farm was looking especially sumptuous that year after the rainy season and there were snakes everywhere. Jonah killed a mamba in the rockery, a cobra was found in the study, and Frankson came in one day to say that a python had eaten the ducks. We all trooped down to the pen and, sure enough, there was a silky mound which resembled a large, ornate designer bag. The python was only four feet long and, with three fully-grown ducks inside it, almost as wide. When we came back later the ducks had been regurgitated, quite dead, in a heap of moist feathers and the python had disappeared.

If snakes were the most serious discomfort that we faced, the same could not be said of farmers in Matabeleland. I had made regular trips to Bulawayo after attacks in which dozens of ranchers and tourists had been killed by Ndebele dissidents. A number of cases had all the cold-blooded hallmarks of the Rhodesian war. Farmers, their wives and children, living in remote areas like Nyamandhlovu and Inyati, had been ordered to kneel and then shot. Six foreign travellers had been hauled off an overland bus south of Victoria Falls, marched into the bush and killed.

One Friday afternoon Josiah came into my office and said Nkomo had called a press conference. We found the burly old man, surrounded by grim-looking Ndebele. He spoke in his high-pitched voice of a slaughter of civilians in Matabeleland by government troops. To start with, he said, the soldiers of the exclusively Shona Fifth Brigade had swept through rural areas looking for dissidents. Then they had turned on the local people. At least fifty had been killed in the past few days. 'We are hearing of more every hour,' he said. 'This is a tribal massacre.'

That evening I flew down to Bulawayo. On the Monday, 31 January, *The Times* published my story under the headline 'Terror in Matabeleland: Carnage Blamed on Mugabe Troops'. Travelling with colleagues, I found villages abandoned to a handful of people too old to travel who pointed out freshly dug graves and spoke of beatings, detentions and outright atrocities. One elderly man in Mbembezi said he had seen his pregnant granddaughter bayoneted. 'They said she had a dissident in her stomach so she had to die,' he said. Other districts – Tjolotjo, Lupane, Nkayi – were also being seared by the Fifth Brigade, or *Gukurandi*, the wind that blows away the chaff, to use its Shona name.

Over the following days and weeks, the Holiday Inn on the outskirts of Bulawayo became a base from which correspondents ventured out into the bush to collect evidence of the massacres. Angry but frightened, desperately anxious to avoid roadblocks of hostile soldiers in the distinctive red berets of the Fifth Brigade, we would return from the panic-stricken countryside to be confronted by the stark madness of the Holiday Inn, where a game of mixed doubles was in progress on the tennis court and families were gathered at the buffet *braai* around the swimming pool.

All through February, the killing continued. I would return from the inferno to the idyll of the farm, driving out on a late afternoon with the grass swaying high and golden beside the road, the dams brimming, to my family and my own pregnant wife. Then once more back to Matabeleland. In my reports, I wrote that in a month between 1,000 and 2,000 Ndebele civilians had been killed. This turned out to be conservative; the only comprehensive inquiry, fourteen years later, found the latter figure to have been closer the mark.

The fantastic thing was that the government was getting away with it. Mugabe described the Fifth Brigade as 'a first-class fighting unit', and denounced 'reactionary foreign journalists'. British academics who should have known better joined in the criticism, saying that as tribal identities in Zimbabwe were a colonial invention it was absurd to suggest the Shona harboured hostility towards the Ndebele, and that the press was clearly over-reacting to a little local difficulty.

At the Holiday Inn one night in March, we heard that the Fifth Brigade had descended on Nkomo's house in the township of Highfields. Driving out in the dark, we found it deserted and a bloody body lying in the road outside. Suddenly we were surrounded by troops pointing guns. 'Leave, now,' said a lieutenant who looked as scared as we were.

Later that night, we were taken to a secret meeting with Nkomo. He looked grey and terribly tired. 'They have gone mad. They are trying to kill me,' he said. Then he was driven to the Botswana border by bodyguards and taken across into exile. I remember feeling an absurd surge of exultation when I heard he had got away.

Finally, two weeks later, the Roman Catholic Commission for Justice and Peace, the most vocal internal critic of Smith's war, issued a statement censuring 'the frightful consequences' of army brutality in Matabeleland. A spokesman admitted privately that they had been concerned about speaking out earlier in case it only inflamed the situation, which sounded like just another way of saying that it was actually less risky to denounce atrocities by whites than atrocities by blacks.

Soon after that the Fifth Brigade was withdrawn from Matabeleland but the abuse of rights, torture and detention without trial were by now standard tools of authority. For brutality by the security forces and contempt for civil liberties, there was now little to distinguish Zimbabwe from South Africa. Somehow, the world seemed not to care greatly. While Sharpville still had immense international resonance, the name Tjolotjo was quite unknown, although the scale of that crime was certainly far greater.

In Harare's now diminishing circle of white liberals, attempts were made to argue that this was not so, that even if the situation was not being distorted by the foreign media it was simply a case of individual ministers and officials abusing their authority. Mugabe, it was said, would find out what was going on; he would pull the renegades into line.

We were at a crossroads. A *Guardian* correspondent had just been declared an enemy of the state and expelled for his reporting and, according to the rumour mill, my name was next on the list. If we were to stay in Zimbabwe the likelihood was that it could only be if I was prepared to give up journalism and become a proper farmer. Whatever the allure of the life, the idea of enforced silence was obnoxious. Racial tyranny had made it impossible for us to live in South Africa; how, then, could we turn a blind eye while living under an ethnic tyranny. It had begun to appear that the African environment, whether under white or black rule, was not one in which our values – a confused amalgam of colonial Englishness, modern Britain and, yes, something of Africa as well – could survive.

A few months later, the Fifth Brigade was unleashed again. When, on

1 March, 1984, *The Times* published my report under the headline 'Brutality Returns to Matabeleland', we had already decided to leave.

I HAD ONE last friend to see before taking the train to Bulawayo. I will call him Pete. Unlike me, Pete was a true African. When he saw us off at the airport in 1984, he had grinned and embraced me. 'I'm just a white kaffir, I can't live anywhere else,' he said. So long as he had beer and *dagga*, a fire on which to cook some meat and a place to stretch out his huge, bare feet, he was content.

We met again at a dive run by old Portuguese refugees from Mozambique. It came out in a burst. 'I'm sick of it,' he said. 'I'm sick of the corruption, the cynicism. The worst thing though is the racism. They won't admit failure so they have to find scapegoats, and it is always us, it is always whitey. They've fucked up on agriculture – they took farms and turned them into disaster stories. So what do they do? They want to take over in business. We've got indigenous business initiatives, everyone has got to get behind the black businessman. It's going horribly wrong already and we're starting to hear the threats – "if whites don't give us business, we'll burn down their buildings," says Phillip Chiyangwa, and he's not the only one. Always bluster.

'You know the real problem? Well, this is racist, but the fact is that no one here with any power has the slightest interest in how business works or farming works. Instead of looking at how whitey has made it, and trying to emulate him, they make out that he is part of some magical secret society which excludes blacks. Then they take over the society, and what happens? It turns to shit in their hands. And that, my friend, is why this country is going down the tubes.'

He looked up from his beer, glowering. 'We've had seventeen years under Mugabe, each one worse than the last. You've heard the blacks say it – "better under Smith". Who would ever have thought there could be worse than Smith? Now even Mugabe is corrupt. Mugabe! You remember how we used to talk about him – too intelligent, not enough common sense, but an African leader who had broken the mould. And whatever else you thought about him, he was honest.'

A look of recognition passed between us. 'You know what I mean,' he said, suddenly weary. 'When you left, you were finished with this place – *klaar*. Well, now it's me who wants out. I can't hack it in England – went once, hated it. All I can think of is finding some place, maybe a *dorp* in the Cape, where I can keep my head down and not have to listen to what a fuck-up I am, because I'm white.'

17. The *Kraal*

THE TRAVELLING WAS EASY now and comfortable. Rail had always been the most gracious way of covering the great distances of southern Africa and from Harare the line ran down to Bulawayo, the Clapham Junction of the region, along the spine of eastern Botswana, skirting the Kalahari desert, to Mafeking and on past the Diamond Fields of Kimberley through another arid flatland, the Great Karroo, to the Cape. The total distance was about 1,700 miles.

A car was independence but the train was something wonderful. Board a carriage and you entered a sleek, teak-lined passage off which opened a series of wooden doors. Slide back a door and you entered a compact little cabin of green leather and more teak. As the train lumbered out of the station, you might shut out the world with a book. Later, in the heat of the day with the vast expanse of the empty veld passing by, you could open a sliding window to cool the air, or step into the passage to stand for a while; then in the evening make your way to the dining-car or possibly, if you were fortunate and the journey was a long one, to an observation car with comfy seats and a long bar, and come back later as the train bored on through the night, up the swaying carriages, to find your cosy room with the seats pulled down and a bedding roll of clean white sheets and blue blankets laid out, and above each bunk a reading light. Not even the atrocious food, mutton or beef roasted down to the fibres and served with flaccid potatoes and Bisto gravy by surly waiters in stiff collars and stained white waistcoats, could spoil it. When I was a boy, heaven was two nights on the slow train to Cape Town.

My father was a real rail traveller. He was a water treatment specialist for Imperial Chemical Industries, and in his job travelled on trains, giving out advice and bottles of chemicals to keep the old steam locomotives, the Fairlies and Mallets, and the great Garratts, the workhorse of the African railways, from seizing up. His patch was the network that extended from Cape Town via Bulawayo to the Copperbelt and ultimately arrived at Benguela on the Atlantic Ocean, a distance of well over 3,000 miles. He would set off with his samples for the Rhodesias, Belgian Congo and Angola, and I would envy him all those nights in a little teak cabin as the train rattled north. He had a hard-drinking friend named Tom Travers, and I could imagine them, on the haul up from Bulawayo to the Victoria Falls, or on the line from Ndola to Elisabethville, dispensing beakers of anti-corrosive chemicals to the train driver and large measures of gin to one another.

Harare station looked just as it did in those days, a long, low-slung colonial building with a clock tower and tin roof, and a platform strangely deserted on which stood a wooden information board with a typed list showing the occupants of each carriage for the overnight train to Bulawayo. I had a last drink with Alan and his wife, Lesley, at the bar, feeling a sense of regret that there was little reason to come back again to the place we had once so loved. Then I boarded a carriage – these days the passage was lined with grey Formica instead of teak – and found my compartment.

He had a lugubrious, rubbery face with barely a hair on his head, and wore a navy blue blazer and a guilty expression. The smoke of a cigarette trailed up towards the No Smoking sign. 'Hello there, old boy,' he said, extending his hand. 'Gerry.' He sounded like Terry-Thomas. 'Gerry Arnfield. Don't mind if I smoke, do you?'

'Not if I can cadge one off you.'

His face lit up and he produced a pack of Madisons. 'Help yourself, old boy.' A single small leather suitcase was stashed under the seat. In another age, one would have put him down as a remittance man. Now he might have been a salesman or a conman, but I knew almost instinctively that he was a journalist.

Gerry was in his late fifties, an old Fleet Street hand whose last assignment in the Gulf had soured when his wife ran off and he was sacked by the TV outfit he was working for. Quite what it was that had brought him to Matabeleland was never spelt out, but he had been in Bulawayo for a few months and liked the town – 'my sort of place, plenty of sun, nice old houses, and cheap drink'. He was just about getting by freelancing for British television. 'Soft features, old boy,' he drawled. 'Wildlife, steam trains – you know the sort of thing.'

We went off to find the bar. It turned out we had many mutual acquaintances in the business and so had many reasons to order more beers to go with the stories and gossip. Outside the window, stations came and went in the night . . . Norton . . . Selous . . . Chegutu . . . The barman didn't bother to ask, but each time the glasses emptied he brought two more Zambezis. Apart from us the car was deserted, a dimly lit tube with a bored barman and two dishevelled Englishmen talking excitedly and laughing foolishly.

In the early hours we swayed up the swaying carriages and, when we woke in our bunks, it was a sunny morning in Bulawayo. We exchanged addresses, knowing we would never see each other again. The last I saw of Gerry, he was trailing up the platform, an old hack in a creased blazer with a leather suitcase. Oddly, he looked more at home there than he could ever have done at Euston or Paddington.

Bulawayo: Thursday, 15 May

BACK AGAIN AFTER all these years, I buy a newspaper and am hit like a hammer by a headline from the past. On the front page, the *Zimbabwe Standard* proclaims 'Matabele Slaughter'. It reads: 'The *Standard* reveals details of a chilling report on Matabeleland atrocities, compiled by the Catholic Commission for Justice and Peace.' At first it seems this must be some new outrage. Then it dawns: after fourteen years of cover-up and denial, the massacres are finally being reported in the country where they occurred.

During the day, the sense of unreality deepens. Mike Auret, the commission's chairman, is in Bulawayo and he confirms that investigators have produced a meticulous report, *Breaking the Silence, Building True Peace*, based on the testimony of 1,000 witnesses. The hope of the Catholics is that the document will serve the same purpose as the Truth Commission into apartheid-era crimes and that, by bringing the atrocities into the open, reconciliation and healing can begin.

There are some signs of the ghosts being laid to rest. One of the investigators tells me that in the worst-affected district, Tjolotjo, relatives have at last started to exhume bones from mass graves and rebury them in accordance with Ndebele custom. I also hear that, in recent years, a few Fifth Brigade soldiers, troubled by the spirits of their victims, have returned to the scene of massacres and sought forgiveness.

I ALWAYS LIKED the name Bulawayo. It had a full, masculine sound, like a hearty burp. The town itself still had the rough, open feel of the frontier. Streets were broad enough for a twelve-span of oxen to execute a full turn, and the centre was composed largely of older buildings, like the Selborne Hotel with its latticed first-floor balcony overlooking the street, and on the corner a bar with bat-wing doors leading to a long teak counter worn to marble smoothness by generations of elbows. On the edge of town stood the official residence, Government House, built in 1894 for the man old-timers called Mr Rhodes, although he hardly ever visited the place.

The white settlement was laid out fifteen miles south of the last Ndebele king's *kraal* and seemed not to have learned to think of itself as a proper town. The original residential area, for instance, continued to be called Suburbs and, if such things existed, it might well have been designated a colonial heritage site. Many of the handsome old homes were built soon after the turn of the century; each was individually designed although veran-dahs and big gardens were standard features. My eyes, accustomed by now to imperial decay, were startled by the brightness of whitewash, the absence of rust on corrugated iron roofs, the crispness of freshly mowed lawns.

Just south of Bulawayo lay the Matopos hills, where both blacks and whites had their sacred sites. In the midst of thousands of square miles of unbroken savannah, the Matopos appeared suddenly like an aberration, a granite playground for whimsical giants – here, a turmoil of immense, smooth-backed boulders piled willy-nilly on top of one another; there, a precariously compiled structure of the same honey-coloured stone, each boulder balanced more impossibly on top of the last; and above the silent hills, black eagles wheeling in contemplation. When Mzilikazi brought his Ndebele here at the end of their migration from Zululand, he called it Matobo, meaning the bald heads. When Rhodes came to the spot as the conqueror of the Ndebele, he called it the View of the World, and left instructions that he was to be buried here in a ceremony 'big and simple, barbaric if you like'.

It used to be a shrine for white Rhodesians, a settler Valhalla, but the day I went up to the grave again the only other visitors were an African family who were coming down as I climbed the ridge and who smiled shyly in passing. Up this same way, to the pile of granite boulders as big as barns at the top of the ridge, the gun carriage drawn by oxen bore the coffin at the end of a journey of 1,200 miles from the Cape. Rhodes's early biogra-pher, Sarah Gertrude Millin, evoked the symbolism and the period:

Rhodes began in the little greenness of a place called Bishop's Stortford and he ended in the granite desolation of a land called after himself . . . His body passed along the path of his spirit: from Cape Town where he had ruled, through the Western Province of his vineyards, to Kimberley that had begotten his dreams and his wealth, along his own railway in Bechuanaland, through the country of his name, to the hills where he had made peace with the sons of Mzilikazi.

The place was magisterially unblemished by almost a century – the land-scape elemental, mile after mile of rocky hills, the grave with the simple brass plaque, 'Here lie the remains of Cecil John Rhodes'. It was typical of the man – grand, solitary and ultimately a little hollow in the way he presumed to match his own accomplishments with those of nature. Rhodes was always bigger on myth than substance. A few yards away stood a similar grave with a similar plaque, 'Here lies Leander Starr Jameson'; just that subtle difference of epitaph, the offset position at Rhodes's right hand, hinting at deference. In this place Jameson, the love of Rhodes's life and his ruin, had his reward.

They lived together in Jameson's corrugated iron shanty opposite the Kimberley Club from 1886, just after Rhodes's first intimate friendship ended with the death of Neville Pickering and as Rhodes's star was about to begin its blaze. In many respects 'the Doctor' was the most attractive of Rhodes's associates. A slight, dapper man – something of a dandy – he had a jaunty charm and a reputation in that frontier town as a gambler. Beneath a cynical exterior, however, Jameson was utterly in thrall to Rhodes. There is no evidence that there was ever a physical side to their love; rather, their feelings were channelled into a bond marked on Rhodes's side by a dangerously undiscriminating trust, and on Jameson's by an almost total absence of scruple when it came to carrying out his friend's big schemes. These elements produced the touchstone moments of triumph and disaster in their lives, the creation of Rhodesia and the invasion of the Transvaal.

Mzilikazi, too, was an invader and nation builder, and he was buried in the Matopos just thirty years before Rhodes. He had been forced to flee from Shaka with his small clan but his arrival on the highveld of the Transvaal coincided with that of Boer trekkers escaping British rule at the Cape. Like their Zulu kin, the Ndebele were a warrior people who made a grand and theatrical appearance, draped in animal skins and ostrich plumes, and Mzilikazi was as great a leader in his way as Shaka. But the discipline and raw courage of the Ndebele *impis* was no match for Boer cavalry and firearms, and the migrant tribe were forced to resume their wanderings.

Twenty years passed between Mzilikazi's flight and his arrival north of the Matopos. The Ndebele, meaning 'the people of the long shields', regularly raided their Shona neighbours. They were not interested solely in cattle. Mzilikazi was building a nation and, like all successful African monarchs, did so by winning adherents. Men, women and children brought back by raiding parties were incorporated into the tribe. A class system evolved of the *abezansi*, the original Khumalo clan from Zululand, the *abenhla*, or those mainly of Sotho extraction who were absorbed during the migration north, and the Shona *amaholi*, the lowest caste. All were citizens, however, and prospered under Mzilikazi. On his death in 1868, the Ndebele were a secure and powerful nation, rich in cattle and secure against any outside threat. The king was walled up in a cave in the Matopos.

His successor was also a capable ruler, as well as being familiar with the ways of the whites just starting to make their way to the Far Interior, as the area of modern Zimbabwe was known. Before becoming king, Lobengula had befriended George 'Elephant' Phillips, a dissolute but popular Englishman whom he joined on hunting expeditions, George Wood, a leathery adventurer from the West Riding, and the legendary George Westbeech who founded an ivory-trading empire on the Zambezi. For these 'gentlemen by birth and education but Bohemians by nature', as a visiting Indian Army officer described them, Lobengula's *kraal* at Bulawayo was home. Most had at least one native wife, while Phillips enjoyed a liaison with the King's gargantuan sister, Nini.

The epochal event that spelt the undoing of this society was the discovery of gold on the Rand. From the mid-1880s, a new breed of adventurers started to wend their way up the Missionary Road from the Cape to Bulawayo. Brash and ruthless, they had as little regard for the old-timers and their easygoing ways as they had for blacks. They were gamblers scenting the big break, and they were after mineral concessions. An instinctive diplomat, Lobengula played for time. But as the clamouring became more insistent, and as uniformed and bemedalled envoys joined the procession with greetings from the 'great white queen', he sensed his peril. 'England is the chameleon, and I am the fly,' he once said.

Lobengula's downfall is among the shabbiest episodes in colonial history. Jameson used morphine to ease the king's gout and to try – unsuccessfully – to win his consent to the settlement of Mashonaland, then found a pretext for a *casus belli*. The king sent peace envoys. They were shot. Two battles in which an Ndebele army of 8,000 men tried to repel Jameson's force led to the virtual annihilation of Lobengula's best regiments and may well have served as the inspiration for Belloc's grim little couplet:

> *Whatever happens, we have got,*
> *The Maxim gun, and they have not.*

Jameson entered the smouldering ruins of Bulawayo to find that the king had fled. Lobengula kept faith with two whites who stayed with him to the end, ordering that they were not to be harmed. A fugitive in his own land, he continued to head north with a small band. It is sometimes represented, in a final poetic touch to the tragedy, that the king took poison. The most reliable story, told later by an *induna* named Mjaan to one of the Bulawayo whites, was that he died of disease, possibly smallpox or malaria.

Such is conquerors' justice, and being conquerors themselves the Ndebele had no difficulty in recognising superior power and bending the knee – in the expectation that the whites would then conduct themselves in African fashion. But instead of absorbing the Ndebele – as they themselves had absorbed the Sotho *abenhla* and the Shona *amaholi* – the whites kept them at arm's length while plundering their land and cattle. The curious thing is that an empathy grew up between white and Ndebele, and that Bulawayo retained its relatively easygoing racial ways. It is easy of course to take a mistily romantic view of a defeated foe, and there were no doubt plenty of whites whose regard for the Ndebele extended only insofar as they 'knew their place'. There were also those who took an interest in their history, culture and language, and generally esteemed them as a people.

MALCOLM KING'S CLOSEST friends were Ndebele. Peter Khumalo, the last great-grandson of Lobengula and head of the royal Khumalo clan, said: 'He is one of us. He is a Khumalo.'

Malcolm was a former white hunter, the quintessential Rhodesian with the burly build and weatherbeaten countenance of the outdoorsman. His intimacy with Ndebele ways had been forged in the bush and around the campfire, with trackers and skinners. I asked him the reason for the empathy between Briton and Ndebele. 'We are both intrinsically conservative, with all the virtues and vices that go with the condition,' he said. 'Both of us are drawn to ritual and neither is very good at accepting progress.'

So strongly had he felt about his friends that, during Rhodesia's bush war, he went over to their side, and acted as an agent for Zapu, the party of the most prominent nationalist leader, Joshua Nkomo. First he went to Lusaka to volunteer his services, and was detained for four weeks for his pains. Then, after being accepted, he went to Johannesburg where, behind the screen of running a Soweto football team, he acted until the end of the war as a conduit for young Ndebele whom he provided with money, contacts and routes for reaching Zapu bases.

'The reason most whites fail to appreciate African culture is that they have never bothered to learn a language,' he said. 'They learn our language, we don't learn theirs. Language is the very basis of understanding African tradition, oral history, storytelling. For me it opened the door to rituals, values, the spirit world of the ancestors, the *amadlozi*. I can only say I was drawn to the culture. It is so different from ours, but so . . .' he paused, searching for the word, '. . . so *embraceable*.'

I asked how the massacres had affected him. 'We will never forget the

Fifth Brigade,' Malcolm said. 'That time has become part of our folklore.'
So how did he feel about the Shona? 'They are an imaginative people,' he
said woodenly, 'impressive as writers and artists. But they don't endear
themselves to me for all that.'

THE TODDS WERE not the kind of people you felt pity for. They were dignified,
gracious and self-contained. Sir Garfield, missionary, rancher and the only
liberal white politician ever to hold power in southern Africa, was now
almost ninety. Judith, his daughter, ally, confidante and a campaigner in her
own right, lived a few blocks away along the tree-lined avenues of Suburbs.
It was a tranquil spot for a venerable figure to be seeing out his days. But
a thread of deep sadness ran through their lives. Both had seen the dream
of a life's work come true, only to turn to ashes.

Todd came to Southern Rhodesia from New Zealand with his wife,
Grace, in 1934, and founded Christ Mission at Dadaya, out in the bush on
the edge of the Ndebele country. Here Judith was born and Garfield taught,
doctored, married and buried three generations. The doctoring was pretty
basic. Once he was called to a woman whose womb had been inverted as she
gave birth. All he could do was wash it with soap and push it back in. He
thought she would not survive, but she went on to have more children. The
first, also named Todd, was now a middle-aged man still living at Dadaya.

Sir Garfield entered politics by chance. At a public meeting, he took issue
with the prime minister, Godfrey Huggins, and on the strength of his speaking
skills was invited to stand for parliament. He was elected in 1946 and went on
to the backbenches with a neighbouring farmer named Ian Smith.

For all its rugged settler ethos, Rhodesia had adopted elements of the old
Cape Colony's constitution, which was among the most racially enlightened
anywhere in the colonial world and from 1853 elected its legislators by a
qualified franchise of voters of all races. Rhodesia, too, had a qualified vote
and, in the post-war period, saw a significant flowering of liberal opinion
represented by the Capricorn Africa Society, founded by a war hero, Colonel
David Stirling, DSO, to foster partnership between the races. Todd, who
combined startling oratory with missionary zeal – he had what the historian,
Robert Blake, thought an 'intriguing combination of other-worldliness and
realism' – was the natural leader of this group, and he became prime minister
in 1953. There were then roughly 1,000 Africans entitled to vote on the
basis of literacy or income. Todd's policies were directed at accelerating
black political rights but he was not an advocate of universal suffrage which,
he once said, 'would lead to universal chaos'. All the same, he was seen

by blacks as something of a saviour, described in the *African Weekly* as 'the Moses of our age', and as a dangerous radical by conservatives. Although few realised it, southern Africa was at a crossroads.

In his ninetieth year, Todd remained a handsome man of striking presence. Looking back, he acknowledged that he had misjudged the white mood himself. 'Until the late 1950s, Africans were asking for improvements in health and education rather than political power. They just wanted to share in the civilisation of the country. I did not realise how deep was the determination of the majority of whites to deny them even that.'

I reminded him of what he once told Robert Blake: 'Living as we do, all of us [whites] are guilty. But I think it is asking for a generation of white saints to hope that they will voluntarily abandon what they hold.'

He laughed. 'That's true, but Africans were very ready to negotiate early on, and their demands were quite reasonable. It was because the whites were so obdurate that the whole tone changed.'

Two issues brought him into conflict with his colleagues. The first was his opposition to a Cabinet resolution to make sex between white men and black women illegal outside marriage. (It was already illegal between black men and white women.) The second were his efforts to broaden the African franchise. Soon afterwards, in 1958, he was toppled in a Cabinet revolt. An African wrote a lament – 'Todd has left us, Go well, old man' – which became a best-selling township record.

'I had anticipated a slow transition to multiracial power through the qualified franchise,' he said. 'When I was thrown out, it was a turning-point. The whites turned their backs on the idea of partnership with blacks, and that was the signal for a tremendous surge in support for African nationalism.' Todd's successors moved steadily to the right, until by 1964 the stage was set for the downright reactionary Smith, a man described by one of his predecessors as 'devious, parochial and suspicious', and UDI.

The truly remarkable thing is that even then there might have been another way. The name of HMS *Tiger*, as the scene of talks between Harold Wilson and Smith the year after UDI, is almost forgotten now, the details of the agreement they reached even more so. What it amounted to was a return to the principle of an incremental enfranchisement of blacks, albeit at a pace that would only have led – in the estimation of Smith's intelligence chief, Ken Flower – to full universal suffrage around the turn of the century, while Rhodesia would have been brought back into the international community. If Smith had held to his side of the bargain, the history of southern Africa might have been much altered. But the hardliners behind him could not bear to think they might ever be ruled by 'a bunch of munts' and the only chance for a middle way was lost.

In the rush towards disaster, Todd was put under house arrest. Judith had meanwhile joined Zapu. In 1970 both Garfield and Judith were held in solitary confinement until an international outcry obliged Smith to release them. Todd was taken to see his former neighbour for a curious audience. 'He didn't get up, just sat there and said, "You're looking well, Garfield." I said, "No thanks to you, Ian."'

By the time Smith finally admitted defeat, Rhodesia had been ruined by seven years of war. When the negotiating parties assembled at Lancaster House, Todd was a member of Nkomo's delegation. Later he was appointed to the Senate but his relationship with Mugabe had never been close. 'I went to see him, and said I'd like to maintain the tradition of the old prime minister seeing the new prime minister. He was not really interested.'

Perhaps unkindly, I asked him if he now thought Mugabe – whom he once described as a great man – a bigger monster than Smith. 'What was better under Smith was honesty in administration. Now it is totally corrupt. People suffered discrimination then but they were not robbed blind.'

Had his dream been despoiled? 'Everything was wrecked by the war,' he said. 'So many dead. What is happening now is very distressing. At the same time, we can't expect that after the war blacks would embrace what whites want. And we can't complain because . . .' and he gestured round at our surroundings, the house, the swimming pool and garden '. . . we still have a good life. Perhaps we should feel ashamed about that, but it was honestly made. The basic trouble is we are all human beings.'

Circumstances had made Todd a farmer, then a politician. But, first and foremost, he remained a missionary. When I met him, there had been some suggestion that the government might want to give him a symbolic burial at Hero's Acre, the first white to be thus honoured. But he had told Judith that when the time came, his place was at Dadaya.

THE NDEBELE ELDERS, descendants of Lobengula, were gathered under his *indaba* tree. Judith had driven me out to the site of the last royal *kraal* and it was a cool day with the pale light of early winter on the veld. There was little sign of the great enclosure of beehive huts where once up to 12,000 warriors gathered for the annual *inxwala*, the first fruits festival – just the ruins of the king's house, built by two white traders, and the *indaba* tree, a luxuriant example of *pappea capensis*.

The elders were *mntwana*, princes of Mzilikazi's original Khumalo clan.

Not that there was anything in their appearance to distinguish them. Indeed, apart from one lean old man in a waistcoat and threadbare jacket, they were a rather ragged group in workclothes and overalls. Each had a wooden stick and sat on a small stool. Gravely they rose to shake hands. They spoke through Peter Khumalo.

Lobengula's legacy was alive, they said, but dormant. It had been suppressed but could not be destroyed. An old man named Msongelona said: 'People do not vote for a culture. To destroy it you would have to destroy our lineage, but you cannot do that because it lives among our people.'

Another, Mcindo, said: 'Our time is coming again. We have seen the revival among our brothers in Zululand. On this site we will rebuild our old *kraal* as it was.' Peter explained that the previous year, the Khumalo had welcomed Chief Mangosuthu Buthelezi, the Zulu leader, and slaughtered an ox and feasted at a ceremony to symbolise this idea of rebirth.

There was a pause. Msongelona, who had been looking intently at Judith, spoke to Peter. 'He asks who you are,' Peter said.

'Judith Todd.'

'Garfield's daughter?'

'Yes.'

He relayed this information, which was greeted with appreciative exclamations of 'Todd!' and 'Hauw!' and 'Aah, Garfield!' Judith smiled pinkly with embarrassed pleasure. One of the elders indicated that I should take a picture of her with them under the *indaba* tree. It was a touching reminder of the importance of reputation.

THERE WAS A case to be made that, having come to Africa in the first place, the British fault was in not staying longer. An African anthropologist, John Mbiti, had noted that Africans lived two half cultures which never quite formed a whole. But holding on would probably have involved unpleasantness and taken more energy than a war-tired nation had left. As far back as 1852, Livingstone wrote of a time when Britain's colonies would start to exercise their will, and he gave a warning then that to perpetuate subordination would only engender hatred.

In the end, Livingstone's legacy lasted better than the rest of the colonial heritage. Neither democracy nor industrialisation took root, but a love of learning and Christianity ran like a seam through the upheavals of post-colonial times. Africa might never become entirely Christianised, but a spiritual hunger continued to attract new adherents. My own feeling was that it was on the spiritual – not necessarily Christian – level that Africans and Europeans had most frequently recognised one another. And yet how often a cultural divide still came between us. Take the story of Musa Zulu and Archbishop Milingo.

Musa grew up in a rural district north of Bulawayo. His parents ran a country store and the Zulu family were prosperous pillars of the Catholic church in Lupane, with a second home in the Khumalo suburb of Bulawayo. Musa was a bright boy and no cloud darkened his childhood until, in 1981, soon after his tenth birthday, his mother fell ill and died. His father, utterly bereft, brooded on his loss. And he came back to the traditional conviction that premature death must have an external agent.

'Dad became sure she had been bewitched by someone jealous about their success,' Musa said. 'He started consulting *nangas* to sniff out the witch who had caused this. From that time things became worse for our family. The *nangas* came to our house and they would speak with our ancestors' spirits. I saw the spirits take possession of them. Dad became obsessed with these people. He never got any answers, but he kept calling in the *nangas*. Each one gave him a different story. He neglected the store and business went down. He stopped going to church. All the things he and Mum had achieved were the effect of the light. After she died, he turned to the dark. The practice of ancestor worship is very strong with us, but it brings out negative forces in our society. To achieve a lot in his life, a man needs to devote himself to the positive. I was trying to fulfil my potential. I found the presence of these spirits had a bad effect on me. They did not come to our home in love. I didn't know if I was possessed, but I was very troubled.'

A spiral of disaster led to the loss of the family business, a shooting accident involving one of Musa's brothers and the jailing of another. At his lowest point, Musa got to hear of Emmanuel Milingo. This turbulent prelate, appointed Roman Catholic Archbishop of Lusaka in 1969, invoked the Holy Spirit in a healing and exorcising ministry that was spectacularly successful in attracting congregants who believed themselves possessed. Milingo who, in the words of his biographer, thought the Church in the West had lost its ability to communicate with the spirit world and, therefore, its capacity to combat evil, came into conflict with the European missionaries who still dominated church leadership in Zambia. In 1982 he was summoned to the Vatican, and had never been allowed to go home.*

---

* At the time of writing, Milingo was still exiled in the Vatican. His view that 'demons exist among us. They are like wild cats which tear chickens to pieces and which the farmer cannot catch', had made him unpopular with senior clergy, but he had acquired an Italian following of some thousands who believed he possessed miraculous healing powers.

As a result of reading a book by Milingo in which he addressed the African beliefs in ancestor worship and possession, Musa decided to make a pilgrimage to the Vatican and seek his help. He reached Britain and stayed with a Catholic community in Brentwood. However, his request for a visa was rejected by the Italian authorities who suspected he would claim refugee status, and eventually he returned home fortified only by the sympathy of some good people in Essex. When I met him, he was still troubled, his face occasionally gripped by what appeared an almost physical pain, but he was no longer fearful. His experience, he said, had persuaded him to enter the Church and follow the example of Milingo. 'He identified the negative practices that are harming our society. He is very gifted and very much loved. What the Church has done is unfortunate for all of Africa.

'Some people believe that Christianity is a means of white oppression. But if you look at the effects of African traditions and Christianity, you see the contrast. Why is there so much suffering, so much darkness on our continent? Why is Europe so advanced? You are not better people. Maybe it is because you have the benefit of centuries of living with the Gospels. They made you believe in hope and improvement. You take that for granted. Maybe now you forget it. Africans are very spiritual people. If we can turn our spirituality to the positive, we can accomplish much. If we feed only off the negative, we will stay as we are.'

I had this affecting conversation after meeting Malcolm King and it brought back his explanation of how he had been drawn to a culture 'so different from ours but so . . . so *embraceable*'. Musa and Malcolm did as much as anything to show me how the souls of our peoples had touched.

Bulawayo–Mafeking Line: Sunday, 18 May

THE RAILWAY LINE through Botswana follows the route of what used to be called the Missionary Road. Until the completion of the line to Bulawayo, the journey from the Cape was made by the excrutiating agency of the Zeederburg Mail Coach. This mule-drawn contraption, made in America and resembling the stagecoaches featured in Western films, carried twelve passengers and the Royal Mail at 6 mph over ten days for the 500 miles between Mafeking and Bulawayo. Seats and leg room compared unfavourably with the modern *matatu*. Baden Powell, who travelled on the Zeederburg a century ago, thought it an abomination.

The cost of undergoing this form of licensed torture was about £50, roughly £500 at today's prices. I am covering the route in a single overnight journey in the comfort of a Botswana Railways first class compartment, which I have all to myself, for £23.

It is 5 p.m. and the tiny town of Plumtree – remarkable only for Rhodesia's most famous school – is approaching as the sun sinks. The scene touches me powerfully, although it is hard to say why. The terrain, like so much of Matabeleland, is flat as far as the eye can see, with straggly mopane trees and thorn bushes little higher than a man and grass quickly turning flaxen under the dry winter sun. Yet, especially now in the evening light, which burns and glows even as it fades and dies, its unchanging tranquillity seems to reflect eternity.

The siding at Plumtree is ageless in another way – a deserted platform, the stationmaster's little bungalow with a verandah enclosed by wire mesh, a roof of red corrugated iron and a bed of limp flowers. The sun has gone and against a pink horizon the grey is falling. I am surprised by the pain of accepting that my journey is nearly over.

18. The Reef

THE BUS TO JOHANNESBURG took a road running like a line of gunmetal across a burnt orange land. Telephone lines drooped from rusted poles, casting hard shadows in the clean, pale light of early winter. Only a day back, and already a brush with the law.

Among the things I still missed about my native land was the immanence of absurdity. There was little appetite for eccentricity in South Africa, but plain craziness was another matter. Crazy was the condition with which we were most familiar. Mostly this was tied up with the inherent violence of the place, and gave rise to a humour as black as the grave, but there was also a strong strand of the utterly absurd. It was entirely natural that anyone carrying rocks in a rucksack should be detained on suspicion of high crimes.

The train had halted that morning at the tiny Botswana town of Lobatse, where I caught a *matatu* crossing to Mafeking. At the border a tubby South African customs official rooted around in the bottom of the bag and came up with about 6 lb of rocks. I had been carrying them since Kenya. Walking at Soysambu one morning, Lord Delamere showed me a seam of lava rock containing fossils. He gave an entertaining account of a volcano exploding, causing the animals grazing on the valley floor to shit themselves in panic and flee, leaving their dung to be fossilised in the lava. He picked out examples. This large flat pat was a buffalo, that round fist-size lump a zebra, and so on. I decided to take some of these intriguing objects home as presents.

As the rocks emerged from the rucksack and were laid on the counter, the official's expression went from puzzlement to astonishment – then suspicion. He looked at me narrowly. 'Okay, what is this?' he demanded.

I should have shrugged and said 'rocks' as though it were the most natural and obvious thing to be carrying in a rucksack. Instead, I tried to explain it as Delamere had done. Halfway through, I started to falter. 'I am just interested in these rocks,' I ended lamely.

'We must call to Mmabatho for police,' said the plump man. He had taken the case in hand. 'You will have to stay. We need a second opinion.'

'A second opinion? What on earth do you mean? Look . . .' I picked up two fossils and knocked them together . . . 'they are just old stones.'

He looked smug. 'Ah, but maybe they are not just stones.' Knowingly, he added: 'What happens if you put them in boiling water?'

There was no answer to that, so I watched the *matatu* depart for Mafeking without me and sat down to wait for the police. Two hours went by. No traffic came. Perhaps they had picked on me to keep up their statistics: 19 May, one Englishman detained on suspicion of . . . of what? Narcotics, perhaps. South Africa had acquired a serious heavy drug habit.

Eventually a van drew up and a plainclothes cop entered, tall and businesslike. My fossils were studied in silence, then popped into a super-market plastic bag. The plump man, pleased with his day's work, surrendered me to police custody. Shouldering my rucksack, I followed the cop out to the van and we set off for Mmabatho.

'What happens now?' I asked.

'I must have these samples analysed,' he said. 'They will be sent to Pretoria.'

I tried to stay calm. Pretoria was 200 miles away and, if the new bureau-cracy was anything like the old, I would be languishing in Mmabatho for weeks. I said I needed to be in Johannesburg in two days. 'Anyway, what are you looking for?' I asked. He shrugged.

It was fifteen miles from the border to Mmabatho. We drew up outside a modern high-rise block. The cop, carrying the supermarket bag of contra-band, motioned me to a seat, while he made a call. He murmured a few words, ending 'We'll be right over.' To me he said: 'The government geologist will see us now.' I felt an absurd sense of relief.

Once again my rocks were spread out. The geologist picked one up, scratched it.

'Stromatolites,' he pronounced with an Italian accent. The cop and I looked equally blank. 'Thees ees stromatolites – ees a kind of dolomite.'

I jumped in quickly. 'So they could not contain any drugs?'

He and the cop looked at me as though I were deranged.

'So they have no commercial value?' asked the cop.

The geologist and I looked at him as though he were demented.

My rocks were swept up for the last time. We walked out into the sunny day. 'Can I help, take you anywhere?' the cop asked.

'Well, I'm trying to get to Mafeking,' I said.

'I've got nothing else on. I'll drive you,' he said. It was five miles. He dropped me at a hotel and gave me a phone number. 'You have any more trouble about this, give me a ring – Inspector Madito, diamond unit.'

Diamonds were the last thing I had thought buffaloes capable of shitting. I would like to put it on record, though, that Inspector Madito was a gentle-

man, the first of his kind I had ever encountered among the South African
police.

THE EFFECT OF this episode was to make me feel immediately home in my
native land, while depriving me of any sense of arrival. Only when I looked
around Mafeking, and was suddenly struck by the dazzling newness of the
cars and the shop windows full of consumer goods, did I recognise that I
had reached my destination. I was back in South Africa.

There was one other striking feature as well. For the first time, many of
the faces around me were white. That night I found a place called Bugs's,
where the local youngsters went to *jol*, and met a young man named Sammy,
who was an illegal immigrant from Ethiopia. A long-haired youth in shorts
and sandals ran the disco and the pretty white girls shrieked and giggled.
Sammy, the only black in the place, was high on a subtly intoxicating leaf
called *khat*, which he obtained from the Nigerians who ran the narcotics
trade in Jo'burg. Despite his state, he was a wizard at the pool table, making
short work of all comers. I tried the *khat*, to no effect, and instead had too
much to drink and lost a few rands at the table, then lurched back to
my hotel marvelling at having played pool in post-imperial, post-apartheid
Mafeking with a stoned Ethiopian and the youth of the New South Africa.

I would have lingered, but time was now very short. In a week it would
be over and I would be leaving Cape Town. I felt something was wrong,
as if this final return should take the form of an extended climax in which
the lessons of the journey might be considered and absorbed. Instead, I
knew I would be racing through scenes of childhood, trying to recapture a
sense of the past rather than anticipate the future. As the bus to Jo'burg
passed mile after mile of maize, farm gates with names like Snyman, De
Wet and Van Zyl, and dusty tracks leading to little homesteads buried in
the green bob of willow groves, and signs pointed across the veld to *dorps*
like Vlakdrif and Blesbokfontein, the place reflected the nostalgia of my
mood back at me.

This was western Transvaal, landscape of the murderer-poet, Herman
Charles Bosman, whose life story was quintessential bittersweet South
Africa. Aged twenty-one, Bosman shot his step-brother after a violent quarrel and was sentenced to death but reprieved. His stories of prison life
established a style in which the expectation of tragedy is laced with wry
humour; the tales that made his reputation, of Oom Schalk Lourens and the
Boers of the Groot Marico district, conjure up a harsh world redeemed by

irony and humanity. He was a romantic, too, translating *The Rubaiyat of Omar Khayyam* into Afrikaans before he died at the age of forty-six. The author, according to the poet Roy Campbell, of the best stories ever to come out of South Africa, he had been eking out a living as a newspaper proof-reader.

Here, too, was another typically South African ending. Here, galloping across these golden plains to the Rand, Jameson finally over-reached himself. The invasion of Matabeleland had been a dress rehearsal. Now came the real thing, charging into the Transvaal at the head of a small army, while Rhodes's cronies in Johannesburg launched an uprising against that old ox Paul Kruger. The Boers would crumble and the Rand and its goldfields would fall to Rhodes. Game, set and match. Only there was no rising, and the Boers did not crumble. Instead, they rode out against Jameson and ambushed him. He did not even put up much of a show. Sixteen of his 600 men had been picked off before a native maid's apron was raised in surrender.

There was a terrific fuss. Kruger would have been well within his rights to carry out the death sentence passed on Jameson by a Transvaal court. Instead, he was handed over to the British, who tried him and sentenced him to fifteen months in Holloway. Having disgraced himself and ruined his friend Rhodes, that ought to have been the end of Jameson. But within a decade he had been elected prime minister of the Cape and made a member of the Privy Council.

The day after arriving in Johannesburg, I set out down the road from Roodepoort to Krugersdorp, to a point where the map showed the monument to be. There was no signpost nor any other indication beside a road swarming with cars on that flat plain, so I stopped at what turned out to be a cement factory. A large woman behind a counter looked baffled for a moment when I asked her.

'Hey, Cassie,' she shouted. 'Where's that Jameson memorial *dingus* again?'

A head poked out from a door. 'It's out the back,' he said. 'There's another one also but you can't get there because it's in the yard and, man, those dogs bite.'

I went round the back, where a film of powdery dust from the factory gave the veld a deathly bleach. In a small enclosure overgrown by blackjack weeds stood an obelisk marking the spot where Jameson surrendered. It is perhaps stretching a point, but not very greatly, to call it the birthplace of modern South Africa. Smuts it was who described the Jameson Raid as the opening shots in the Boer War, and the process by which the colonies of the Cape and Natal were joined with the Boer republics of the Transvaal and Orange Free State.

PERHAPS THE REASON I kept going back to Africa was that Britain turned out to be not quite what I expected. Childhood reading was partly to blame. All that love of English popular fiction stunted my understanding. An impression based on Conan Doyle and Charteris, *Comet* and *Chums*, was bound to be defective in a country gripped by imperial guilt and class struggle. Besides, leaving Africa had never been an act of finality. I was no refugee and, unlike the small group of white South Africans who made their homes in London in the 1960s, I could not summon any enthusiasm for exile politics. I attended one meeting of the Anti-Apartheid Movement and went on a couple of protest marches, but found the rhetoric so stupefying that I never went back.

Of course, there were benefits to living in England while not actually being English. A colonial background helped to frustrate the beady-eyed categorisation of class. After a while you realised that this gave you a social mobility that was denied to others. The drawback was that you were not entirely a part of any one group. At first I assumed that this was temporary, that I would assimilate imperceptibly until one day I found that, without realising it, I had become English. This sense of not quite belonging was no great bother, and no obstacle to friendships. But gradually I realised that the condition was probably permanent.

I wondered how my grandfathers, one from Norfolk, the other from the East End, had assimilated in South Africa. The one from Norfolk was a Presbyterian pastor who went out in a missionary capacity to the Dutch Reformed Church because not enough indigenous *predikants* could be found in the Cape. The East Ender went out to make a new life after the promise of a land fit for heroes remained unfulfilled. They remained Englishmen to the core. Did they not long for some glimpse of their old lives – grandfather Taylor for the spires of Norwich Cathedral and the Broads, grandfather Hollyer for the gaiety of his beloved music hall? It was not as if these were worlds beyond reach. The Union Castle line was one of the great institutions of the Empire, with vessels that carried the mail weekly between Cape Town and Southampton via Madeira. Yet neither ever saw England again.

Ours is a more restless age. Once more, like an adolescent with a ragged childhood teddy that I could not learn to live without, I had come back. Almost twenty years after we left South Africa, De Klerk announced he was freeing Mandela, and we dragged ourselves back one last time. We rode the exhilarating, hair-raising roller-coaster to the election we had been so sure we would never see. It was epic and grand, and the memory of it still had the power to move me, for it was about so much more than politics. Never in my life did I cry like I cried when it all came together in a single moment, when Mandela and François Pienaar united us all that day on the turf of Ellis Park, and for the first time since I was a boy I felt free again to love men in jerseys of green and gold.

On the day multiracial democracy was achieved, I was in a dusty little town in the arid far northern Cape. The name Kuruman had long since ceased to have resonance but once it was Britain's final frontier in Africa, an outpost planted in 1820 by Robert Moffat, the pioneer missionary. Moffat's mud-brick cottage and the stone church on the outskirts of town were improbable cradles for a crusade, but I had chosen to be there that day because in a sense it marked the starting-point of the era that was just ending. Moffat's son-in-law was Livingstone, and Kuruman was the explorer's first African home. Here began his wanderings, north to the Tswana country, through the Kalahari to Lake Ngami and the Zambezi.

The spirit of apartheid endured to the end at Kuruman's two polling stations. The town hall was intended for whites – burly farmers and their ample wives – the marqee on an open stretch of ground was for blacks. The queue outside the tent stretched for hundreds of yards until word spread that voting was quicker at the white station. Slowly at first, and then with growing confidence, blacks made their way to the town hall, so that by mid-morning the races were sharing a two-hour wait to vote in the sweltering Kalahari sun.

I had wondered about my own vote. I had never cast a ballot in a South African election. Surely I was entitled to take my place in the queues beside all those others who had waited a lifetime. But where would I put my cross? Next to the people's choice, the ANC, or where my English democratic nurturing prompted, the healthy opposition of the liberal Democratic Party? The longer I considered it, the more it seemed an empty gesture. I think the moment I accepted finally that England really was my home was when I decided not to vote at all.

I STEPPED OFF the bus and went to stay with Mike, my oldest friend, the only person with whom I still shared childhood memories. He was quite grey now, a doctor, married with three daughters, and the stand-up shouting matches when I lived in Zimbabwe and he in South Africa were a thing of the past. As boys we had a fight which he won and there were times when we met that we raged at one another like kids again. Usually we ended up weeping with laughter at ourselves.

We set out in Mike's rusty white Volkswagen. We took the road north through familiar suburbs, sumptuous Parktown, comfortable Parkview, past Zoo Lake, Rosebank where we used to go to bioscope, and my old school at Inanda. As we got closer to the landscape of childhood I started to get lost. Where once the bus taking us home in the afternoon took a long gentle sweep around a few odd houses on the crest at Morningside before dropping away across the veld for the last few miles – there now a city had arisen.

There was nothing that I recognised. Even the contours of the land seemed to have changed shape. For a while we drove on in bewildered silence. Then, sandwiched between a new shopping mall and an office block, we saw the stone walls of the old Carmelite convent. It was only then that we realised that we were back in Rivonia.

When we were boys, there were perhaps a score of tin-roof bungalows scattered over the veld on our side of the main road. As well as a few English there was a smattering of other Europeans – like the Radziwills, said to be exiled Polish aristocrats, who were almost as reclusive as the Carmelite nuns and rarely emerged from a house on the other side of a vast bougainvillea hedge. More sinister rumours concerned the Schmidts, a childless and ill-tempered German couple who tended a smallholding. Herr Schmidt, it was whispered, was an old Nazi who had taken refuge in South Africa, where few questions were asked about such things.

Wizened old Mrs Cohen, on the other hand, had been a refugee from the Nazis, and ran, with a firm hand and sharp tongue, the native store. With its walls of faded whitewash, red-polished floor and smell of hessian sacks and Lifebuoy soap, the old place was long gone. When we were kids it had been almost an embarrassment, so humiliatingly *backward* compared with proper shops.

The road that ran down to our old house was equally unfamiliar. In the place of the old tin roofs were houses grand and luxurious, with pools and tennis courts. More disconcerting still was the fact that most of this new world was out of reach. Our little settlement had been absorbed into a new *laager* of the wealthy known as Sandton. All the resources of a highly evolved security industry had been thrown into protecting this imperium. Each house was surrounded by a high security fence, topped with razor wire or jagged spikes. Some were electrified. Gates were emblazoned with the emblems of various armed response units or signs showing savagely salivating dogs.

I searched in vain. Eventually, surveying a wall twelve feet high, I decided that our old house might have been on the other side. A sign on the gate showed a smoking gun with the legend 'Go Ahead, Make My Day'. Briefly I considered pressing the intercom buzzer. What would I say? 'Excuse me, I used to live here long ago, I just wanted to see the place where I used to play cricket with our servant'?

Other areas of our boyhood were equally out of reach. The river where we camped at the bottom of Liliesleaf Farm seemed somehow to have been sucked up by an invisible sponge. Mandela's old hideout was gone too, the land subdivided for more houses. While we were still wandering lost in this way, one sight leapt out; in that moment we were taken back to adolescence. There was the wooden fence, the row of pine trees, the house where we used to call in the hope of seeing Margaret.

We walked up the drive. Margaret's mother answered the door; her father showed us to the sitting-room. It was just as it had always been – lace curtains, parquet floors, pressed-steel ceiling, even the same 1950s leather-ette armchairs. Then I spotted the old walnut gramophone in the corner, and felt weak. Once, when we were thirteen and their parents were out, Margaret and her brother invited me over to listen to a record of risqué army ballads belonging to their father, which included a rendition of *Foggy, foggy dew*. We played it half a dozen times on the old gramophone, feigning comprehension and hilarity, and I almost died of pleasure.

Her parents were welcoming, as if it were every day that ghostly visitors stepped out of the past. They had always been kindly folk, even to infuriating adolescents, with the very English manners of a grainy black-and-white war film. Her mother was into her seventies, but still doing good works, serving Meals on Wheels among the poor whites of Doornfontein and Mayfair. 'It's a little hairy these days,' she said in the genteel tones of an elderly Deborah Kerr. 'It's the kaffirs. The kaffirs are everywhere now.'

IN MY FINAL year at school, I went to clubs in Hillbrow to sing anthems to equality and freedom with other well-heeled white kids. I started work as a trainee reporter on the *Rand Daily Mail*, a newspaper resolutely antagon-istic to apartheid. Later I worked for the *World*, the Soweto paper edited by the late Percy Qoboza, and for the first time met blacks as colleagues. Sometimes we could even pretend that we were equals. With my girlfriend, another reporter, I went to plays in bleak Soweto halls as theatre was just starting to emerge as South Africa's *samizdat* art form. Going into the townships was an adventure, a form of defiance even. We were supposed to have permits, but never did. Once we persuaded Mike to come with us. His father, a sociologist, worked in Soweto.

But if I fancied myself as a bit of a nonconformist, I had also to admit that, for all practical purposes, this was mere posturing. White obduracy had hardened and apartheid appeared impregnable. Not in our lifetimes, the saying went, and it certainly looked that way. With the girlfriend who was now my wife, I started my first journey through Africa to Britain.

Some time later, Mike's father was on his way to work in Soweto. As he drove to the juvenile employment centre where he was chief welfare officer, a crowd of high school pupils about 15,000 strong was marching in protest at a decree forcing them to study in Afrikaans. It is not known whether he heard the police gunfire which killed a thirteen-year-old named Hector Petersen, but, as Mike's father neared the Morris Isaacson High School, he saw a mob coming his way and realised it meant trouble. He drove into the yard at the West Rand Administration Board just ahead of them and took shelter in his office. Pupils poured into the yard behind him, setting fire to cars, then attacked the office.

According to court records, as they hammered on the door, one shouted: '*Jou bloody wit kaffir, vandag vrek jy*' (You bloody white kaffir, today you die). A black colleague told him to hide under a desk and, as the mob broke in demanding to know where the white man was, he bravely told them the whites had fled. But they found Mike's father. As he ran from the office into the yard, he was stoned. Later, a police captain named Engelbrecht found him lying face down in the dirt, dead, his clothes torn, his head bloodied.

Hector Petersen, as is widely known – the picture of his body being borne from the scene by weeping friends is one of the indelible images of South Africa – was the first to die in the Soweto Uprising of 1976. Melville Edelstein, now forgotten, was the second. He was an earnest, well-meaning man. There is a keen poignancy to his sociology doctorate, a thesis on attitudes among matriculation students in Soweto entitled *What Do Young Africans Think?* It anticipated a time when race hostility might lead to upheaval, and was conducted among the same age group that stoned and kicked him to death.

Later, when the struggle was in full swing and the Hippos roared through blazing townships bristling with riflemen in blue who picked off blacks at random, Mike started to behave oddly. After he qualified, he opened a practice in Diagonal Street, among the *nangas* and witchdoctors, who displayed animal skins and vegetable roots and God knows what else in their windows. Then he fell in with the White Right, and the oddballs and crazies who talked about white survival and demanded a homeland of their own where things would be as they once were. Friends said then this was a delayed reaction to his father's death. To his credit, he always denied it.

I HAD BEEN expecting to hear about crime. Every press report about South Africa mentioned rates of murder and rape which were the highest in the world. I told myself that there was probably an element of hysteria in this. By now I was used to being wrong, so was not all that surprised to find my own internal alarm system ringing furiously as I walked in Johannesburg.

The financial district of what used to be called the Golden City had a post-apocalyptic air. The high-rise canyons of glass and steel had been abandoned by the great corporations and mining houses. Within a few months the Stock Exchange was to join a wholesale exodus to Sandton, while Anglo-American went so far as to shift its headquarters to London. The city had been taken over by a new form of entrepreneurial activity. Pavement traders ran what was known as the Cardboard Economy, the most vibrant sector in virtually every major African city. From a shy-faced Zairean, I bought a heart-warming object to take home to my family: a tray of miniature fruit and vegetables, deftly carved from wood and exquisitely coloured – melon, mango, pineapple, avocado. On the tray was carved a passage from Joshua 24:15. *Moi et ma maison Nous servirons l'éternal.*

But gangsters and *tsotsis* were out on the streets as well. Squatters had taken over empty buildings and underground car parks were best avoided. The old temples of wealth, five-star hotels like the Carlton, were boarding up luxury wings and providing security guards for the few remaining guests who ventured out on foot. Tourists were advised to avoid the city altogether.

Everyone had personal knowledge of someone who had died violently. Not someone they had heard about, but someone they knew. At a dinner at Mike's they all had a story, and the theme was not of crime, but revenge. One, quite common, went like this: a woman picked up her child from school and drove home. The Mercedes was approaching the gate, and the woman was reaching for the control pad to open it when she saw a man who had been standing across the road swiftly cross and produce a gun. Without hesitation she and the child got out. 'The keys are there,' she said. 'Take it, take the car.' Then he shot her.

It remained the case that most victims of crime were black. Violent robbery had ever been the bane of the townships, and Soweto had been one of the most dangerous places in the world at a time when Sandton was one of the safest. Then, the cops used to keep watch on the wealthy white suburbs while turning a blind eye to mayhem in the black areas. Now the cops, overwhelmed and understaffed, mistrusted and demoralised (more than 200 had been killed in a year) had given up the struggle, while crime against whites had for some the respectability conferred by the struggle against apartheid. The fear expressed by the author Alan Paton in *Cry, the Beloved Country* – 'When we turn to loving, they will have turned to hating' – had acquired the resonance of prophecy.*

Virtually all those I spoke to had considered emigrating, many had made applications. Few saw Britain as their first choice of destination but, should it come to an exodus, a million of South Africa's 5 million whites could claim the right of British residence. The brain-drain of young professionals was becoming more catastrophic and the country was so short of doctors that hospitals were recruiting replacements from Cuba.

Mike seemed distant from all this. Although a doctor himself, he had avoided both the trappings of prosperity and the long hours normally associated with the medical profession in South Africa. He and his family lived in a curious A-frame house which he had built himself and which had never quite been finished. Surrounded by palatial fortresses on a ridge south of Johannesburg, they had not even a fence or burglar alarm, let alone armed protection. His Volkswagen was so beat up it would not have looked out of place in Tanzania. '*Priceless* car,' he said, patting it affectionately. 'Buy a wreck and save your life.'

The night before I left Johannesburg, we went out for a last beer. The hotel in Booysens was typical of the working-class white watering holes across South Africa, where serious drinking was done by men who sat at the bar on stools nursing double brandies and Coke. Nobody stayed in these hotels any more, unless it was involuntarily, after falling off a stool and passing out, and the staircase led to rooms with a Gideon's Bible and a narrow bed unslept in since the demise of what used to be called the commercial traveller. These were places heavy with sadness and failure.

On our second beer Mike said he had been granted immigration papers for Canada. I don't know why I was surprised, probably because I had

---

* Paton died in April 1988. Ten years later, a few months after my journey ended, his widow announced she was emigrating after being hijacked and mugged. The headline read 'Flee, the Beloved Country'.

always thought of him as so utterly South African. It was the children, of course. Almost always it was the children.

The next day, before boarding the train for Cape Town, I bought a copy of the *Star* and turned to a column called Crime Count, a chilling distillation of the previous twenty-four hours of mayhem. Under one-paragraph items about the murder of a motorist by a gunman with an AK47, and the killing of a security guard in an armed robbery, was an equally brief report on the Booysens hotel. An hour after we left, two men had entered, poured petrol over the receptionist and threatened to set her on fire until the contents of the safe were handed over. They fled with about £900.

I WAS ON the final leg, but I left Johannesburg feeling that here another journey was just starting. Forty years ago, with Kenya's independence approaching, Elspeth Huxley posed the question in a book, *White Africans*, whether black and white could 'unite together to form a modern, reasonably well conducted state ... In short, is a multiracial state a possibility or a chimera?'

The prospects now looked a good deal gloomier than they did then. All the way south, the evidence had pointed to the eventual extinction of whites as a species capable of enduring in Africa. In Tanzania, Uganda, Malawi and Zambia they had all but died out. Although these were countries which never had large white populations, the problem was even more evident in the two places which had started off with significant numbers of whites and comparatively developed economies, Kenya and Zimbabwe. Neither could any longer claim to be a modern, reasonably well conducted state and in both the white populations had been so whittled away that there was now insufficient regeneration to ensure survival. Ultimately, it would all come down to South Africa.

This magnificent, tragic and ultimately baffling country had repeatedly confounded the prophets of doom. Like democracy in India, the often-unsuspected depths of humanity in South Africa continued to defy analysis. Although the miraculous political transition was now a part of history, nothing could take away from the majesty of that accomplishment. Talk of an African renaissance in which South Africa would lead a revival by the whole continent had started to sound hopelessly wishful, but the underlying strength of its economic institutions was undiminished.

Some whites were starting to speak of their own Africanness. Yet I could not help wondering how many knew just what that meant. The cultural experience of white South Africans had been based not only on segregation, privilege and prosperity, but on an industrial revolution unique in the continent. While a great many had been overseas and had visited the cultural and consumer capitals of Europe and America, few knew any other part of Africa. Their influences remained those of the West and although South African society was changing fast, there was an underlying assumption that the values which had assured white privilege would continue to prevail.

The new core of black leaders, on the other hand, felt the call of an older world, more truly African. The acquisition of power had given rise to a trend – it was too early to talk of a pattern – towards opportunism and sensitivity to criticism. Little credit was accorded the Afrikaner nationalists who, when faced with a choice between going down the path to all-out totalitarianism, or surrendering with grace, had, almost without precedent, opted for the latter. In the end, there had been just too many decent Afrikaners to permit a Wagnerian finale. Perhaps it was too early for this contribution to African history to be acknowledged. More worrying was an inclination to treat white alarm over crime as though pathological violence was part of some payback for apartheid, rather than a national shame requiring immediate action. The sharpness of the racial rhetoric on both sides filled me with foreboding.

For myself, I felt weary of the burdens of race. Whites had plenty to feel guilty about, but white guilt had usually served African politicians far better than it had those over whom they ruled. Elsewhere expiation had mostly involved an old white corporate elite buying favour with a new black political elite; the result had entrenched the worst elements on either side of the racial divide.

Richard Leakey had spoken of a transition in majority-rule states, a turning point at which blacks acknowledged the white contribution to development, and whites learnt their place. That meant equality, not privilege. It was the hardest of all Africa's lessons, but Afrikaners knew it instinctively. They had negotiated themselves out of power, and for many the consequences had been traumatic. You saw them increasingly now, the poor whites who had shed their previous status like an old skin. Times were hard, jobs were short, and there was no segregation among those who lived rough – dossing, hitch-hiking, picking up a few rands by panhandling and casual work. Afrikaners had no bolt hole and they understood the cardinal rule – that to survive an African tribe must constantly adapt to new priorities. In their short history they had already made huge adjustments. An adventurous few were embracing a new destiny. Instead of packing for Perth or Toronto, they were modern-day trekkers, heading with *bakkies* rather than ox-wagons into Zambia and Mozambique, where land was plentiful, or further north in search of other opportunities.

We, the British, had failed. Beyond the Zambezi, only that diminishing, ghostly little band of old hands, the remnants of Livingstone's tribe, had loved and understood Africa well enough to allow themselves to be treated as one of its own. It was only in retrospect that I realised what it was that had drawn me to them. They were not simply intriguing and gallant for the way they had gone against the tide of privilege in colonial times, but in a way enviable too, for they now lived in a world in which there was room for neither guilt nor prejudice.

I recalled an elderly white woman queuing for a *matatu* in a grimy swamp of refuse and slosh in Nairobi. She had the air of the well-to-do but her print frock was worn and spattered with mud. I could imagine how her old friends – secure in Guildford or Reigate with their memories of the Muthaiga Club and the Norfolk Hotel – might have found the sight distressing. She stood there with an air of serene dignity, her feet planted firmly in a pair of large green galoshes.

And I recalled what Daudi Ricardo told me just as I was setting out. Before *uhuru*, he said, other whites used to come and ask if he thought things were going to be all right. 'What I always said was "Only you can answer that. I know that *I* am going to be all right."'

That was all very well, I said, but he had lost everything, farm and possessions, and was left with only his books, sharing a beach shanty with an African family. He just looked at me, nodding and smiling.

19. The Bay

I N DEFERENCE TO OLD sensibilities, Spoornet, as the South African Railways was now called, tried to avoid mixing the races. There were three other whites in the compartment, two elderly men and a stocky youth barely out of his teens. The old fellows were going home to Cape Town after a bowls tournament; the youth was leaving Johannesburg for a job, and what looked like all his possessions were in suitcases and cardboard boxes stacked around the compartment.

At one of the early stops, Roodepoort it might have been, a black man in rags shambled past the carriage. The youth, whose name was Flip, said: 'Hey you guys, you can take the monkey out of the jungle, but you can't take the jungle out of the monkey, hey?' He must have made this ice-breaking jest before, for he looked around expectantly, chortling. The old Capetonians, looking out another window, said nothing.

Maybe I should have risen to the challenge. But I felt tired and ready to get home, and was thinking about seeing my wife and children again. Anyway, there were some people you could not tell anything, and he would be learning a thing or two for himself in due course. So I looked at him briefly and went back to my book and a long silence descended.

The two bowlers were keen to get home as well. Afrikaner gentlemen from the gentler climes of the Cape, they had been shaken by a week in Gauteng, as the Witwatersrand was now called. At the hostel where they had stayed with teams from all over the country, daily anecdotes about the horrors on the streets had evidently left the bowling fraternity with a traumatised determination that a national tournament should never be played there again.

The next morning, Flip got out at Touws River without saying goodbye. The train meandered down through the slow majesty of the Hex River Pass before crawling into Paarl, a sleepy, historic town in the wine country set beneath a vast tortoise hump of granite. A man in a felt hat and khaki shirt sauntered up to the window and asked: '*Kom julle van Guateng af?*' (Have you come from Gauteng?)

They nodded glumly.

'*Jislaik, man,*' he said. '*Ek sal nooit 'n visa soek nie vir daardie mal plek.*' Which roughly translates as, There's no way you'll ever catch me going near that mad place.

*   *   *

THERE was one last train journey. I went out to Sea Point, where I was born, and found the little apartment block with a balcony overlooking the sea where my parents lived for a year or so before we moved to Johannesburg. The slopes leading down to the beaches of Clifton and Camps Bay were now studded with high-rise towers fashionable among a breed of European expatriates whose pounds or marks bought a lot of luxury in rands. I had to go further back. So I bought a train ticket to my mother's childhood.

I always had mixed feelings about Cape Town. It was a beautiful city, with a setting at the base of its magnificently moody mountain that to my mind overshadowed any rival feature of the world's other great harbour cities. The fast-talking, wisecracking, street culture of the Coloureds, a unique ethnic fusion of African, European and Asian, gave parts of it a certain wild *joie*. But the over-riding character of white society was a vapid smugness. Capetonians were blithely disinterested in just about everything, and most particularly the rest of the country. What made them proud was their city's beauty and its colonial pedigree, but what pleased them above all was its remoteness from the rest of Africa. The author, Christopher Hope, elegantly summed up Cape Town as 'a piece of Europe strapped to the bottom of Africa . . . a ballet shoe on a boxer'.

Isolation had made it attractive to others as well. Traumatised executives from Johannesburg were removing their households en masse to the Cape to escape crime. They joined the new European hedonists on the Atlantic coast and wealthy English émigrés like Earl Spencer and Mark Thatcher who had acquired cut-price palaces among the wine-producing vales of Constantia. And so a new wave of refugees had decamped to the final extremity of Africa. Whites had been retreating southwards since the 1950s. Here, surely, must be the very last redoubt.

However, Africa was no longer remote. Since the demise of apartheid, other migrants had come to the peninsula, from the failed bantustans of the eastern Cape, and taken up residence on the Flats, the sandy wastes leading out to the airport where a lawless metropolis of plastic sheeting, corrugated iron and cardboard burgeoned. The squatter camps of Khayelitsha were as dispiriting as any Nairobi shantytown, and all the more glaring for the loveliness and opulence that surrounded them. Resentment bred among these hopeless hovels and it had become quite common for traffic on the airport road to be pelted with missiles by youths.

The train wound round the base of Devil's Peak, where the white temple of Herbert Baker's memorial to Rhodes sat amid a pine forest, through the garden suburbs of Mowbray and Rondebosch. Against the heavy winter sky, the great flat-topped mountain cast its shadow over the city. Each day its nature altered according to the light – by turns alluring, imperious, benign, aloof. As Table Mountain fell behind, the land trailed off into the mossy green slopes, the thatch roofs and white gables of Constantia. Then, quite suddenly, the train emerged by the sea and started to follow the creamy line of False Bay, sweeping down the peninsula. Grey breakers fell on boulders piled below the railway line, disintegrating in shards that spattered the carriage window. Here, beside the line at Muizenburg, was the thatch cottage where Rhodes gasped his last, asphyxiated by a heart swollen to the size of a baby's head, with Jameson at his side.

The brightly painted wooden beach huts at St James might have been an image drawn from Anthony Trollope's visit in 1877, when the novelist noted how the ladies of Cape Town had started to retreat to False Bay for the bathing, the fresh air and 'the generally improved sanitary arrangements'. The line wormed its way through snooty St James and dull Fish Hoek before taking one last curve in the great semicircle of the bay, and the train came to a slow stop in Simonstown.

WE HAVE TWO pictures of my grandfather, Reg Hollyer. The first, taken before he went off to the trenches, shows an insouciant young corporal in leggings, with the spurs and riding crop of the mounted artillery. In the second, soon after he was invalided out with shrapnel wounds, he is in his best civilian outfit, velvet-collared morning coat, Homberg and necktie. My grandmother, Bertha, her long face emphasised by a wide hat – she had a fine soprano voice but was certainly no beauty – is seated beside him in a fur coat. My mother, a tiny bundle of white lace with huge eyes, hence her nickname, Inky, is on her lap. Their prosperity, due to a photo studio in the East End, did not last. The demand for portraits fell off after the Armistice and the business collapsed.

In 1922, Reg bought a third-class ticket on the Union Castle ship *Armadale* from Southampton for Cape Town, to start a new life for them. On a cold November day he was seen off by Bertha and Inky, and watched as their figures on the quay faded from view. To console himself in the lonely hours, he started a journal in a neat hand which ran to thirty-two pages by the end of the voyage and which he sent back to Leyton, marked 'Dear Kiddie, This is a slight idea of how we went along on board.'

He had sound advice on shipboard pastimes such as deck quoits – 'that's a game, Bertha, that you will be tidy ready to dodge when you make the trip' – and etiquette – 'Try as much as possible to keep a liking for everybody you have to meet, even though you may not exactly like them ... As a lady, do not under any condition visit different places in the ship at any of the crew's invitation.'

He liked company and the music hall, and was made chairman of the third-class activities committee. He was glad to be kept occupied. 'Often I have regretted my action in coming away from you,' he confided to the journal. 'I have felt our parting very much.' There was plenty to do, from patching up a quarrel when some second-class passengers tried to take over the third-class saloon, to venturing into first class to ask Lord Ormeston and Mme Pennequin, a handsome Frenchwoman, to judge the third-class fancy dress. He struck up a friendship with a Mr Green, a schoolmaster whose comic version of *Widecombe Fair* was the star turn of the concert evening and who turned out to be a student of telepathy.

> He got me so interested with what appeared to be conclusive proofs that I promised him I would follow his reasoning and concentrate on the person with whom I wanted to communicate with. Naturally you Bertha was my subject when I did attempt it, but of course I got no results. My imagination is not large enough for these sort of things.

The *Armadale* berthed two weeks before Christmas and Reg went directly to Simonstown. The port, twenty miles down the peninsula from Cape Town, was a Royal Navy base and, as an ex-serviceman, he was hoping to find work in a military milieu. He took lodgings at the British Hotel overlooking the docks and got a job as manager of E. K. Green's bottle store. Bertha and my mother sailed to join him a few months later. They stayed at the British Hotel until moving to the apartment over the bottle store, where my mother grew up.

I remember Reg as a curious mixture of sternness and gregariousness. He was extremely fond of Bass ale and could turn a dead party around with a song at the piano, but was often quiet and almost stiff in his bearing. He remained completely an Englishman, the first I ever knew. He died of tuberculosis in 1957. He had been very ill for years and the night before he fell into a coma, my mother found him trying to load his service revolver.

I TOOK THE rucksack down from the train for the last time, and hefted it on to my back. That first morning in Dar es Salaam, I had been bathed in sweat as I humped it down to the ferry for Zanzibar. Now the gentle weight on my shoulders and hips was almost comforting, like an old leather coat, as I swung along St George's Street. On a Sunday afternoon, Simonstown was deserted. Rain came sweeping off the bay in cloudy gusts.

It was here, just over 200 years earlier, that the British took their first hesitant steps as an African colonial power. Acting on the orders of William of Orange, a British fleet landed near Simonstown in 1795 to secure the passage to the Indies, and after a skirmish at Muizenburg seized the fort in Cape Town. The embryo colony was returned briefly to the Dutch, but on the emergence of the threat of Napoleon was occupied by the British again in 1806 and this time they stayed. Simonstown remained a strategic bastion long after the opening of the Suez Canal. It was a little corner of England until 1955 when the naval base was handed over and, although by then my mother had lived almost her entire life in South Africa, I remember she cried in the cinema during the Movietone film of the ceremony.

Even at a distance, the British Hotel was unmistakable. It was a broad-fronted Victorian colonial building with a balcony of fine, wrought-iron filigree freshly painted in white and had a Red Ensign drooping from a flagstaff. I pushed through the heavy double doors to a darkened lobby that was as deserted as the street. For some time I stood there alone in the gloom with the ghosts. Eventually, I went through to a courtyard and halloed. A pleasant young man came down and signed me in. I was the only guest.

I mounted the stained oak staircase. The door opened on to a large sitting-room with a polished wooden floor and tiled fireplace. French doors led to the balcony overlooking the docks. Off the passage there were three bedrooms. I had no idea in which our family had stayed so, rather presumptuously, I chose the narrow, single one used by Mary Kingsley. A niece of the novelist, Mary was one of the most indomitable of that extraordinary breed of Victorian women travellers. Her adventures and investigations of native fetishes in Congo and Angola in the 1890s were published in *Travels in West Africa*. She was no lover of missionaries and advocated a form of colonial governance that would leave the African 'a free, unsmashed man not a whitewashed slave or an enemy'. She came to Simonstown as a volunteer nurse in 1900, and was staying at the British Hotel while caring for Boer prisoners when she died in a typhoid outbreak, aged thirty-eight.

I was almost home now. I ran an enormous bath in a cast iron tub and soaked in it for half an hour. Outside, it was still raining and the streets were still deserted. I had a drink at a cosy pub called the Jolly Roger where a man and his son were nursing a beer and a cola, and three Xhosas were talking about football. The Pescado restaurant had no customers at all. I ordered chicken livers in a hot piri-piri sauce, followed by a lightly grilled kabeljou, a succulent Cape fish, in butter and parsley, and a bottle and a half of sauvignon blanc. Afterwards, I had a large brandy and a cigar.

Then I went back and turned out all the lights, and sat down on the balcony. I dozed off, listening for the voices of Reg and Bertha and Inky, as the sea swirled round the bay and out to the Cape of Good Hope.

Glossary

amadlozi *Sindebele* the shades of departed ancestors who may act as intermediaries with the spirit world

badza *Shona* a short-handled hoe typically used by peasant growers

bakkie *Afrikaans* an open-backed, light van used by farmers to transport men and materials

bibi *Ki-Swahili* a woman. The sense may vary. At the coast it suggests respect; among inland people it does not

bittereinders *Afrikaans* bitter-enders, meaning the Afrikaner diehards who held out against peace with Britain in the Boer War. The word is a nice example of the flexibility of Afrikaans to expropriate from other languages. See also *hensoppers*.

boerewors *Afrikaans* Literally, farmers' sausage. A distinctively meaty and spicy sausage for which white and black South Africans have an inordinate appetite, and for which exiles used to pine

braai *Afrikaans* a barbecue

bulogi *Ki-Sukuma* witchcraft

bundu *settler slang* the African bush

dagga *Afrikaans* marijuana. Grown and used all over East and southern Africa

dorp *Afrikaans* a small town or village

hensoppers *Afrikaans* hands-uppers. A term of opprobrium for those who surrendered to the British in the Boer War

houts *Afrikaans* literally, wood, but also an insulting terms for blacks, indicating block-headed stupidity

indaba *Sindebele* a discussion of any weighty matter, usually involving a number of elders, to arrive at a consensus

induna *Sindebele* formerly a military commander, now also a man of standing

inxwala *Sindebele* the first-fruits ceremony characteristic of the Zulu and Ndebele peoples. Used by a ruling head as a symbol and instrument of authority

jol *Afrikaans* to go out on the town; to drink, dance and party

jukskei *Afrikaans* a quoit-like game involving the tossing of wooden pegs at a stake

kaffirboetie *Afrikaans* an insult for one who is friendly, or at least not actively hostile, to blacks

kaffirboom *Afrikaans* a scarlet-blossoming tree, *erethrina lysistemon*. Probably the species referred to in Kipling's lines 'The great grey-green, greasy Limpopo River/ All set about with fever trees'

koeksusters *Afrikaans* a doughnut-like confection soaked in syrup

kopje *Afrikaans* a hill

kraal *Afrikaans* a tribal village or settlement

laager *Afrikaans* a defensive ring of wagons drawn up in a circle against attack

manyatta *settler slang* demented. A condition arising from living too long in the *bundu*

matatu *Ki-Swahili* a minibus, usually of Japanese make, designed to carry between ten and fifteen people but usually packed to contain more than double the intended number. *Matatus* are ubiquitous through East and southern Africa and, as the transport system used by the masses, have been an agent of almost revolutionary social change over the past decade

matoke *Luganda* a large, green plantain which is the staple of the lakes region

melktert *Afrikaans* milk tart. Like *koeksusters*, a traditional delicacy

mntwana *Sindebele* a prince of the royal Khumalo clan of the Ndebele people

moran *Maasai* a young man or warrior

munt *settler slang* insulting term commonly used by white Rhodesians for blacks. Derived from, but not to be confused with, *muntu*.

muntu the word in a number of languages for an individual African. The plural is *bantu*, meaning people

mzee *Ki-Swahili* an elderly man. A term indicating respect

mzungu *Ki-Swahili* a white man. Apparently derived from the verb *kuzunguka*, meaning 'to surround', and thus suggesting 'those who surround us'. Many Swahili names for individual whites are derived from verbs. Livingstone, for example, was known as *Kitokezi*, meaning 'the one who is always leaving', from the verb *kutoka*, 'to leave'

nanga *Shona* one of the numerous terms in African languages for a traditional healer or herbalist

nfumu *Ki-Sukuma* also the word for a diviner. In Sindebele and Zulu the word is *issanusi*

pombe *Ki-Swahili* beer

povo *Shona* the people. Term used by Zimbabwean politicians to simulate an attitude of respect for the masses. See also *wananchi*

shamba *Ki-Swahili* a plot or small farm

skokkian illegal South African home-brew of indeterminate ingredients and variable potency

tikkiedraai *Afrikaans* a traditional dance

tsotsi a colloquial term used in South Africa for a thug or criminal

uhuru *Ki-Swahili* freedom, or independence. Like many Ki-Swahili words, derived from Arabic

ujamaa *Ki-Swahili* literally, the community, but synonymous with the package of socialist policies pursued by Julius Nyerere in Tanzania

wananchi *Ki-Swahili* 'children of the land'. A term for the masses used by the political class in Kenya to suggest esteem for the common folk, but in reality – like *povo* in Zimbabwe – indicative of quite the reverse

Bibliography

General

Atieno Odhiambo, E. S., Ouso, T. I., and Williams, J. F. M., *A History of East Africa*, Essex, 1977

Blake, Robert, *A History of Rhodesia*, London, 1977

Cockcroft, Laurence, *Africa's Way: A Journey From the Past*, London, 1990

Davenport, T. R. H., *South Africa: A Modern History*, London, 1991

De Klerk, W. A., *The Puritans in Africa: A Story of Afrikanerdom*, London, 1975

Diamond, Jared, *Guns, Germs and Steel: A Short History of Everybody*, London, 1997

Harden, Blaine, *Africa: Dispatches from a Fragile Continent*, London, 1991

Hastings, Adrian, *Church and Mission in Modern Africa*, London, 1967

Hodd, Michael (ed.), *East African Handbook*, Bath, 1995

Holman, Michael, *African Deadlines*, privately published, London, 1995

Hyam, Ronald, *Empire and Sexuality: The British Experience*, Manchester, 1990

Iliffe, John, *Africans: The History of a Continent*, Cambridge, 1995

Ingham, Kenneth, *A History of East Africa*, London, 1966

McLynn, Frank, *Hearts of Darkness: The Exploration of Africa*, London, 1992

Macmillan, W. M., *Africa Emergent: A Survey of Trends in British Africa*, London, 1938

Marnham, Patrick, *Fantastic Invasion*, London, 1980

Miller, Charles, *The Lunatic Express*, New York, 1974

Moorhouse, Geoffrey, *The Missionaries*, London, 1973

Morris, Jan, *Pax Britannica: The Empire Trilogy*, London, 1968–72

Oliver, Roland, and Atmore, Anthony, *Africa since 1800*, Cambridge, 1972

Pakenham, Thomas, *The Scramble for Africa*, London, 1991

Robinson, Ronald, and Gallagher, John, *Africa and the Victorians*, London, 1961

Royle, Trevor, *Winds of Change: The End of Empire in Africa*, London, 1996

Walvin, James, *Black Ivory: A History of British Slavery*, London, 1992

Chapter One

Burton, Richard F., *Zanzibar – City, Island and Coast*, London, 1872

Crofton, R. H., *Zanzibar Affairs 1914–1933*, London, 1953

Heanley, R. M., *Edward Steere: A Memoir*, London, 1888

Jeal, Tim, *Livingstone*, London, 1973

Voules, Eleanor, *African Witchcraft in Pemba Island* (in *Witchcraft*, by Voules and Munday, J. T.), London, 1951

Maynard Smith, H., *Frank, Bishop of Zanzibar*, London, 1926

Ruete, Emily, *An Arabian Princess Between Two Worlds*, Leiden, 1993

Chapter Two

Moorehead, Alan, *The White Nile*, London, 1960

Stanley, Henry M., *In Darkest Africa: The Emin Expedition*, London, 1890

Chapter Three

Brodie, Fawn, *The Devil Drives: A Life of Richard Burton*, London, 1967

Burton, Richard F., *The Lake Regions of Central Africa*, London, 1866

Gregory, J. W., *The Great Rift Valley*, London, 1896

Lovett, R., *History of the London Missionary Society*, two vols, London, 1899

Morell, Virginia, *Ancestral Passion: The Leakey Family and the Quest for Human Beginnings*, New York, 1995

Stanley, Henry M., *How I Found Livingstone*, London, 1872

Stanley, Henry M., *Through The Dark Continent*, two vols, London, 1899

Waugh, Evelyn, *A Tourist in Africa*, London, 1960

Chapter Four

Abrahams, Ray (ed.), *Witchcraft in Contemporary Tanzania*, Cambridge, 1994

Roscoe, John, *Twenty-five Years in East Africa*, Cambridge, 1921

Speke, John H., *Journal of the Discovery of the Source of the Nile*, London, 1872

Chapter Five

De Bunsen, Bernard, *Adventures in Education* [at Makerere], privately published, London, 1995

Goldschmidt, Tijs, *Darwin's Dreampond: Drama in Lake Victoria*, Cambridge, 1997

Miller, Charles, *The Battle for the Bundu*, New York, 1974

Perham, Margery, *East African Journey: Kenya and Tanganyika in 1929*, London, 1976

Thomson, Joseph, *Through Masai-Land*, London, 1882

Chapter Six

Grahame, Ian, *Amin and Uganda: A Memoir*, London, 1980

Hills, Denis, *The Rock of the Wind*, London, 1984

Hooper, Ed, *Slim: A Reporter's Story of Aids in East Africa*, London, 1990

The Kabaka of Buganda, *Desecration of My Kingdom*, London, 1967

Low, D. Anthony, and Pratt, R. Cranford, *Buganda and British Overrule 1900–1955*, Oxford, 1960

Roscoe, John, *The Baganda*, London, 1911

Chapter Seven

Hall, Richard, *Lovers on the Nile*, London, 1980

Speke, John H., *Journal of the Discovery of the Source of the Nile*, London, 1872

Chapter Eight

Brown, D. and M., *Looking Back at the Uganda Protectorate: Recollections of District Officers*, privately published, Perth, 1996

Stanley, Henry M., *In Darkest Africa: The Emin Expedition*, two vols, London, 1890

Chapter Nine

Farrant, Leda, *Lady Delamere and the Lord Erroll Murder*, Nairobi, 1997

Fox, James, *White Mischief*, London, 1982

Huxley, Elspeth, *White Man's Country: Lord Delamere and the Making of Modern Kenya*, two vols, London, 1953

Huxley, Elspeth and Perham, Margery, *Race and Politics in Kenya: A Correspondence*, London, 1955

Markham, Beryl, *West With the Night*, London, 1943

Pakenham, Thomas, *The Boer War*, London, 1979

Trzebinski, Errol, *The Kenya Pioneers*, London, 1985

Chapter Ten

Blixen, Karen, *Out of Africa*, London, 1937

Huxley, Elspeth, *The Flame Trees of Thika: Memories of an African Childhood*, London, 1959

Huxley, Elspeth, *Out in the Midday Sun*, London, 1985

Kenyatta, Jomo, *Facing Mount Kenya*, London, 1938

Roosevelt, Theodore, *African Game Trails*, London, 1910

Chapter Twelve

Hall, Richard and Peyman, Hugh, *The Great Uhuru Railway: China's Showpiece in Africa*, London 1976

Patterson, J. H., *The Man-eaters of Tsavo*, London, 1912

Ransford, Oliver, *Livingstone's Lake: The Drama of Nyasa*, London, 1966
Wallis, J. P. R. (ed.), *Journals of the Zambezi Expedition of David Livingstone*, two vols, London, 1956

Chapter Thirteen
Banda, H. and Young, C., *Our African Way of Life*, London, 1946
Jeal, Tim, *Livingstone*, London, 1973
Livingstone, W.P., *Laws of Livingstonia*, London, 1921
Van der Post, Laurens, *Venture to the Interior*, London, 1952

Chapter Fifteen
Baines, Thomas, *The Gold Regions of South Eastern Africa*, Bulawayo, 1968 (reprint of 1877 edn)
Bent, J. T., *The Ruined Cities of Mashonaland*, London, 1895
Caute, David, *Under the Skin: The Death of White Rhodesia*, London, 1983
Mason, Philip, *The Birth of a Dilemma: The Conquest and Settlement of Rhodesia*, Oxford, 1958
Meredith, Martin, *The Past is Another Country. Rhodesia: UDI to Zimbabwe*, London, 1979
Ranger, T. O., *Revolt in Southern Rhodesia 1896–7*, London, 1967
Tabler, E. C. *The Far Interior: Chronicles of Pioneering*, Cape Town 1955

Chapter Sixteen
Catholic Commission for Justice and Peace in Zimbabwe, *Breaking the Silence: A Report on the Disturbances in Matabeleland 1980 to 1988*, Harare, 1997
Godwin, Peter, *Mukiwa: A White Boy in Africa*, London, 1996
Mungoshi, Charles, *Coming of the Dry Season*, Oxford, 1972
Rasmussen, R. Kent, *Migrant Kingdom: Mzilikazi's Ndebele in South Africa*, London, 1978

Chapter Seventeen
Flower, Ken, *Serving Secretly: Rhodesia into Zimbabwe, 1964–1981*, London, 1987
Hole, H. M., *The Passing of the Black Kings*, Bulawayo, 1978 (reprint of 1932 edn)
Millin, Sarah Gertrude, *Rhodes*, London, 1933
Ransford, Oliver, *Bulawayo: Historic Battleground of Rhodesia*, Cape Town, 1968
Selous, Frederick Courteney, *A Hunter's Wanderings in Africa*, Bulawayo, 1970 (reprint of 1881 edn)
Summers, R. and Pagden, C. W., *The Warriors*, Cape Town, 1970

Tabler, E. C., *To the Victoria Falls: The Diary of Major Henry Stabb*, Cape Town, 1970

Ter Haar, Gerrie, *Spirit of Africa: The Healing Ministry of Archbishop Milingo of Zambia*, London, 1992

Thomas, Thomas Morgan, *Eleven Years in Central South Africa*, Bulawayo, 1970 (reprint of 1873 edn)

Chapter Eighteen

Bosman, Herman Charles, *Mafeking Road*, Johannesburg, 1947

Hope, Christopher, *White Boy Running*, London, 1988

Lewin, Hugh, *Bandiet: Seven Years in a South African Prison*, London, 1974

Livingstone, David, *Missionary Travels and Researches in Africa*, London, 1857

Longford, Elizabeth, *Jameson's Raid*, London, 1982

Luthuli, Albert, *Let My People Go*, London, 1962

Malan, Riaan, *My Traitor's Heart*, London, 1990

Mandela, Nelson, *Long Walk to Freedom*, London, 1994

Pakenham, Thomas, *The Boer War*, London, 1979

Paton, Alan, *Cry, the Beloved Country*, London, 1948

Waldmeir, Patti, *Anatomy of a Miracle: The End of Apartheid and the Birth of the New South Africa*, London, 1997

Chapter Nineteen

Mostert, Noel, *Frontiers: The Epic of South Africa's Creation and the Tragedy of the Xhosa People*, London, 1992

Rotberg, Robert, *The Founder: Cecil Rhodes and the Pursuit of Power*, Oxford, 1988

Trollope, Anthony, *South Africa*, Cape Town, 1973 (reprint of 1878 edn)

Index